Trends in American Economic Growth, 1929–1982

EDWARD F. DENISON

→»×««-

Trends in American Economic Growth, 1929–1982

→»×««-

THE BROOKINGS INSTITUTION
Washington, D.C.

Copyright © 1985
THE BROOKINGS INSTITUTION
1775 Massachusetts Avenue, N.W., Washington, D.C. 20036

Library of Congress Cataloging in Publication data:
Denison, Edward Fulton, 1915–
    Trends in American economic growth, 1929–1982.
    Includes index.
    1. United States—Economic conditions.   I. Title.
HC106.3.D3668   1985   338.973   85-17413
ISBN 0-8157-1801-1
ISBN 0-8157-1809-8 (pbk.)

1 2 3 4 5 6 7 8 9

THE BROOKINGS INSTITUTION is an independent organization devoted to nonpartisan research, education, and publication in economics, government, foreign policy, and the social sciences generally. Its principal purposes are to aid in the development of sound public policies and to promote public understanding of issues of national importance.

The Institution was founded on December 8, 1927, to merge the activities of the Institute for Government Research, founded in 1916, the Institute of Economics, founded in 1922, and the Robert Brookings Graduate School of Economics and Government, founded in 1924.

The Board of Trustees is responsible for the general administration of the Institution, while the immediate direction of the policies, program, and staff is vested in the President, assisted by an advisory committee of the officers and staff. The by-laws of the Institution state: "It is the function of the Trustees to make possible the conduct of scientific research, and publication, under the most favorable conditions, and to safeguard the independence of the research staff in the pursuit of their studies and in the publication of the results of such studies. It is not a part of their function to determine, control, or influence the conduct of particular investigations or the conclusions reached."

The President bears final responsibility for the decision to publish a manuscript as a Brookings book. In reaching his judgment on the competence, accuracy, and objectivity of each study, the President is advised by the director of the appropriate research program and weighs the views of a panel of expert outside readers who report to him in confidence on the quality of the work. Publication of a work signifies that it is deemed a competent treatment worthy of public consideration but does not imply endorsement of conclusions or recommendations.

The Institution maintains its position of neutrality on issues of public policy in order to safeguard the intellectual freedom of the staff. Hence interpretations or conclusions in Brookings publications should be understood to be solely those of the authors and should not be attributed to the Institution, to its trustees, officers, or other staff members, or to the organizations that support its research.

In memory of Dwight B. Yntema
Professor of Economics, Hope College
Analyst of national income

‑⇶⟫⟪⇷

Foreword

‑⇶⟫⟪⇷

A new dimension was added to the analysis of economic growth when, in 1962, Edward F. Denison introduced his system of growth accounting, centered on quantitative estimates of the sources of growth. This is the sixth book in which Denison uses growth accounting to analyze growth in industrial countries. The first four studies were completed during the buoyant quarter-century, ending in 1973, that followed the completion of reconversion and recovery from World War II—a period in which the whole industrial world enjoyed vigorous growth. In those investigations Denison identified the determinants of growth, quantified their contributions in the United States and abroad, and examined the sources of international differences in both growth rates and levels of output per person employed. The fifth study, confined to the United States, was already under way when rates of growth suddenly turned sharply downward in 1974. Denison was among the first to recognize that a basic change had occurred and to attempt a systematic and comprehensive analysis. In *Accounting for Slower Economic Growth: The United States in the 1970s,* published in 1979, he observed that slow growth threatened to persist indefinitely.

Six years later Denison's appraisal is no more optimistic. In the present volume Denison carries his growth accounting estimates forward, describes developments impinging on growth, and discusses critically America's response to slow growth. Not only has the growth rate of potential output failed to recover, he finds, but beginning in 1980 it appears to have fallen even more. In addition, ever since 1969 actual output has slipped further below potential output with each business cycle.

Denison has investigated economic growth as a senior fellow, and now senior fellow emeritus, in the Brookings Institution's Economic Studies program since 1962, and before that with the Committee for Economic Development and the U.S. Department of Commerce. He has also devoted many years to national income and product measurement, most recently (1979–81) as associate director of the U.S. Bureau of Economic Analysis.

The author acknowledges with gratitude the assistance in this study of the staff of that bureau, particularly Robert P. Parker, and of the staff of the U.S. Bureau of Labor Statistics, particularly Jerome A. Mark. Growth could be neither measured nor analyzed without the competent economists and statisticians in these and other agencies of the federal government and their devotion to the provision of accurate, objective information.

The manuscript benefited importantly from comments on a preliminary draft by Moses Abramovitz, Jack Alterman, Peter K. Clark, John W. Kendrick, and Solomon Fabricant. Several writers quoted in chapter 3 were kind enough to verify statements of their views. Frederick J. Dreiling provided a revised and updated series for the effect on output of diverting resources to pollution abatement. The author is grateful to all of them, as well as to research assistant Paula R. DeMasi, research secretaries Constance S. Koutris, Charlotte Kaiser, and Meropi R. Antoniadou-McCoy, technical assistant Kirk W. Kimmel, and Whitney Watriss, who edited the manuscript.

A much appreciated grant from Citibank helped defray the cost of the project. Articles flowing from the project were presented at the 1982 annual meeting of the Royal Economic Society in London (published in the *Economic Journal,* March 1983) and a 1982 conference of the American Enterprise Institute in Washington (published in John W. Kendrick, ed., *International Comparisons of Productivity and Causes of the Slowdown,* American Enterprise Institute/ Ballinger, 1984).

The views expressed in this book are those of the author and should not be ascribed to the officers, trustees, or other staff members of the Brookings Institution, nor to those whose assistance is acknowledged.

BRUCE K. MAC LAURY
President

August 1985
Washington, D.C.

Contents

Tables

-»>«<-

Preface

-»>«<-

This, my sixth book about economic growth, updates the measures of growth and its sources that were introduced in substantially their present form in *Accounting for United States Economic Growth, 1929–1969* (Brookings, 1974) and *Accounting for Slower Economic Growth: The United States in the 1970s* (Brookings, 1979). The detailed estimates previously ended with 1976. The present book extends them through 1982. In addition, revisions have been made in the previous estimates to incorporate corrections of the data that enter into their derivation, particularly the national income and product accounts (NIPA) of the Bureau of Economic Analysis, U.S. Department of Commerce. In December 1980 the NIPA were revised back to 1929, although most of the detailed series remain unchanged before 1967.

The addition of six years to the growth tables and the revision of estimates for earlier years result in a set of complete and comparable estimates that span the fifty-four years from 1929 through 1982. Data are provided for thirty-nine of the individual years in this span: 1929, 1940, 1941, and all years from 1947 through 1982. Data covering a long period, as these do, are needed not just to satisfy curiosity about the past, but also to provide a base against which to appraise recent developments.

The tables have characteristics that are highly valuable for growth analysis.

1. They quantify not only annual changes in total output, output per person employed, output per hour at work, and output per unit of input but also, to the greatest extent possible, annual changes in the determinants of output and the effects of these changes upon output.

2. The tables permit the analyst to divide changes in output between those resulting from changes in the economy's ability to produce and those resulting from changes in the extent to which the resources

available for use in production are actually used. All output series are presented on both "actual" and "potential" bases. All series for the determinants of output, and all tables providing the sources of growth of output, are presented for both actual and potential output. In addition, and importantly, the differences between actual and potential values are made available every year, not only for output but also for its determinants.

3. All pertinent data, both actual and potential, are provided for the whole economy and, separately, for each of four sectors: nonresidential business; services of dwellings; general government, households, and institutions; and international assets. Data by sector are especially important for productivity analysis, because productivity series have the most meaning when confined to nonresidential business.

4. The tables and analysis rest upon a comprehensive classification of growth sources that has been carefully described and is internally consistent.[1]

This classification, or a very similar one, has also been used in estimating the sources of growth in other countries and the sources of the differences in the levels of output per person employed in various countries.[2] Consistent classification makes international comparisons possible, although the present book does not provide them. Estimates for most other countries are not up-to-date, and their extension could help in the interpretation of recent developments throughout the industrial world.

Selected Findings

My preceding book described the beginnings of a period, starting after 1973, in which the growth rates

---

1. Besides my books, see my "Classification of Sources of Growth," *Review of Income and Wealth* (March 1972), pp. 1–26. The article points out (p. 4) that "the primary characteristic of a desirable classification is that it identify effect with cause. . . . It is convenient to be able to identify changes in the contribution of capital with changes in saving and investment, changes in the allocation of resources with changes in the way that labor and capital are allocated, and so on."

2. Edward F. Denison, assisted by Jean-Pierre Poullier, in *Why Growth Rates Differ: Postwar Experience in Nine Western Countries* (Brookings, 1967) (hereafter *Why Growth Rates Differ*), provides 1950–62 estimates for Belgium, Denmark, France, the Federal Republic of Germany, Italy, the Netherlands, and Norway. Edward F. Denison and William K. Chung, in *How Japan's Economy Grew So Fast: The Sources of Postwar Expansion* (Brookings, 1976) (hereafter *How Japan's Economy Grew So Fast*), provide 1952–71 estimates for Japan. Dorothy Walters, in *Canadian Growth Revisited, 1950–67* (Economic Council of Canada, 1970), provides 1950–67 estimates for Canada. Bakul H. Dholakis, in *The Sources of Economic Growth in India* (Good Companions, 1974), provides 1948–49 to 1968–69 estimates for India. Kwang Suk Kim and Joon Kyung Park, in *Sources of Economic Growth in Korea: 1963–1982* (Korea Development Institute, 1985), provide 1963–82 estimates for the Republic of Korea.

of both potential and actual output were much reduced and the previous persistent increase in output per person employed had stalled. This slowdown in growth has continued, and more than a decade has now elapsed since it began.

The continuation of slow growth for more than a decade has created an increasingly serious situation. As time has passed, the annual losses from slow growth of potential output have swelled. In addition, actual output has fallen further below potential output with each succeeding business cycle. The lengthening duration of slow growth has also strengthened the case for believing that its causes are deep-seated.

Output and productivity have not merely continued to perform poorly, however. After 1979 their record deteriorated further. My estimates on a potential basis indicate that the growth rate of potential national income, measured in constant prices, fell from 3.9 percent a year over the whole 1948–73 period and 4.3 percent in 1964–73 to 3.0 percent in 1973–79 and 1.8 percent in both 1979–82 and 1979–83. The reductions occurred despite very fast growth of potential employment after 1973. The estimated growth rate of potential national income per person potentially employed fell from 2.3 percent a year over the whole 1948–73 period and 2.0 percent in 1964–73 to 0.5 percent in 1973–79 and then to zero or less in 1979–82 and 1979–83.

The twice-reduced growth rate of potential output has been accompanied by a widening gap between actual output and potential output. Actual national income averaged only 0.9 percent less than my estimates of potential national income from 1948 through 1969, but 4.2 percent less from 1970 through 1973, 6.5 percent less from 1974 through 1979, and 9.8 percent less from 1980 through 1983.

Although no pattern is typical of the sources of growth in all times and places, estimates for the world's largest economy over a fifty-three year period condense a great deal of experience. The growth rate from 1929 to 1982 of the potential national income of the United States was 3.2 percent. As shown on page 30, changes in the amount of work done and the composition of workers (except for their education) were responsible for 34 percent of this growth rate; advances in technological, managerial, and organizational knowledge, 26 percent; the increase in private capital, 17 percent; the increase in education of employed persons, 13 percent; economies of scale, 8 percent; improved allocation of labor among uses, 8 percent; reductions in output per unit of input deriving from pollution and safety regulations and crime against business, –1 percent; and other output determinants, –5 percent.

A similar allocation of the 1.6 percent growth rate from 1929 to 1982 of potential national income per person potentially employed shows that advances in knowledge were responsible for 54 percent of this growth rate; education, 26 percent; economies of scale, 17 percent; improved allocation of labor, 16 percent; the increase in capital per worker, 15 percent; pollution and safety regulations and crime against business, –3 percent; the reduction in land available per worker, –3 percent; labor input per worker except education, –13 percent (reflecting shorter working hours and a changing demographic composition); and other determinants, –10 percent.

The informal table on page 35 summarizes the sources of the 1.49 percentage point decline in the growth rate of potential national income per person potentially employed from the 1964–73 period to the 1973–79 period. Based on the amount of detail used there, eighteen determinants of this series, which are identified in the table, were separately calculated annually. Eleven of the eighteen contributed a total of 0.70 percentage points to this decline, three were neutral, and changes in only four were more favorable in the later period; the latter offset a total of 0.12 percentage points of the adverse effects of changes in the other determinants. Determinants whose individual effects could not be isolated on an annual basis contributed 0.91 percentage points to the slowdown. Less than 0.1 percentage point of this latter amount is ascribed in chapter 3 to the increase in energy prices and controls, and little or nothing to changes in organized research and development (R&D) in this country or abroad. There is no reasonably reliable way to allocate the rest among changes in the remaining determinants. Evidence concerning several that may plausibly be thought to have changed adversely and been responsible for at least some of the rest is evaluated in chapter 3. The topics discussed include technological knowledge not stemming from organized R&D; managerial knowledge and the quality of management; work effort; misallocation of individual workers stemming from reduced testing of job applicants; misallocation of capital stemming from economic change or from discrimination in the tax structure; and misallocation of resources resulting from barriers to international trade.

Changes in contributions from the 1973–79 period to the 1979–82 period, when the growth rate of potential national income per person potentially employed fell an additional 0.77 percentage points, were not nearly so close to being uniformly adverse as they had been in the preceding period. As shown in the table on page 35, many earlier changes were reversed. Nine of the output determinants estimated annually that had contributed 0.35 percentage points to the growth rate decline in 1973–79 contributed 0.43 points toward an increase from 1973–79 to 1979–82. A tenth, the age-sex composition of labor, after contributing only 0.02 percentage points toward increased growth from 1964–73 to 1973–79, contributed an appreciable 0.16 points toward an increase from 1973–79 to 1979–82. On the other hand, three determinants that had changed favorably in 1973–79 contributed 0.33 percentage points to the decline from 1973–79 to 1979–82. More important, the contributions of the determinants whose effects were not separately estimated annually fell by an additional 0.8 percentage points, of which perhaps 0.2 points can be ascribed to energy prices.

Information up to the end of 1984 does not indicate, in my opinion, that the economy has moved out of the pattern of the slow growth of potential output and potential output per person employed that has characterized it since 1973. The improvement since the 1982 recession that is shown by series calculated on an "actual" basis appears to reflect the rising utilization of resources during the recovery phase of the business cycle. The future, as always, is unknown, and prospects for future development are mixed. But the fact that the growth rate of potential output per person potentially employed dropped after 1979, despite improvement in many of the determinants contributing to the initial slowdown, is worrisome.

The federal government's response to the slowdown in growth since 1973 has concentrated on raising saving and investment, even though capital is only one of several major sources of growth and was responsible for only a little of the slowdown. The mechanism chosen was general tax reductions and the introduction of special preferences to discriminate in favor of saving and investment. The nation's saving and investment did not increase in response to the government's actions—after 1981 they dropped, as dissaving by the federal government itself became huge. The new tax preferences greatly intensified the lack of horizontal equity in the tax system and stimulated the misallocation of investment.

Meanwhile, the government did not—perhaps it could not—meet its primary economic responsibility: to enable business to operate within an environment in which the nation's actual output stays close to potential output and prices are acceptably stable. The country may now be moving toward a position in which this condition could be achieved if a way were found for a smooth transition to a balanced federal budget position. But such a transition is unlikely in the near future.

The growth of potential output itself depends mainly on a myriad of private decisions and actions. These are divided among nearly all individuals and organizations, but in the short and medium run the course of output per unit of input will depend particularly on business management, which is in the most strategic position to affect events.

This section has suggested some of the topics discussed in this book and a few of the conclusions and views to which the analysis has led me. It is by no means a comprehensive summary.

The Tables and Their Derivation

The fact that the data and analysis presented here are extensions of those previously published and described permits a smaller volume than would otherwise be possible. The reader can turn to the earlier books for amplification of concepts, definitions, and classifications, and my reasons for selecting them. When required at all, explanations need only be sufficient to serve as reminders for those familiar with my earlier writings and to convey the main points to those who are not.

The method by which every series was derived in 1929–76 is fully described in *Accounting for Slower Economic Growth: The United States in the 1970s* (hereafter *Slower Growth*), sometimes in part by reference to descriptions in *Accounting for United States Economic Growth, 1929–1969* (hereafter *Accounting for Growth*) or elsewhere. Methods used in *Slower Growth* have been changed in this volume when required by changes in the availability of source data or by the nature of recent economic changes. The appendix, "Derivations of the Estimates" (hereafter referred to as "Derivations"), and the sources of the tables together describe the derivation of the estimates fully, for the most part by reference to *Slower Growth*. All changes from *Slower Growth* are fully described. The most important tables provide data for all years. Other tables sometimes omit some years for which the data are unchanged and can be obtained from *Slower Growth*. Text references to these tables are meant to include these years. Subject to the constraints just described, this book is self-contained.

For convenience, the tables are assigned the same numbers as in *Slower Growth,* where each table is identified by a number or letter that corresponds to the chapter or appendix in which it appears, followed by a number representing its order of appearance in the chapter or appendix. Thus table 8-7 is the seventh table in chapter 8 of *Slower Growth* and table L-4 is the fourth table in appendix L. In the present volume, which is organized differently, all formal tables except table 1-1 are grouped and placed after the appendix. The format of most tables is the same as in *Slower Growth*, except for the years covered. In some tables columns or rows have been added to provide additional information or have been deleted to eliminate information that is not available or of little interest. One table is added, while a number are omitted, either because no new data were available, or because the tables were not needed for the present study, were not pertinent to the present estimates, or were deemed unnecessary.

Selected Definitions

The value of the nation's output of goods and services is measured in this study by *national income*, which is also known as net national product valued at factor cost. The nation's net national product consists of personal consumption expenditures, net private domestic investment, and government purchases of goods and services (the three of which together account for domestic use of net product), plus the amount by which exports of goods and services exceed imports. National income is the value of the nation's net national product when each product is valued by the factor cost of producing it. The factor cost of producing a product is the earnings of labor and property that are derived from its production. Total national income in current prices is thus equal to the aggregate earnings of labor and property accruing from current production.

National income in constant prices, which I use to measure changes in real output, is the value obtained for net national product when each product is valued at its factor cost in 1972, the base year selected by the Bureau of Economic Analysis (BEA). National income, it should be understood, measures exactly the same bundle of goods and services as net national product at market prices. Further, an index of the quantity of any individual product is the same whether one is measuring national income or net national product. Indexes of national income and net national product in constant 1972 prices differ only because they weight products differently as a result of the fact that the 1972 prices of most goods and services were different at factor cost and at market prices.[3]

To facilitate analysis of the sources of growth of real national income, I divide national income among the following four sectors.

Nonresidential business. This sector covers all production by business within the geographic area of the United States, except that the services provided by dwellings are excluded. It includes corporations, partnerships, sole proprietorships, mutual financial institutions, government enterprises, cooperatives, and other miscellaneous forms of business, as well as organizations such as trade associations or chambers of commerce that primarily serve business. The distinguishing feature of the sector as a whole is that it sells its products for a price. Output in this sector is, with minor exceptions, measured as the sum of series for the various types of output, which are obtained either by dividing expenditures in current prices by a price index or, less often, by multiplying a physical quantity series by a base-year price. Output is only rarely inferred from the behavior of labor, capital, or land input. Changes in the output of the nonresidential business sector result from changes in the quantities of all types of input and from changes in a great variety of determinants of output per unit of input.

Services of dwellings. The output of this sector consists of the services provided by the nation's stock of dwellings. The establishments in the sector are owner-occupied and tenant-occupied nonfarm and farm dwellings. By definition, all residential structures and residential land (except nonhousekeeping units such as hotels) are used in this sector. Factor input in this sector consists only of residential structures and land.[4] Consequently, changes in the output of this sector provide a direct measure of the contribution that residential capital and land have made to the growth of total real national income. A minor exception is that changes in the proportion of dwellings that are unoccupied have had a slight effect.

General government, households, institutions, and labor in the rest-of-the-world industry. The national income in current prices that originates in this sector is the compensation of the labor that is hired directly by final purchasers of the nation's output. It includes the compensation of (1) civilian and military employees of federal, state, and local governments (except government enterprises), including Ameri-

---

3. Factor-cost valuation is a little more convenient for analysis of productivity changes. The reason is that a mere shift in the

allocation of resources from a lightly taxed to a heavily taxed commodity (or from a subsidized to an unsubsidized one) raises the real product at market prices but leaves the product at factor cost unchanged if the earnings of resources are the same in all activities.

4. The small amount of labor employed in apartment houses is classified under nonresidential business.

cans but not foreigners that the federal government employs abroad; (2) domestic servants and baby-sitters employed by private households; (3) employees of nonprofit organizations that provide services to individuals; and (4) labor in the rest-of-the-world industry. The fourth component is very small and, for brevity, is omitted from the table stubs.[5] The national income in constant prices that originates in this sector is simply the value that is assigned to the "output" of the individuals employed in the sector. To obtain this value for each group of employees that is distinguished, the BEA extrapolates their compensation in 1972 by a series measuring the quantity of such labor that is used each year. Consequently, changes in the measured output of this sector result exclusively from changes in the quantity of labor that it uses, and directly measure the contribution of this labor to the growth of total real national income.

International assets. The national income originating in this sector consists of the excess of property income received by U.S. residents from abroad over the property income paid by U.S. residents to foreign residents.[6] This net inflow must be separately included because total national income is meant to measure the earnings of the factors of production that are supplied by residents of the United States, not earnings from production that takes place within the United States (as is the case with national income originating in the business sectors). When national income is viewed as an output measure, the addition of the inflow results in the inclusion of the value of production in foreign countries that is attributable to U.S. capital and the exclusion of the value of production within the United States that is attributable to foreign capital. After the publication of *Slower Growth,* the BEA estimates of the international flows of property income (and therefore of total national income) were much improved by the addition of reinvested earnings of incorporated affiliates of direct investors, the elimination (beginning only in 1978) of capital gains and losses, and the introduction of a better deflation procedure.

Based on averages of 1981 and 1982 data, nonresidential business contributed 75 percent of national income in both current and constant prices; the services of dwellings, 6 percent; general government, households, and institutions, 17 percent; and inter-national assets, 2 percent. Tables 2-5 through 2-8 show national income and employment by sector.

These and most other tables that show absolute numbers, as distinguished from indexes, exclude Alaska and Hawaii up to 1960 and include them thereafter. The data for 1960 are shown both ways. In the construction of indexes, such as those in table 3-1, the series are linked at 1960 so that the additional coverage does not raise the index. The same practice is followed in computing growth rates.

Data for 1940 and 1941 are shown both inclusive and exclusive of persons employed on government work relief programs and their compensation. The average compensation of these workers, and therefore their average measured output, was much below the average of other workers.

The BEA deflates imports by import prices and exports by export prices in obtaining national income and its other production measures in constant prices. Net exports in constant prices are then calculated by subtracting deflated imports from deflated exports. Changes in the terms of trade (the ratio of the export price index to the import price index) do not directly affect real national income because they are not viewed as altering U.S. production. Productivity changes, computed with national income as the numerator, consequently reflect only changes in the productivity of domestic resources. They are not directly affected by the terms of trade. A rise in import prices relative to export prices does reduce the quantity of foreign goods the country can purchase with the proceeds of any given quantity of exports. This effect is taken into account in a series that provides a measure of the *quantity of goods and services over which the nation has command as a result of its current production.* To obtain this series, net exports in constant prices are calculated by deflating *net* exports in current prices by import prices. When imports and exports are equal in current prices, they are also equal in constant prices, whereas they may take a large positive or negative value by the regular procedure. Command over goods and services is now published each quarter by the BEA.[7]

Employment. Employment is defined as the number of persons employed, full-time or part-time,

5. It includes compensation of U.S. citizens employed within the United States by foreign governments and international organizations and the amount by which the compensation of Americans employed abroad by U.S. business firms exceeds the compensation of foreign residents employed here by U.S. business firms.

6. Interest paid and received by the U.S. government is excluded from these income flows.

7. The command series I use is the counterpart to national income. The BEA also prepares command counterparts to gross and net national product at market prices. The command series, the geographic aspects of the concept of national income, the deflation of exports and imports, and the measurement of the net inflow of property income from abroad in current and constant prices are discussed in detail in Edward F. Denison, "International Transactions in Measures of the Nation's Production," *Survey of Current Business,* vol. 61 (May 1981), pp. 17–28.

during an average week. For maximum statistical consistency between the national income and employment series, the movement of the employment series is based mainly on estimates compiled by the BEA as part of the national income and product accounts. The BEA series is based mainly on establishment reports. Series so constructed initially measure jobs rather than people, but the level of my series has been adjusted to correspond to the average level of a count of employed persons rather than a count of jobs.[8] The series for *total and average hours* of employed persons attempt to measure hours "at work." Hours for which persons are paid when they are not at work are excluded, but the time they spend at the workplace without actually working is not eliminated. *National income per person employed* and *national income per hour at work* are the ratios of national income in constant prices to employment and total hours at work, respectively.

Total factor input. This series measures the combined amount of labor, capital, and land used in production; the various types of labor, capital, and land are weighted by their marginal products, as indicated by their earnings, to obtain a combined index. *Output per unit of input* measures the output obtained for each unit of input. These series are calculated for only two of the sectors, nonresidential business and the services of dwellings.[9] By method of measurement, the indexes of labor input, total factor input, and output are identical in the general government, households, and institutions sector, while the indexes of capital input, total factor input, and output are identical in the international assets sector; in neither of these sectors does measured output per unit of input change. Annual indexes of total factor input and output per unit of input, as such, are not shown for the economy as a whole, but the growth rates of total output in selected periods are divided between the two.

Concept of Potential Output

The concept of potential output and estimates of its size have been important ingredients of economic

analysis in the United States for decades.[10] They have entered into both discussions of economic stabilization—that is, the consideration of pressures toward unemployment or inflation, and policies for demand management—and analyses of long-term growth. Any serious investigation of changes in output, whether focused on business cycles or growth, must separate changes in the economy's capacity to produce from changes in the extent to which that capacity is used. High and fluctuating unemployment in the last fifteen years has made the separation even more vital than at any time since the 1930s. The present book stresses changes in output and input that are calculated on a potential basis. For this reason, and because the concept of potential output has been given various meanings in recent years, it is necessary to review my own use of the term and my derivation of the estimates.

Potential output was originally considered, in a general way, to be the largest output that could be obtained without inflation. But such a definition was acceptable only if it implied low unemployment because, more fundamentally, potential output was considered a measure of what output would be if the economy were using its supply capabilities fully. Indeed, the term "output at high employment" was often used as a synonym. Potential output was also regarded as a desirable level of output that provided a suitable target for fiscal and monetary policy.[11]

One output level could satisfy all these meanings only in the presence of a beneficent Phillips curve that equated price stability with low unemployment.[12] In the 1950s and 1960s such a curve was implicitly assumed. Thus potential output was envis-

---

8. A problem arises because the ratio of the number enumerated in the Census of Population to the true population was apparently higher in 1980 than in 1970. My resolution is described in "Derivations."

9. In the services of dwellings sector, the index of total factor input is the same as that of "sector national income at constant (1972) occupancy ratio," and the index of output per unit of input is the same as that of "effects of changes in occupancy ratio," both shown in table 6-4.

10. I have discussed potential output more fully not only in *Slower Growth* and *Accounting for Growth* (which provides the most complete discussion of my methods of estimation, subject to slight amendment in *Slower Growth* and the "Derivations" section of the present book), but also in Edward F. Denison, "Changes in the Concept and Measurement of Potential Output in the United States of America," which appears in the Festschrift für Rolf Krengel, entitled *Empirische Wirtschaftsforschung: Konzeptionen, Verfahren und Ergebnisse*, Joachim Frohn and Reiner Stäglin, eds. (Berlin: Duncker and Humblot, 1980) (Brookings Reprint 367). The latter includes a history of potential output measurement by the federal government.

11. Potential output came to have special significance with respect to the budget of the federal government because the government surplus or deficit that would emerge at potential output became a guide to interpretation and formulation of fiscal policy.

12. The Phillips curve (named for A. W. Phillips, who presented it in a November 1958 article in *Economica*) connected points on a scatter diagram for the United Kingdom that related the unemployment rate to the rate of change in money wage rates (which, in turn, was thought to govern the rate of price change). To make all the concepts of potential output consistent, there would have to have been a stable Phillips curve, and on the curve

aged as a desirable level of production that would be consistent with low unemployment and price stability. Higher output would cause inflation, while lower output would result in excessive unemployment.

The conditions determining the appropriate level of unemployment were not precisely formulated. Some regarded unemployment present under potential conditions as consisting of types of unemployment that would not be reduced much by stronger demand—at least not quickly and without exerting strong upward pressure on wages and prices. Included in such unemployment were persons who had recently entered or reentered the labor force, or quit their jobs, for the duration of the period normally required to find a satisfactory new position; those seasonally unemployed; those "structurally" unemployed in depressed areas or displaced from declining industries or occupations; and those frictionally unemployed for other reasons. Others regarded the unemployment rate corresponding to potential conditions as simply a rate low enough to be generally acceptable. The president's Council of Economic Advisers (CEA), which became the custodian of the government series for potential output, considered potential output to be the output that would be obtained if 4 percent of the civilian labor force were unemployed.

Price stability was not closely defined either. Often price increases of 1 or even 2 percent a year were considered to qualify as price stability. From 1951 to 1965 annual increases averaged 1.4 percent in the consumer price index, 0.4 percent in the producers' price index, and 1.9 percent in the implicit deflator for gross national product (GNP). Meanwhile, unemployment was above 4 percent most of the time, and from 1958 to 1965 it was continuously in the 4.5 to 6.8 percent range. Although there never was a showing that 4 percent unemployment was consistent with truly stable prices, and the record just summarized indicates it was not, any inconsistency was not sufficiently glaring to make the concept of potential output a major problem up to 1965. From 1966 to 1969 price increases broke above the range that could conceivably be described as price stability, but in this period unemployment was below 4 percent, and demand was clearly excessive. It was not until the 1970s that large price increases and unemployment rates well above 4 percent occurred together.

4 percent (or less) unemployment would have had to correspond (approximately) to a change in average hourly earnings that equaled the change in output per hour (assuming the labor share of national income to be constant).

The 1970s and 1980s created confusion in the use of the term "potential output" because one series of numbers could no longer have all the old meanings and serve all the old purposes. Different users retained the meaning that appealed to them, but discussion sometimes proceeded as if everyone still had the same meaning in mind.

Definition of Potential Output

Before discussing this dilemma, I repeat my own definition of potential output, which adheres to the 4 percent criterion but is more precise.

I define potential national income in 1972 prices in any year as the value that national income in 1972 prices would have taken if (1) unemployment had been at 4 percent of the civilian labor force sixteen years of age and over; (2) the intensity of utilization of resources that were in use had been at the same rate every year, namely, that which on the average would be associated with a 4 percent unemployment rate; and (3) other conditions had been those that actually prevailed in that year. The term "on the average" in the second part of the definition refers to the average of a hypothetical random sample of years in which unemployment is 4 percent but output is changing by amounts larger than, the same as, or smaller than the trend rate of change at the time.

I stress that the specification of an unemployment rate, as in the first part of this definition, is insufficient to define potential output. The second part—which refers to the relationship between the strength of demand, intensity of utilization, and productivity—is essential because the output that is obtained per unit of labor, capital, and land in use is greatly affected by the *rate of change* in output as well as by the *level* of unemployment or output. At any unemployment rate productivity is usually much higher, relative to its trend, when output is rising rapidly than when it is stable or falling. However, the pattern is complex. The third part of my definition means that the weather, labor disputes, the size of the armed forces, and all other conditions except demand are taken to be the same under potential conditions as under actual conditions. Many determinants of output are subject to erratic changes that are neither the consequences of changes in demand nor controllable by macroeconomic policy. I regard these determinants as affecting both actual and potential output, not the difference between them. This is so even though many determinants of output not only move erratically but also might have been different if the history of business cycles and wars had been different.

Capital stock, an important output determinant, requires special mention in this context because investment moves with the business cycle. The estimates of potential output that I present for each year are based on the capital stock that actually existed that year, not the stock that might have existed if investment had been different in previous periods (either the preceding years of the same business cycle or unusual periods such as the Depression of the 1930s).

I obtain potential national income each year by adjusting actual national income to take account of the differences between actual and potential conditions (tables 2-4, 8-7, and L-5). There are two main components of this adjustment.

The first eliminates the effect of fluctuations in intensity of demand upon output per unit of input in nonresidential business. The objective is to obtain the output that the resources measured as actually in use would have produced under standardized demand conditions corresponding to the definition of potential output.

The second component measures the effect on output of the difference between actual and potential labor input. The calculation is a refined one that takes account of not only the difference between actual and potential employment, but also (separately for employed persons and persons making up the difference between actual and potential employment) the division of workers of each sex between full-time and part-time, the difference between actual and potential hours for each group, the age, sex, and education of workers, and the percentage allocation of workers among sectors of the economy. Only the labor component of total input must be changed in moving from actual to potential output, because my series for other inputs refer to capital and land available for business use, while the effects of demand-related changes in their actual utilization are included in the first adjustment.

The simplifying assumption is made that if the unemployment rate had been 4 percent rather than its actual rate, the entire difference in employment would have appeared among nonfarm wage and salary workers in the business sector. This assumption is satisfactory because farm employment, employment of nonfarm proprietors and unpaid family workers, employment in general government, and even employment in households and institutions are not, in fact, much affected by short-term changes in the strength of total demand. In addition, a moderate error in the assumption adopted would have little effect on the results for the whole economy because

of offsets. The assumption is modified in 1940–41 with respect to persons employed on government work relief programs, because there would have been no work relief programs if unemployment had been at 4 percent. In the adjustment of actual national income to a potential basis, the value of the output of work relief workers is therefore first eliminated from general government national income. In deriving potential output in nonresidential business, these workers are then treated as if they had been unemployed (except in the estimation of the labor force response to unemployment).

Weighted Unemployment Standard Not Used

In 1970–71 two important articles by George L. Perry pointed out that unemployment and the gap between the actual and the potential labor force were concentrated among women and teenagers more than had been the case in the 1950s.[13] When employed, these groups work shorter average hours and earn less per hour than adult males, an indication that on average their marginal products are lower. Consequently, if the unemployment rate had been only as high in 1971 as in 1955, the proportion of labor input that was not in use would have been lower in 1971. Using earnings as weights to combine demographic groups, Perry computed a ratio of actual to potential labor input. He proposed that the standard for potential output should not be 4 percent unemployment in all years, but a constant ratio of actual to potential labor input, with the level of the ratio being set to correspond to a 4 percent unemployment rate in the mid-1950s. Perry also constructed a potential output series that conformed to this proposal. The effect in the late 1960s and the 1970s was to raise the unemployment rate that he considered to correspond to potential output and to lower the estimate of potential output accordingly.

The CEA incorporated the Perry suggestion into its estimates beginning in January 1977. In its January 1979 annual report the CEA used 5.1 percent as the potential unemployment rate in each of the years from 1975 through 1978. The main justification for the change was the belief, correct in itself, that the weighted unemployment rate provides a better measure of the tightness of labor markets than the simple unemployment rate. But tightness of labor markets never has been a criterion for CEA estimates of potential output, and substitution of the new measure

13. George L. Perry, "Changing Labor Markets and Inflation," *Brookings Papers on Economic Activity*, 3:1970, pp. 411–41 (hereafter *BPEA*), and "Labor Force Structure, Potential Output, and Productivity," *BPEA*, 3:1971, pp. 533–65.

for unemployment does not reconcile labor market tightness and price stability. With unemployment rates far above even the new higher CEA standard, inflation greatly exceeded both the acceptable range and previous experience. Use of the weighted unemployment rate to define potential output does not make it possible to regard potential output as consistent with price stability, or even as being much closer to consistency with price stability than if the unweighted unemployment measure is retained.

I have not myself adopted the weighted unemployment rate, because I think the loss in simplicity of definition and analysis outweighs any gain. But it is a close choice, and I do not criticize use of the weighted measure. Moreover, my preference is conditioned by the view expressed below concerning the meaning to be attached to potential output in the future. In any case the composition of unemployment relative to that of employment has moved back toward the relationship prevailing in the early 1950s.

Present Meaning of Potential Output

Almost no one believes that after 1973 an unemployment rate of 4.0 percent or 5.1 percent would have been consistent with price stability.

Faced with the incompatibility of high employment and price stability, some economists chose to retain price behavior as a criterion for potential output and to discard low unemployment. However, none attempted to measure potential output as the largest output obtainable with price stability. Such a figure may not even have existed, and if it did exist, it was so small and implied so high an unemployment rate as to be uninteresting as either a goal or an analytical tool. Instead, this group of economists introduced a wholly new criterion, regarding potential unemployment as the unemployment that would not change the "present" rate of inflation, whatever that rate might be, and potential output as the output consistent with that unemployment rate.[14]

Since potential price change is the same as actual price change by this definition, it might seem that potential values of output and unemployment should also be equal to actual values. The estimates provided

by adherents of this definition did sometimes have a tendency to equal actual values. But they were not identical, because adherents of this definition seem to have introduced a second innovation in the potential output concept: they had the underlying rate of inflation rather than the actual rate in mind. They attempted to examine conditions (notably, labor markets) considered pertinent to the underlying rate of price change and to eliminate the effect on price of erratic factors such as changes in farm prices and OPEC oil prices.

After 1973 the rate of inflation fluctuated so widely and with so little direct correspondence to the unemployment rate that one might have expected to find similar wide fluctuations in potential output and unemployment when they were defined as the output and unemployment that would keep the present inflation rate unchanged. One might also have expected the estimates to have been highly sensitive to the interpretation of "present"—did it mean this year, this quarter, or this month? Adherents of this definition apparently saw the matter differently. Their model seems to have been an economy in which, if a 7 percent unemployment rate would keep this year's 10 percent inflation rate constant, it would also keep next year's 6 percent or the following year's 12 percent inflation rate constant. Hence they did not envisage potential output and employment as a highly jumpy series. The series conforming to this definition estimated by Jeffrey Perloff and Michael L. Wachter were quite smooth.[15]

The definition based on stable inflation had little resemblance to either the original idea of potential output as the highest output consistent with price stability or the commonsense meaning attached to the words, which was related to supply possibilities and high employment. It was related to only one of the uses to which potential output is put—to serve as an objective of policy—and even this use must be modified, because adherents of this definition tended to advocate as a target not potential values themselves, but an unemployment rate moderately above, and output moderately below, the potential rates as defined.[16] Their hope was that adherence to this target would gradually reduce the rate of inflation associated with a particular unemployment rate and even-

14. See Phillip Cagan, "The Reduction of Inflation and the Magnitude of Unemployment," and William Fellner, "Guide to the Volume," both in *Contemporary Economic Problems, 1977* (Washington, D.C.: American Enterprise Institute for Public Policy Research, 1977); and Phillip Cagan, "The Reduction of Inflation by Slack Demand," and William Fellner, "The Core of the Controversy about Reducing Inflation," both in *Contemporary Economic Problems, 1978* (Washington, D.C.: American Enterprise Institute for Public Policy Research, 1978).

15. Jeffrey Perloff and Michael L. Wachter, "A Production Function-Nonaccelerating Inflation Approach to Potential Output: Is Measured Potential Output Too High?" Center for the Study of Organizational Innovation, University of Pennsylvania, revised July 1978, charts 6.5 and 6.6.

16. In 1977 Cagan described the objective as something between "very mild restraint" and "the opposite extreme." See Cagan, "The Reduction of Inflation."

tually restore conditions in which an acceptable rate of inflation would be compatible with low unemployment.

Stable inflation does not provide the basis for a useful time series. Given the erratic relationship that has prevailed between the unemployment rate and price changes, a series that really reflected the requirements of stable inflation would be too volatile to be useful if it were accurately estimated, and in any case there is no way to estimate it accurately. However, there is no need for such a time series. This statement is not meant to deny the usefulness of simply asking what levels of unemployment and output in the period immediately ahead would maintain the present rate of inflation unchanged. But answering this question does not require a time series, and such appraisals should not be identified as potential output or confused with the more common meaning of that term.

The CEA, and probably most other organizations and economists, continued to define potential output in terms of the economy's ability to produce. The January 1977 CEA report, the last by President Gerald R. Ford's council, states: "Potential GNP is a measure of the aggregate supply capability of the economy, or the amount of output that could be expected at full employment. More precisely, potential GNP is the output the economy could produce with the existing technology under assumed conditions of high but sustainable utilization of the factors of production—labor, capital, and natural resources. It does not represent the absolute maximum level of production that could be generated by wartime or other abnormal levels of aggregate demand, but rather that which could be expected from high utilization rates obtainable under more normal circumstances."[17] The description, it is to be noted, makes no reference to prices.

Two years later, President Jimmy Carter's CEA stated: "Potential GNP is defined as the level of real output that the economy could produce at high rates of resource utilization."[18] Again, in the definition of potential output there is no reference to prices.[19]

I agree with this definition. To analyze either economic growth or business fluctuations, a measure of potential output based on supply capability at high employment is needed. I urge that the term potential output be confined to such series. Prices should not enter its definition.[20] But when such series are presented, it must be made clear, as I now stress, that no particular price behavior is assumed or implied and that the validity of the estimates does not depend on their implications for prices. The unemployment criterion for such a potential output series ought conceptually to be the amount of seasonal, structural, and frictional unemployment that is present, but as a simplification I retain the customary (and higher) 4 percent unemployment rate.

The value of potential output each year does not necessarily represent a short-term target for demand management policy, and this point, too, should be clearly understood. Most economists consider it desirable at present to operate the economy below its potential output, thus defined, in order to moderate inflation and to facilitate the growth of potential output itself. Potential output retains normative significance only in the long run. A long-term goal must be price behavior that permits the economy once more to operate at the potential level. The amount by which actual output falls below potential output remains a measure of policy failure, but in a new sense. This gap measures not only failures of short-term demand management or stabilization policy, but also failure to establish conditions under which the economy can utilize its productive potential and still enjoy price stability.

This conclusion is, indeed, accepted by the federal government. As stated by President Ronald W. Reagan's CEA in its February 1984 report: "A central economic goal of the Congress, as indicated by the title 'Full Employment and Balanced Growth Act,'

17. *Economic Report of the President Together with the Annual Report of the Council of Economic Advisers, January 1977*, p. 52.
18. *Economic Report of the President Together with the Annual Report of the Council of Economic Advisers, January 1979*, p. 72.
19. This time, however, the report continues: "The *level* of potential output is less meaningful than its *rate of growth*. The latter gives the best estimate of how much the economy can actually grow over the next few years without putting additional pressure on labor or product markets." The last sentence clearly hints at the idea of potential output as output that would not raise

the rate of inflation. It illustrates a terminological confusion, or perhaps a deliberately ambiguous use of language, that became widespread. It was still common to refer to potential output as if there were one potential output figure that could serve all the old purposes, either as they were originally envisaged or, as in this example, if the price standard were amended to refer to stable inflation rather than stable prices. This practice gave rise to confusion and to pointless argument. Stable inflation is different from price stability and both are different standards than high employment. In the 1970s and early 1980s stable inflation probably required an unemployment rate well above the limit to which the high employment or aggregate supply capability criterion could be stretched, even if Perry's weighted unemployment concept were adopted. Certainly the two criteria could yield the same figure only by chance, and this statement applies to rates of change as well as to levels.
20. Terms such as "output at the natural rate of unemployment" are available to identify concepts that incorporate price.

was and is the achievement of full employment. That goal is also a high priority for this administration.''[21] The report notes: ''The Balanced Growth Act set a goal that unemployment not exceed . . . 4 percent among individuals aged 16 and over, by 1983. The act also set an inflation goal of 3 percent by 1983 and zero by 1988, *provided that achieving the inflation goal did not impede achieving the unemployment goal*. Finally, the act provided that the President could, if he deemed necessary, recommend modification of the timetables for reaching these goals.''[22]

21. *Economic Report of the President Together with the Annual Report of the Council of Economic Advisers, February 1984*, p. 201.
22. *Ibid.*, p. 202. Emphasis added.

The definition of potential output used in the present study and its two predecessors makes it possible to distinguish changes in the economy's capacity to produce from changes in the extent to which it uses that capacity. The definition is satisfactory for this purpose. Substitution of a different constant unemployment rate for 4 percent in the definition of potential national income would have almost no effect on the analysis of growth and its sources. A change of 1 percentage point in either direction in the unemployment rate used in the definition would change the level of potential national income by about 1.8 percent in the opposite direction and the level of potential GNP (which is shown in table 8-7 to facilitate comparisons with other estimates) by about 1.6 percent.

CHAPTER ONE

-»»<«<-

The Record of Output and Productivity

-»»<«<-

Growth of United States national income fell off sharply after 1973 and even more, it appears, after 1979. This is reason for serious concern because national income measures the output that our economy makes available each year for private consumption, for public consumption including provision for education and national security, and for additions to the capital stock. Expenditures for one or more of these purposes must be curtailed when there is less output to be distributed, and in practice all are likely to be reduced.

To be sure, there would be no reason for criticism or complaint if slow growth had been caused by a decision of the American people, made freely and with knowledge of its consequences, to devote less time to work and more to leisure, or to consume more of their income immediately and save less. But this description does not apply to the situation following 1973. Not since the World War II years has the total time spent at work increased as rapidly as it did from 1973 to 1979, and it was involuntary unemployment rather than free choice that caused a decline in total working time later on. The nation's saving did not decline until the 1980s, and even then it was a huge undesired government deficit, not decisions by individuals and businesses, that was responsible. The growth slowdown after 1973 was caused mainly by two developments that were neither desirable nor desired. First, the persistent increase that business firms had experienced historically in their output per unit of labor, capital, and land input nearly stopped from 1973 to 1979 and then turned into a decrease. Second, the proportion of the

resources available to the nation that was actually used in production fell. These two developments will be quantified later in this chapter. Although it is also true that the country adopted social programs that required the sacrifice of some growth to advance other objectives, these programs account for only a small part of the slowdown.

Identification of Time Periods

The first year covered by the growth data is 1929. It was the last year before the Great Depression. From 1925 to 1929 actual national income had risen an average of 3.2 percent a year, and the growth rate of potential national income may not have been much different.

The more than one-half century since 1929 must be condensed into a manageable number of periods if past growth and its sources are to be described without exhausting the reader. In addition to the whole 1929–82 time span covered by the analysis, I distinguish three long periods that are further subdivided into seven shorter periods, as described below. Growth rates of potential and actual national income in the whole economy and in nonresidential business, and growth rates of corresponding series for national income per person employed and national income per hour at work, are shown in table 2-9 for all periods distinguished.

Economic history from 1929 to 1948 was dominated by depression and war, and this situation dictates both the separation of the 1929–48 period from later years and its subdivision into two shorter periods: 1929–41, spanning the years of the Great Depression, and 1941–48, spanning the years of U.S. participation in World War II and the immediate postwar reconversion. From 1929 to 1948, my first long period, the growth rate of potential national income was 2.6 percent, with rates of 2.4 percent in 1929–41 and 2.9 percent in 1941–48.

My second long period is 1948–73, when the growth rate of potential national income was 3.9 percent. What gives this period homogeneity is a sustained high rate of growth of productivity computed on a potential basis, whether measured by output per person employed, output per hour, or output per unit of input, both in the economy as a whole and in nonresidential business. Particularly striking is the stability of the rate of growth of an index that measures the effect of advances in knowledge and changes in miscellaneous determinants (output determinants that are not separately measured) upon output per unit of input in nonresidential business (column 12 of tables 5-1 and 5-3). This series is calculated as a residual by eliminating from output per unit of input the effects of several conditions (which are detailed in the next chapter) that are beyond the control of individual firms. This series for "residual productivity" comes closest to providing a measure of the changes in productivity that result from new knowledge of how to produce at low cost, together with changes in firms' internal efficiency. Residual productivity rose 1.4 percent a year from 1948 to 1973, with little variation in the rate.

The period 1948 to 1973, a quarter-century, is divided into three shorter periods: 1948–53, 1953–64, and 1964–73. The first and last periods, when growth of potential national income was very fast, are separated by a period of less growth. Growth rates of potential output were 4.8 percent in 1948–53, 3.2 percent in 1953–64, and 4.3 percent in 1964–73.[1] Differences between these periods largely mirror differences in the rates of growth of total input, although components of output per unit of input other than residual efficiency also contributed to the high 1948–53 growth rate.

A fundamental change in the pattern of growth after 1973 marks the beginning of a third long period that was still continuing at the latest date for which information is available. Deterioration of productivity growth is its main characteristic. There was also a less pronounced lowering of the growth rate of total output. The annual productivity data unequivocally mark 1973 as the dividing point between the second and third long periods. While potential employment and other input measures grew much more rapidly in 1973–82 than in 1948–73, the growth rate of potential national income per person potentially employed fell from 2.3 percent a year to a mere 0.2 percent. Growth rates of other productivity measures showed similarly dramatic drops.

The near cessation of productivity growth after 1973 provided my main theme in 1977 when I was writing *Slower Growth*. The situation would be more serious today than in 1977 even if continuation of poor performance for a full decade had been the only subsequent development, for the annual losses in output would have swollen as each year of slow

growth passed. Moreover, the passage of additional time without any improvement progressively strengthened the case for believing that the causes of the slowdown, whatever they might be, were deep-seated and resistant to improvement, rather than reflections of some transitory development that would quickly be reversed, perhaps even permitting the lost ground to be made up. In the years after *Slower Growth* was written, I often described the adverse implications of the lengthening period of slowdown.

The present study presents a still darker picture. It indicates that since 1979 output and productivity performance has deteriorated further, even on a potential basis. From 1973–79 to 1979–82 the growth rate of total potential national income fell from 3.0 percent to 1.8 percent, that of potential national income per person potentially employed from 0.5 percent to − 0.3 percent, and that of potential national income per potential hour at work from 1.1 percent to 0.2 percent. The declines in the comparable rates for nonresidential business are similar. The declines in all "actual" rates are bigger.

It is true that I have myself regarded three years as the shortest period from which it is possible to detect a change in trend, and 1979–82 only barely meets this test. Moreover, the possibility of error in deriving potential output from actual output is maximized by the fact that whereas 1979 was a business cycle peak, 1982 was an exceptionally deep trough. And for such recent years there is a possibility of significant revisions in actual national income or in the data used to derive potential output from actual output. These considerations suggest the need for caution in concluding that a second growth decline occurred. It is possible that, when looking back from the perspective of some later year, the two subperiods may seem less distinct.

On the other hand, the reductions in growth rates are big. They are also consistent: in every year of the later period the percentage increase in potential national income fell below the 1973–79 growth rate. Further, a preliminary estimate of potential national income for 1983 (based in part on a shortcut method) yields about the same growth rate for 1979–83 as for 1979–82. As the data stand, they compel me to divide the years after 1973 into two short periods, 1973–79 and an unfinished period from 1979 to 1982 or, where data permit, 1983. Without such a division it is not possible to describe accurately the events portrayed by the data for the years after 1973.[2] I regard it as a

---

1. I formerly recognized 1964–69 and 1969–73 as separate periods, the former having a somewhat higher growth rate. However, relative to other periods, rates of potential output growth were high in both 1964–69 (4.6 percent) and 1969–73 (3.9 percent). On a potential basis, output per person and output per hour in nonresidential business also grew faster in 1964–69 than in 1969–73, but output per unit of input grew at almost the same rate, and residual productivity grew a little less. The two time spans are combined in the present study in the interest of restricting the number of periods and, when possible, avoiding very short periods.

2. Not only growth rates but also their division among the sources of growth changed from 1973–79 to 1979–82.

dismal probability, although not a certainty, that the second slowdown is a reality.

A Comparison of the 1948–73 Period with 1973–79 and 1979–82

I turn now to a more systematic description of recent changes in economic growth and related series. Table 1-1 compares selected growth rates in 1948–73, 1973–79, 1979–82, and, when preliminary 1983 estimates are available, 1979–83. Rates for the longer 1973–82 period are also shown.

Growth of Potential Output in the Whole Economy

Potential national income measures the underlying growth trend and provides an appropriate starting point for this description. Its growth rate is not affected by the cyclical position of the economy in the particular years compared.

The 3.9 percent growth rate of potential output from 1948 to 1973 was high by U.S. historical standards and, indeed, by those of other countries before World War II.[3] Even before 1973 the higher current growth rates achieved by industrial countries with lower *levels* of productivity than the United States gave rise to complaints that our growth rate was unsatisfactory, but my own studies of the reasons for growth rate differences do not support the complaint. Instead, they indicate that the differences in the conditions under which growth was taking place, mostly related to the stage of development, were responsible for faster growth abroad. In no meaningful sense was higher growth in other countries the result of their doing more than we to achieve growth.[4]

Our 3.9 percent growth rate in 1948–73 was achieved by a 1.6 percent growth rate of potential employment and a 2.3 percent growth rate of potential national income per person potentially employed. All these rates exceeded those in the preceding long period, 1929–48, when potential output grew 2.6 percent a year, potential employment 1.3 percent, and potential national income per person potentially employed 1.2 percent.

3. In the immediate postwar period 3 percent was widely accepted as the long-term U.S. growth rate achieved in the past and foreseeable for the long-term future. It is curious that the rate for potential national income has fallen back to 3.2 percent when computed over the whole 1929–82 period and the rate for actual national income to 2.9 percent.

4. See Denison, *Why Growth Rates Differ,* especially pp. 342–45; and Denison and Chung, *How Japan's Economy Grew So Fast.*

The growth rate of total potential output fell by nearly one-fourth from 1948–73 to 1973–79, or from 3.9 percent to 3.0 percent. Although large, the drop left this growth rate at what had formerly been thought to represent normal long-term growth. More startling is the fact that the growth of potential output fell off at the same time that the growth of potential employment jumped from 1.6 percent to an almost unprecedentedly high 2.5 percent. Growth of potential output per person potentially employed fell by nearly four-fifths, from a rate of 2.3 percent in 1948–73 to 0.5 percent in 1973–79. Similarly, when also measured on a potential basis, the growth rate of total hours at work rose from 1.1 percent to 1.9 percent, while that of output per hour fell from 2.8 percent to 1.1 percent. The growth rates of potential output per person and potential output per hour were, respectively, only two-fifths and one-half as high as they had been even in the low-growth period from 1929 to 1948.

Even while analysts were trying to establish the reasons for the collapse of productivity growth, and while many observers were anticipating that growth would recover and perhaps even make up the ground that had been lost, the situation deteriorated further. The growth rate of total potential output fell from 3.0 percent in 1973–79 to 1.8 percent in 1979–82 (and 1.7 percent in 1979–83). The growth rate of potential employment receded from 2.5 percent in 1973–79 to a still very high 2.1 percent in 1979–82 (1.7 percent in 1979–83), and that of total potential hours at work from 1.9 percent to 1.6 percent. But again, the more striking changes were in productivity. From 1979 to 1982 potential output per person actually declined, and even potential output per hour barely more than held its own. The growth rate of potential output per person fell from 0.5 percent in 1973–79 to −0.3 percent in 1979–82 (0.0 percent in 1979–83), and that of potential output per hour from 1.1 percent to 0.2 percent.

Growth of Actual Output in the Whole Economy

Although 1948, 1973, and 1979 all qualify as business cycle peaks if unemployment is used as an indicator, the unemployment rate was higher and employed resources were used less intensively in 1973 than in 1948, and in 1979 than in 1973. Actual national income exceeded potential national income by 1.2 percent in 1948 but fell below potential by 3.2 percent in 1973 and by 5.5 percent in 1979 (table 2-4). Hence, the growth rate of output was lower on an actual than on a potential basis both in 1948–73 and

Table 1-1. 1948–73 Growth Rates Compared with Later Periods, Selected Series[a]

Percent a year

Item	1948–73	1973–79	1979–82	1979–83[b]	1973–82
			Whole economy		
Series referring to potential conditions					
1. Potential national income	3.89	3.01	1.82	1.74	2.61
2. Potential employment	1.59	2.50	2.11	1.73	2.37
3. Potential national income per person potentially employed	2.26	0.49	−0.28	0.00	0.23
4. Total potential hours at work	1.07	1.90	1.62	n.a.	1.81
5. Potential national income per potential hour at work	2.79	1.09	0.19	n.a.	0.79
Series referring to actual conditions					
6. National income	3.70	2.61	−0.54	0.41	1.55
7. Employment	1.51	2.25	−0.01	0.08	1.49
8. National income per person employed	2.16	0.36	−0.54	0.22	0.06
9. Total hours at work	0.97	1.62	−0.83	n.a.	0.79
10. National income per hour at work	2.70	0.98	0.28	n.a.	0.75
11. Command over goods and services (national income basis)	3.70	2.25	−0.32	0.73	1.39
12. Command per person employed	2.15	0.00	−0.31	0.54	−0.10
13. Population	1.46	1.01	1.03	1.03	1.02
14. National income per capita	2.21	1.59	−1.55	−0.62	0.53
15. Command per capita	2.20	1.23	−1.33	−0.30	0.37
16. Personal consumption expenditures per capita	2.15	2.17	0.47	1.09	1.59
17. Implicit price deflator for GNP	2.80	7.52	8.18	7.14	7.79
			Nonresidential business		
Series referring to potential conditions					
18. Potential national income	3.82	3.02	1.94	1.91	2.66
19. Potential employment	1.21	2.75	2.50	n.a.	2.66
20. Potential national income per person potentially employed	2.59	0.27	−0.55	n.a.	0.00
21. Total potential hours at work	0.73	2.08	1.91	n.a.	2.02
22. Potential national income per potential hour at work	3.08	0.93	0.03	n.a.	0.63
Series referring to actual conditions					
23. National income	3.58	2.50	−1.18	0.17	1.26
24. Employment	1.10	2.42	−0.25	n.a.	1.52
25. National income per person employed	2.45	0.08	−0.93	n.a.	−0.26
26. Total hours at work	0.60	1.72	−1.18	−0.43	0.74
27. National income per hour at work	2.96	0.77	0.00	0.60	0.51
28. Input of reproducible capital	3.71	3.65	3.06	2.74	3.45
29. Residual efficiency	1.38	0.28	−0.75	n.a.	−0.07

Sources: Rows 1, 3, 5, 6, 8, 10, 18, 20, 22, 23, 25, 27, table 2-9; rows 2 and 4, computed from table 2-8; rows 7, 9, 11, 12, 13, and 15, computed from table 2-1; row 14, computed from table 2-2; row 16, computed from table 2-1 and national income and product accounts (NIPA), table 2.5; row 17, computed from NIPA, table 7.1; rows 19, 21, 24, and 26, table 3-4; row 28, table 4-7; row 29, table 5-3.

n.a. Not available.

a. Growth rates of series based on value are computed from data expressed in constant (1972) prices.

b. The 1979–83 growth rates use 1983 estimates that are based, in part, on shortcut procedures. The NIPA data used are from the July 1984 issue of the *Survey of Current Business* and are not precisely comparable to the 1982 data from the July 1983 issue that were used to compute 1979–82 rates.

in 1973–79, and growth rates of actual employment and total hours were also below corresponding rates computed on a potential basis. However, the changes in actual growth rates from the earlier to the later of these periods were rather similar to changes in the growth rates of potential. The growth rate of actual national income fell by 1.1 percentage points, the rates of actual employment and hours at work rose by 0.7 and 0.6 percentage points, respectively, and those of output per person employed and output per hour fell by 1.8 and 1.7 percentage points, respectively.

Most series for the present unfinished period end with 1982, a business cycle trough, when the unemployment rate was 9.7 percent of the civilian labor force—the highest since before World War II—and actual output was 11.9 percent below potential. In 1983, for which some estimates are available, the unemployment rate was still 9.6 percent, and actual output was still 10.3 percent below potential. Consequently, the 1979–82 and 1979–83 growth rates of output, employment, and total hours were far lower, and declines from 1973–79 rates were much bigger, on an actual than on a potential basis.

National income, national income per person employed, and total hours at work were actually smaller in 1982 than in 1979, employment was the same, and output per hour was only slightly higher. The growth rate of total actual national income was −0.5 percent in 1979–82; it rises, but only to 1.9 percent, if this period is extended to include the brisk cyclical recovery up to the first quarter of 1985. The preceding sentences make clear the sensitivity of "actual" growth rates to the exact dates compared, but also give an initial hint of the profligacy with which we have been wasting our resources by failing to use them.

The extent of this waste is conveyed better by period averages for the ratio of actual to potential output. From 1948 through 1969 actual national income averaged 99.1 percent of potential national income. The subsequent decline in this percentage is shocking. From 1970 through 1973 the average fell to 95.8 percent, from 1974 through 1979 to 93.5 percent, and from 1980 through 1983 to 90.2 percent. Actual national income had exceeded potential national income in ten of the twenty-two years from 1948 through 1969 but never came within 3 percent of potential after 1969 or within 8 percent from 1980 through 1983.

This increasing gap between actual and potential output accompanied, and to a considerable extent was a consequence of, rising inflation. The average

annual rate of increase in the implicit deflator for GNP was 2.4 percent in 1948–69, 5.1 percent in 1969–73, 7.5 percent in 1973–79, and 8.2 percent in 1979–82. (With the inclusion of much smaller subsequent increases, the annual average from 1979 to the first quarter of 1985 was 6.2 percent.)[5]

Among the many consequences of increased inflation, two affected the ratio of actual to potential output. First, policymakers became persuaded, at least intermittently, that it was desirable to hold actual output below potential output in order to restrain inflation. (Sometimes the aim was to prevent accelerating inflation, at other times to reduce an existing inflation rate.) Second, inflation helped to make it more difficult to formulate and coordinate policies that would attain any desired ratio of actual to potential output and even to judge where the economy stood and was heading. It seems certain that since 1969 policymakers have, on average, aimed at lower rates of output than they would have in the absence of increased inflation and that, on average, the ratio of actual to potential output that was achieved fell even below policymakers' targets. Admittedly, to reach any such judgment one must try to penetrate a fog of verbiage that often obscures goals and policies. Nor do I mean to suggest that escalating inflation has been the only reason for greater underutilization.

From 1948–73 to 1973–79, the nation's command over goods and services resulting from current production fared even worse than current production itself (national income) because the terms of trade in the later period deteriorated as a result of higher prices for oil imports. As previously indicated, the growth rate of actual national income per person employed fell from 2.16 percent in 1948–73 to 0.36 percent in 1973–79.[6] The growth rate of command per person employed fell from 2.15 percent to 0.00 percent.

Two developments cushioned the impact that this drop had on per capita personal consumption expenditures. First, whereas the growth rate of employment rose strongly from 1948–73 to 1973–79,

5. I use the GNP deflator because of its familiarity to readers and the unavailability until 1959 of the fixed weighted price index for GNP, a superior price measure. Changes in the implicit price deflator for national income are very close to those in the GNP deflator over the periods cited.

6. Indexes and growth rates are usually shown rounded to 2 decimal points in the tables of this study because additional rounding would prevent calculating accurately the differences between periods, or reclassifying or combining growth sources whose contributions are small. Henceforth, the same rounding practice is usually followed in the text. No implication as to margins of error in the estimates should be inferred.

that of total population fell from 1.46 percent to 1.01 percent. Second, the share of personal consumption expenditures in real net national product, which had fallen from 1948 to 1973, rose from 1973 to 1979. As a consequence, the growth rate of personal consumption expenditures per capita actually increased a trifle, from 2.15 percent in 1948–73 to 2.17 percent in 1973–79. Thus, remarkably, there was no retardation in this measure of consumer welfare up to 1979, despite the retardation of productivity growth, the increase in unused resources, and the deterioration in the terms of trade.

From 1973–79 to 1979–82, when the growth rate of actual national income per person employed fell from 0.36 percent to − 0.54 percent, these relationships were quite different. The terms of trade turned in favor of the United States, and the growth rate of command per person employed fell only from 0.00 percent to − 0.31 percent. The share of personal consumption expenditures in net national product rose even faster than in 1973–79. But these two developments favorable to per capita consumption were swamped by a third. Whereas the growth rate of employment tumbled from 2.25 percent in 1973–79 to − 0.01 percent in 1979–82, the growth rate of population scarcely changed, increasing from 1.01 percent to 1.03 percent. As a result, the growth rate of personal consumption expenditures per capita fell from 2.17 percent in 1948–73 to 0.47 percent in 1979–82. Partial economic recovery in 1983 raised the rate for 1979–83, but only to 1.09 percent. The sizable increase in the consumption share of net national product that shielded personal consumption per capita from an even sharper decline was made possible by net disinvestment abroad, which became massive in 1983 and still larger in 1984.

Growth in Nonresidential Business

To appraise or analyze productivity changes, it is necessary to consider the nonresidential business sector as well as the whole economy. The growth rate of total potential national income in this sector dropped only slightly less from 1948–73 to 1973–79 and 1979–82 than did the rate for the economy as a whole. However, this similarity was the net result of growth rates of potential employment and potential hours at work that rose even more than the rates in the whole economy offset by growth rates of potential national income per person potentially employed and per potential hour that fell even more. The growth rate of output per person employed, computed on a potential basis, fell from 2.59 percent in 1948–73 to 0.27 percent in 1973–79 and − 0.55 percent in 1979–

82. Potential output per person employed was, in fact, the same in 1982 as it had been in 1973, nine years earlier (table 2-8, column 6). It had, moreover, been nearly flat in the meantime, except for a dip in 1975.[7] Although potential output per person employed was below its 1973 value in 1974–76 and above the 1973 value in 1977–81, its whole range from 1973 to 1982, apart from 1975, was only from 98.3 to 101.5 percent of the 1973 value. This range only slightly exceeds the average one-year percentage increase during the previous quarter century, a period in which the series rose appreciably in every year but one. The growth rate of potential output per hour fell from 3.08 percent in 1948–73 to 0.93 percent in 1973–79 and 0.03 percent in 1979–82.

In all these periods the growth rates of output per person employed and output per hour in nonresidential business computed on an actual basis fell below those computed on a potential basis. The differences were widening, except for the change in the growth of output per hour from 1973–79 to 1979–82. The growth rate of actual output per person employed was 2.45 percent in 1948–73, 0.08 percent in 1973–79, and − 0.93 percent in 1979–82, while that of actual output per hour fell from 2.96 percent in 1948–73 to 0.77 percent in 1973–79 and 0.00 percent in 1979–82.[8] (Table 2-7 provides annual data for these series.) From 1982 to 1983 a cyclical increase in the intensity with which employed resources were used improved actual output per hour and raised its preliminary 1979–83 growth rate, but only to 0.60 percent.

I have already discussed employment and total hours of work. The growth rate of reproducible capital input in nonresidential business, another major type of factor input, barely changed from 3.71 percent in 1948–73 to 3.65 percent in 1973–79, and then slipped to 3.06 percent in 1979–82 (and 2.74 percent in 1979–83).

---

7. Whether the 1975 figure, which is 4.6 percent below the 1973 value, portrays reality or an error in either the "actual" data or my adjustments to a potential basis is uncertain.

8. Some readers may be surprised that the differences between the growth rates of actual and potential output per hour are not larger in nonresidential business than table 1-1 shows them to be. In the case of 1948–73, the explanation is that a substantial difference between the 1948 and 1973 ratios of actual to potential output per hour equates to only 0.12 percentage points when spread over 25 years. The similarity of growth rates in 1973–79 and 1979–82, on the other hand, stems from similar ratios of actual to potential output per hour in 1973 (0.984), 1979 (0.978), and 1982 (0.981). This similarity is happenstance; it should not be inferred that the ratio is always stable. From 1947 to 1982 the ratio has ranged from 0.961 in 1974, 0.968 in 1980, and 0.974 in 1970 to 1.013 in 1964, 1.017 in 1965, and 1.024 in 1950. The growth rates of the two series sometimes differ substantially—by a full one-half percentage point from 1977 to 1982, for example.

Two characteristics of the productivity slowdown are striking. One is its abruptness. The decline in the trend of output per unit of input occurred suddenly in 1974. From 1948 to 1973 there had been cyclical fluctuations but no decline in trend.[9] A second characteristic of the productivity slowdown is that it was pervasive. All advanced countries, not just the United States, were affected.[10] Almost all regions of the United States were affected.[11] Almost all branches of the economy, in both manufacturing and nonmanufacturing sectors, were affected in the United States.[12] This pattern seems also to have prevailed abroad, at least in manufacturing. When Bureau of Labor Statistics (BLS) analysts examined the thirteen branches of manufacturing in four countries (the United States, the United Kingdom, France, and West Germany),

productivity growth was found to have slowed after 1973 in fifty-one of the fifty-two cases.[13]

The Loss of Production

The gap between actual and potential national income, which has already been discussed, is shown on an annual basis in table 2-4. There is also a second gap: that between potential national income and the value that potential national income would have attained in the absence of the slowdown in the growth of "residual" productivity.

To compute this second gap, I use residual productivity rather than output per unit of input because part of the change in the trend of output per unit of input from 1948–73 to the subsequent period resulted from developments that, to quote *Slower Growth:*

were inevitable or even welcome. The transfer of surplus workers from farming to nonfarm jobs in which they produce output of greater value diminished as the pool of such labor approached exhaustion. Great increases in the working-age population under 25 years of age, reinforced by increases in the ratios of employment to population in the young age groups and by the entry of many adult women into the labor force, boosted the proportion of inexperienced workers among the employed. The costs of regulations that Congress presumably felt had benefits in excess of their costs began to impinge on productivity.[14]

The retardation in the growth rate of the residual series labeled "advances in knowledge and miscellaneous" (that is, not elsewhere classified, or n.e.c.) determinants, on the other hand, certainly was not welcome, and if that retardation was inevitable, we do not know why or in what sense. It is of interest to calculate what potential national income would have been if the 1948–73 growth rate of this series had continued unchanged while the other determinants of output per unit of input had behaved as they actually did.

This value may be put at $1,495 billion, at 1972 prices, in the year 1982. This figure is $161 billion more than potential national income, which at $1,334 billion was, in turn, $159 billion greater than actual national income.[15] The combined gap was therefore

9. For any reader who may prefer to rely on data without cyclical adjustment I note that, if the 1948–73 period is divided into approximately equal parts, with the dividing point at either 1960 or 1961, the growth rate even of actual output per *hour* is almost the same in the second half, 2.94 percent, as in the first half, 2.97 percent (computed from table 2-7, column 13), while the growth rate of actual output per unit of input is higher (computed from table 5-1, column 1). The growth rate of potential output per unit of input is the same in the two halves (computed from table 5-2, column 1).

The Bureau of Labor Statistics (BLS) agrees that the trend change began in 1974. (U.S. Bureau of Labor Statistics, *Trends in Multifactor Productivity, 1948–81*, Bulletin 2178, September 1983, p. 1.) Earlier, BLS staff had reported declines in growth of output per hour starting in both 1966 and 1974. (J. R. Norsworthy, Michael R. Harper, and Kent Kunze, "The Slowdown in Productivity Growth: Analysis of Some Contributing Factors," *BPEA*, 2:1979, pp. 387–421.) However, they obtained a substantial decline from 1948–65 to 1965–73 only by dividing 1948–73 at a date when productivity was cyclically very high and omitting a cyclical adjustment. The growth rate of actual output per hour in nonresidential business computed from table 2-7, column 13, also declines, from 3.26 percent in 1948–65 to 2.33 percent in 1965–73, but that of potential output per hour slipped only from 3.16 percent to 2.90 percent (computed from table 2-8, column 10) and that of potential output per unit of input from 2.14 percent to 2.10 percent (computed from table 5-2, column 1). The growth rate of residual productivity increased slightly, from 1.33 percent to 1.48 percent (computed from table 5-1, column 12).

10. See, for example, *Slower Growth*, pp. 146–47; Angus Maddison, "Comparative Analysis of the Productivity Situation in Advanced Capitalist Countries," in John W. Kendrick, ed., *International Comparisons of Productivity and Causes of the Slowdown* (American Enterprise Institute/Ballinger, 1984), pp. 59–108; Thad P. Alton, Elizabeth M. Bass, Krzysztof Badach, Gregor Lazarcik, and George G. Staller, *Economic Growth in Eastern Europe, 1965, 1970, and 1975–1983*, Occasional Paper 80 (New York: L.W. International Financial Research, 1984); U.S. Bureau of Labor Statistics, *Productivity and the Economy: A Chartbook*, Bulletin 2172, June 1983, tables 10 and 12, and "Manufacturing Productivity and Labor Cost Trends in 1983 in 12 Countries," press release, December 31, 1984.

11. Charles R. Hulten and Robert M. Schwab found that there were large drops from 1951–73 and 1965–73 to 1973–78 in the growth rates of both labor productivity and total factor productivity in manufacturing in eight of nine regions. See "Regional Productivity Growth in U.S. Manufacturing 1951–78," *American Economic Review*, vol. 74 (March 1984), pp. 152–62.

12. *Slower Growth*, pp. 145–46.

13. Arthur Neef and Edwin Dean, "Comparative Changes in Labor Productivity and Unit Labor Costs by Manufacturing Industry: United States and Western Europe," in John W. Kendrick, ed., *Interindustry Differences in Productivity Growth* (Washington, D.C.: American Enterprise Institute for Public Policy Research, forthcoming).

14. *Slower Growth*, p. 1. The costs of crime against business also impaired potential output per unit of input, while irregular factors had a small offsetting effect.

15. The figure of $161 billion is the product of potential national income originating in nonresidential business ($1,033.4 billion, from table 2-8) and 15.56 percent. The latter is the percentage (13.83) by which the value of the index for the effect

$319 billion in 1972 prices (which is equivalent to $661 billion in 1982 prices). Actual national income was 21.4 percent less than this expanded potential figure, of which 10.8 percent was due to the slowed growth of residual productivity and 10.6 percent to our failure to produce up to potential in 1982. Even if the growth rate of residual productivity had been maintained, as assumed in this calculation, the growth rate of potential national income per person potentially employed would still have fallen by one-third, from 2.26 percent in 1948–73 to 1.51 percent in 1973–82.

The cumulative combined gap over the nine years from 1974 through 1982 was $1,473 billion in 1972 prices, or 12.8 percent of the expanded potential national income figures for those years. Of this amount, $652 billion resulted from the slackening of residual productivity growth and $821 billion from the gap between actual and potential output. For perspective, it may be noted that in the same nine years federal purchases of goods and services for national defense came to an aggregate $619 billion in 1972 prices.[16]

As long as the growth of residual productivity remains far below its 1948–73 rate, the importance of the gap arising from this deficiency must increase relative to the gap between actual and potential output. This result must ensue, that is to say, in the absence of constantly deepening recessions. Even in the trough recession year of 1982, the residual productivity gap was, by a slight margin, the larger of the two. The difference widened in 1983 and 1984 as a strong cyclical recovery of the economy was apparently not, based on partial data, accompanied by a revived advance in residual productivity.

Substantial underutilization of resources has characterized all advanced market economies in the past decade, while market and centrally planned economies alike have suffered sharp retardation in productivity growth. It is important to stress that in these respects the performance of the U.S. economy has deteriorated no more than that of other national economies and less than most.[17] Also to be stressed is that there is no package of simple panaceas that need only be unwrapped to obtain solutions to our economic problems, and I would be the very last to suggest that there are complete known solutions. It should also be observed that the economy deserves good marks for maintaining its flexibility in adapting to changes in demand patterns, relative supply prices, and labor composition.

Nevertheless, our economic performance since 1973 has been grossly unsatisfactory by any standard except comparisons with countries whose performance has deteriorated even more than ours.

---

of advances in knowledge and n.e.c. would have exceeded its actual value (101.17, from table 5-2) if its 1948–73 growth rate had continued, raised by 12.5 percent to allow for associated gains that would have been obtained from economies of scale. The figure of $159 billion is from table 2-4. Neither figure includes any allowance for the possibility that our 1982 capital stock might have been bigger or that other determinants of potential output might have been different if the period since 1973 had been one of fuller resource utilization.

16. The data are from NIPA, table 3.10. The comparison actually overstates defense expenditures relative to the gaps because 53 percent of defense expenditures were purchases other than employee compensation. These are valued at market prices that are higher than the factor cost values used to measure lost output.

17. Actual rates of productivity growth have continued below those in other countries for reasons that were present before 1973; the text refers to changes in the rate of growth. The United States continues to have the highest level of output per person employed.

-»>«‹-

Determinants of Output Changes since 1929

-»>«‹-

There are many determinants of the nation's output. Since 1929 changes in some of them have been favorable to the growth of potential output all of the time and of actual output most of the time. Consistently favorable determinants include the number of persons employed, their education, the state of knowledge as to how to produce at low cost, and the size of markets served by business. On the other hand, changes in the average hours of work have been as consistently unfavorable to growth. Although both sets of determinants have always moved in the same direction when calculated on a potential basis, they have done so at varying speeds, and this variation has contributed substantially to fluctuations in the growth rate of potential output.

Other determinants have not always moved in the same direction. Most but not all of the time, changes in the amounts of the major types of capital available for production and in the allocation of labor among nonfarm wage and salary workers, farm workers, and the nonfarm self-employed have been favorable to growth. Changes in the composition of labor by age and sex have exhibited long movements unfavorable to growth, but there have also been periods of favorable changes. Annual changes in the weather and in the severity of labor disputes have tended to introduce short-term ups and downs in output per unit of input and hence in total output. Fluctuations in the strength of demand have introduced fluctuations in the intensity with which labor, capital, and land in use are utilized, and these fluctuations have greatly affected actual output per unit of input and actual total output, although not, by definition, po-

tential series.[1] Three of the determinants that I measure—costs to business of regulations to abate pollution and to protect employee safety and health, and costs of crime against business—did not change significantly during the earlier part of the period covered but turned adverse to growth toward its end. My analysis compels me to conclude that there are also determinants among those that I have not measured separately that turned unfavorable after 1973.

This chapter examines trends in individual determinants since 1929, using periods other than the standard periods if they are more appropriate for a particular determinant, while chapter 3 looks specifically at the growth slowdown after 1973.

Labor Input

The output determinants cited in the preceding paragraph include the number of persons employed, the hours they work, and various other attributes of workers that affect the contribution of labor to production.

Two of the four sectors of the economy use labor: nonresidential business, with about four-fifths of the total in recent years, and general government, households, and institutions, with the rest. For each of these sectors a separate index is computed for employment and each pertinent characteristic of labor, and the product of these indexes provides an index of labor input.

The labor input index for nonresidential business measures the amount of labor used in that sector when different groups of workers are weighted by their marginal products, which are inferred from their relative average earnings. Table 3-1 provides this index and indexes of its components computed on an actual basis, while table 3-2 provides similar indexes computed on a potential basis. Because the indexes in both tables are computed with actual values in 1972 equal to 100, the ratio of the value of any entry in table 3-1 to its counterpart in table 3-2 is the ratio of the actual value to the potential value. For example, in 1982 the index of actual labor input shown in table 3-1, column 8, was 118.63, while that of potential labor input shown in table 3-2, column 8, was 133.17. The ratio of 118.63 to 133.17 indicates that 89.1 percent of the potential labor input in nonresidential business was used in 1982—the least since 1940, when the percentage was 86.5. The growth rates of actual and potential labor input in

1. Weather, labor disputes, and demand may affect the amount of labor or capital used, as well as output per unit of input, but such effects are already reflected in the measures of labor and capital input.

nonresidential business and of their components are shown for the standard periods in table 3-4.

Over the whole time span from 1929 to 1982 the growth rate of potential labor input in nonresidential business was 1.58 percent. After fluctuating between the earlier periods, the growth rate more than doubled from a relatively low 0.83 percent in 1953–64 to a high 1.96 percent in 1964–73, then jumped again to 2.53 percent in 1973–79 and 2.56 percent in 1979–82. The amounts that labor contributed to the growth rate of national income in the sector in these periods were smaller, because labor is only one type of factor input, albeit the largest by far.

To clarify the meaning of the contribution of labor to growth (and to get methodology out of the way early), it is helpful to jump to a later part of the story and describe the indexes of total factor input used in production in the nonresidential business sector. These indexes are presented on actual and potential bases in table 4-6, columns 9 and 10. In addition to labor input, their construction requires measures of the input of nonresidential land and two types of business capital (also shown in table 4-6): inventories, and nonresidential structures and equipment. The index of total factor input is a weighted average of the indexes of these four broad categories of inputs.

To combine the four inputs, the weight used for each input is its estimated share of their combined earnings. The principle of proportionality, one of the most powerful in economics, provides the justification for this procedure. The total earnings of each factor can be viewed as equal to the number of units of the factor and its price, or earnings, per unit. If enterprises combine the four factors in such a way as to minimize costs, they will use them in such proportions that the marginal products per unit of the several factors are proportional to their prices, or earnings, per unit.[2] Unless this condition is satisfied, enterprises could reduce costs by substituting one factor for another, and an enterprise's failure to do so would risk its elimination as a result of competition from lower cost competitors. Departures from this situation are assumed to be small or offsetting, so that the total earnings of the four inputs are proportional to the number of units of each times its marginal product.[3]

It follows that if a small percentage increase in the number of units of all of the factors would increase the output of the sector by x percent, then a percentage increase of the same amount in the number of units of only one factor would increase output by x times the share of that factor in the total earnings of the sector.

I measure total input as if a given percentage increase in all inputs would increase output by that same percentage, even though I do not believe this to be the case. The nonresidential business sector actually operates under increasing returns to scale, so that an increase of, say, 1 percent in every input would raise output by more than 1 percent (I put the amount at 1.125 percent). Nevertheless, I prefer to classify this extra gain as an increase in output per unit of input resulting from economies of scale rather than from an increase in total input. Weights summing to 100 percent are therefore used so that if all inputs were to increase by 1 percent, total input would also increase by 1 percent.[4]

The contribution made by all inputs combined to the growth rate of the nonresidential business sector's actual or potential output in any period is the same as the growth rate of the index of total factor input (tables 4-6 and 4-7, columns 9 and 10). The contribution of each separate input is the product of the growth rate of that input and its average share of earnings.[5]

From 1929 to 1982 labor input in nonresidential business grew at an annual rate of 1.58 percent on a potential basis, as stated earlier. Labor's average share of earnings was 80.4 percent. The labor contribution to the growth rate of nonresidential business output was 1.29 percentage points, approximately equal to 80.4 percent of 1.58 percent. Labor's contribution was equal to 41 percent of the 3.14 percent growth rate of potential output that resulted from the

2. The marginal product of each factor is the extra output that would be added by one additional unit of that factor when the quantities of the other factors are held constant.

3. Relative earnings are used not only as weights to combine labor, capital, and land to arrive at a measure of total input, but also as weights to combine different types of input within these broad categories, as already indicated in the case of labor. The justification is the same.

4. The index of total factor input is a chain index of annual percentage changes. The percentage change between each year and the next is a weighted average of the percentage changes in the four input indexes. The weights, which are shown in table G-2, are the averages of the cyclically adjusted earnings shares in the two years compared, and consequently they correspond to average marginal products (at the average postwar level of utilization) during the period in which the changes were taking place. The shares, which are shown before adjustment in table G-1, are adjusted to eliminate cyclical fluctuations, but the average postwar levels of the shares are retained.

In the 1929–40 and 1941–47 periods, for which data for the individual years are not available, the annual growth rates of the input indexes between the terminal dates were substituted for the annual percentage changes, and the average weights in the first and last years of the period were used.

5. These statements are only approximately accurate; interaction terms among the output determinants increase contributions trivially, and the data are also adjusted to eliminate rounding discrepancies. See *Slower Growth*, pp. 91–92.

contributions of all determinants.[6] The contributions of all output determinants, including labor input and its components, to the growth rates of actual and potential national income in nonresidential business are shown for all standard periods in tables 7-1 and 7-2.

Tables 7-3 and 7-4 provide the contributions to the growth rates of national income per person employed in nonresidential business. In the latter tables employment disappears as a growth source, and the contribution of labor refers to the effect upon output per worker of changes in hours, age-sex composition, and education. The contribution in 1929–82 was only 0.12 percentage points on a potential basis, because the large positive effect of rising education (0.51 percentage points) was largely offset by the negative effects of shorter hours (− 0.25 percentage points) and changes in age-sex composition (− 0.14 percentage points).

The contribution of labor to the growth of total potential national income in nonresidential business was variable as well as large. After dropping from 1.10 percentage points in 1948–53 to 0.66 points in 1953–64, it subsequently jumped to 1.62 points in 1964–73, then to 2.10 points in 1973–79 and 2.11 points in 1979–82. The jumps mainly reflect employment changes, but other components also changed, enough to affect output per person employed considerably.

For the sector consisting of general government, households, and institutions, the annual indexes of labor input and its components are shown in table 6-1, and their growth rates in the upper panel of table 6-3. The growth rate of labor input, 3.01 percent over the whole 1929–82 time span, is necessarily the same as that of the sector's output, because the BEA measures the change in output by the change in labor input. Also to be noted is that in this sector the potential series are the same as the actual series. After fluctuating in the early periods, the growth rate of labor input in this sector fell sharply from 2.86 percent in 1964–73 to 1.71 percent in 1973–79 and 0.87 percent in 1979–82. Its growth rate substantially exceeded that of potential labor input in nonresidential business in all standard periods up to 1964–73, but thereafter fell substantially short of it. The change actually dates from 1970, and it apparently continued in 1983–84. Thus, by 1984 business's share of potential labor input had been increasing for well over a

decade, and except during the 1982 employment decline it increased on an actual basis as well.

Tables 8-1 and 8-2 show the contributions of labor and other determinants to the growth rates of actual and potential national income in the economy as a whole.[7] From 1929 to 1982 labor contributed 1.49 percentage points to the 3.20 percent growth rate of potential national income, 47 percent of the total. Recent increases in the labor contribution were much smaller in the whole economy than in nonresidential business. From 1953–64 to 1964–73 the labor contribution did, nevertheless, increase substantially, from 1.01 percentage points to 1.75 points, but the further increase in 1973–79 was only to 1.90 points, and in 1979–82 the contribution slipped back to 1.76 points.

Tables 8-3 and 8-4 show the contributions to the growth rates of actual and potential national income per person employed in the economy as a whole. As in the similar tables for nonresidential business, employment disappears as a growth source, and the contributions of the remaining components of labor input tend to be offsetting. On a potential basis, they made a net contribution of 0.20 percentage points to the 1.55 percent growth rate of national income per person employed from 1929 to 1982.

The components of labor input will now be examined.

Employment[8]

Over the whole 1929–82 span, employment growth was responsible for 1.29 percentage points, or 40 percent, of the growth rate of potential national income in the whole economy, and 1.17 points, or 37 percent, of the growth rate in nonresidential business. In each case employment contributed to the growth rate of output an amount in the neighborhood of four-fifths of the employment growth rate, a proportion corresponding to the labor share of national income. Employment growth usually dominates the rate of change in labor input, and it very importantly affects that of output. The fast growth of potential employment in the economy as a whole after 1973

6. The contribution of an output determinant is the amount by which the growth rate of output would be reduced (or increased, when the contribution is negative) if that determinant had not changed but all other determinants had changed as they actually did. See *Slower Growth*, pp. 91–92.

7. The labor contribution is obtained by adding the contributions made by labor in each sector. The contribution of labor in nonresidential business to the growth rate of total output is obtained by multiplying its contribution to the growth of nonresidential business national income to total national income (shown on an actual basis for each period in table 6-3). A similar calculation, shown in full on an actual basis in table 6-3, is made for general government, households, and institutions.

8. Employment data appear in many of the tables. Besides the tables that cover all types of labor input (3-1, 3-2, 3-4, 6-1, 6-3, 7-1, 7-2, 7-3, 7-4, 8-1, 8-2, 8-3, and 8-4), see tables 1-1, 2-1, 2-2, 2-7, 2-8, 3-7, 3-8, 3-9, 6-2, B-1, H-1, L-1, and L-4.

and its even faster growth in nonresidential business were emphasized in chapter 1.

Employment in nonresidential business has been much affected by changes in the business sector's share of total potential employment. This percentage, after falling irregularly from 86.3 in 1929 to 83.7 in 1948, 79.7 in 1953, and a low of 74.5 in 1968 (when hostilities in Vietnam were boosting federal government employment), rose in every subsequent year, recovering to 78.0 in 1982 (computed from table 2-8).

The rest of employment is in general government, households, and institutions, the sector where measured output per unit of labor input does not change. Table 6-2 shows the division of full-time equivalent employment in this sector among thirteen components in the first and last years of the short postwar periods, and average annual changes during these periods. A more summary view is obtained by comparing 1948–73 changes with 1973–82 changes. Full-time equivalent employment in the sector grew at an annual rate of 2.91 percent in the former period as against 1.27 percent in 1973–82.[9] The average annual increase declined even in absolute amount, from 385,000 in 1948–73 to 251,000 in 1973–82. Almost all components either increased less per year in the latter period, fell more, or switched from an increase to a decrease. The biggest reductions in the absolute annual change occurred in public education, the armed forces, and state and local government non-school employment. The only significant offset was in private nonprofit health services (and even there the *percentage* growth rate fell slightly).

Average Hours of Work[10]

Average hours at work per person employed have declined persistently.[11] Over the whole period from 1929 to 1982 their average growth rate on a potential basis was −0.63 percent in the economy as a whole, −0.60 percent in nonresidential business, and −0.67 percent in government, households, and institutions (tables 3-4 and L-6). In nonresidential business,

almost four-tenths of the total fifty-three-year decline occurred in the first eleven years, from 1929 to 1940, when the growth rate was −1.01 percent; three-tenths in the twenty-three years from 1940 to 1963, when the growth rate was −0.42 percent; and a little over three-tenths in the nineteen years from 1963 to 1982, when the growth rate was −0.58 percent. Much of the decline resulted from changes in the composition of employment, to which I shall return. The average potential hours of the largest relatively homogeneous group, full-time male nonfarm wage and salary workers in nonresidential business, declined less than the average for all groups from 1929 to 1982—the change was at a rate of only −0.38 percent—and the time pattern was different. Of the fifty-three-year decline, well over half occurred in eleven years from 1929 to 1940, when the growth rate was −0.98 percent; little more than one-fifth occurred in the thirty-three years from 1940 to 1973, when the growth rate was −0.14 percent; and the fraction was the same in the nine years from 1973 to 1982, when the growth rate was −0.55 percent (calculated from table L-2). The resumption of a rapid decline in full-time hours after more than three decades of near stability was one of many economic changes that began after 1973.

Because average hours declined, the 1929–82 growth rates of total potential hours were only about three-fifths as large as those of total potential employment: in the whole economy 0.98 percent as compared with 1.63 percent (computed from table 2-2), and in nonresidential business, 0.82 percent as against 1.43 percent (from table 3-4). However, the index of average hours does not measure the effect of changes in average hours upon labor input. I shall return to that subject after examining the distribution of hours worked among demographic groups.

The Age-Sex Distribution of Hours Worked[12]

The proportions of total hours that are worked by males and females, and within each sex by individuals of different ages, change over time. An average hour worked by each demographic group has a different value. Tables 3-1 and 3-2 provide indexes that measure the effect of changes in age-sex proportions upon labor input in nonresidential business, and table 3-4 shows the growth rates of these indexes. Their calculation requires distributions of total hours worked in nonresidential business by age and sex (shown, on

9. The growth rates of the number of persons employed in the sector (calculated from table 2-7) are slightly higher because of an increase in part-time employment, but the change between 1948–73 and 1973–82 growth rates is about the same.

10. Besides the tables that show all the components of labor input (see footnote 8), data referring to average and/or total hours at work and their effects on labor input appear in tables 1-1, 2-1, 2-2, 2-8, 3-7, 3-8, 3-9, C-1, E-1, L-2, L-3, and L-6.

11. The average hours shown in this book refer to employed persons, not persons at work (whose average hours are longer). Persons who have a job but do not work during a week for noneconomic reasons such as vacations or sickness are counted as employed persons working zero hours.

12. Besides the tables that show all the components of labor input (see footnote 8), data referring to the composition of hours worked by age and sex appear in tables 3-5 and 3-6.

an actual basis, for ten groups in table 3-6) and relative hourly earnings of these groups for use as weights (table 3-5, columns 1–3). Males 35–64 years of age have the highest hourly earnings in nonresidential business, followed by males 25–34, males 65 and over, males 20–24, and females 25–34 and 35–64 (both of these earn 54 percent of the highest group). The remaining groups, females 65 and over, females 20–24, and, finally, males 14–19 and females 14–19, have the lowest earnings.

The age-sex index computed on a potential basis declined at an annual rate of −0.17 percent over the whole period from 1929 to 1982, but five distinct swings appear in the data, with the following growth rates: 1929–40, −0.15 percent; 1940–47, 0.17 percent; 1947–49, −0.45 percent; 1949–53, 0.41 percent; and 1953–82, −0.35 percent. If the last time span is divided at 1973, growth rates of −0.34 percent in 1953–73 and −0.38 percent in 1973–82 emerge.[13] Although an influx of inexperienced young and female workers has sometimes been assigned a major role in the post-1973 productivity slowdown, it is evident that it could not have contributed very much if the comparison is between the whole 1973–82 period and the preceding twenty years. Changes in age-sex composition are much more important in explaining why the growth of potential output per person and output per hour were especially high in 1949–53.

In the long run the rise in the female percentage of hours worked in nonresidential business—from 16.5 percent in 1929 and 22.2 percent in 1948 to 36.7 percent in 1982, on an actual basis—has been the dominant factor in the decline in the index. Wide fluctuations in the proportion of young people, including fluctuations ascribable to low birth rates during the Depression and World War II, the baby boom, and the subsequent return to more normal rates—have been a main cause of the reversals in the direction of the index and fluctuations in its rate of change. The annual decline in the index computed on a potential basis was cut by more than half from 1973–79 to 1979–82.

Because young people and, usually, women have been affected more than adult males by cyclical changes in employment, the index on an actual basis rises relative to the index on a potential basis when unemployment increases. As a result, the index on an actual basis was level from 1979 to 1981 and actually increased in 1982, even though the index on

a potential basis continued to fall every year, although at a reduced rate.

Changes in age-sex composition subtracted 0.14 percentage points from the growth rate of potential national income in nonresidential business over the whole 1929–82 period and as much as 0.41 percentage points in 1964–73. The contribution of changes in age-sex composition to growth in general government, households, and institutions cannot be isolated and is included in the "unallocated" component of labor input in the tables for the economy as a whole.

The Effect on Output of Changes in Average Hours

Summary indexes of the net effect of changes in average working hours upon labor input in nonresidential business appear in column 9 of tables 3-1 and 3-2. These indexes are not based upon a supposition that a given percentage change in the average hours worked by all employed persons combined changes labor input proportionately and therefore has the same effect on output as a percentage change in employment of the same size. The results that would be obtained from such an assumption are shown, labeled "average weekly hours," in column 2 of the same tables; the behavior of average hours has already been discussed.

My estimates are based on the belief that the effect of changes in the average hours worked by all persons employed in nonresidential business depends upon the reasons that average hours change. To prepare the estimates, it was first necessary to divide persons employed in nonresidential business among eight categories: full-time workers of each sex who are employed as nonfarm wage and salary workers, as nonfarm self-employed and unpaid family workers, and as farm workers, and part-time workers of each sex. Tables 3-7, 3-8, and 3-9 show employment, total hours, and average hours on an actual basis for each group (with additional detail for part-time workers). Average hours differ greatly among the eight categories, so that changes in employment composition, which have been large, have greatly affected the course of average hours in non-residential business. Three groups of reasons that average hours change are considered.

The first group of reasons includes changes in the relative numbers of full-time and part-time workers, changes in the relative numbers of male and female workers, and changes in the average hours of part-time workers. It is presumed that a change in average hours in the sector as a whole resulting from these causes does indeed mean a proportionate change in

---

13. On an actual basis the rate of decline was greater in 1953–73 than in 1973–82 (−0.29 percent as against −0.23 percent).

labor input, and no adjustment of the results of using the average hours series to measure labor input is required. The percentage of part-time workers rose, on a potential basis, from 7.4 in 1929 and 10.7 in 1948 to 17.5 in 1973 and 18.3 in 1982, and this increase has contributed greatly to the long decline in average hours.[14] However, the annual increase in the percentage was only one-third as large from 1973 to 1982 as it had been from 1948 to 1973. Full-time females work shorter hours than full-time males, and the rising proportion of females in the full-time total also contributed to the decline in the sector's average hours.

Second, a change in the sector's average hours may result from a change in the average hours of one of the six groups of full-time workers. A reduction in the average hours of full-time nonfarm wage and salary workers of either sex is estimated to result in more work done per hour at work because of less fatigue, less absenteeism, and related causes, and hence in a percentage reduction in labor input per worker that is smaller than the percentage reduction in average hours. The amount of this efficiency offset becomes smaller as hours become shorter. The average hours of full-time farm workers and of full-time nonfarm self-employed and unpaid family workers are very long, and from 1940 until recently they fluctuated from year to year with almost no trend. For these groups a change in the reported average hours of either sex is assumed to have no effect on labor input per worker but rather to be fully offset in labor input per hour. These assumptions are incorporated into the labor input series by including the component labeled "efficiency of an hour's work as affected by changes in hours due to intragroup changes" or, for brevity, "efficiency offset." To obtain the offset, the annual percentage changes in indexes constructed for the two sexes separately are weighted by their total earnings and the annual changes are linked. This weighting procedure is consistent with the previous introduction of the age-sex composition index. The weight attached to the female index rose from 10 percent in 1929 to 26 percent in 1982.

When calculated on a potential basis, the efficiency offset index grew at an annual rate of 0.17 percent from 1929 to 1982, an amount that countered the effect on labor input of nearly three-tenths of the reduction in average hours. Its growth rate was as

high as 0.53 percent in 1929–40, when full-time hours fell sharply from very high levels, and then receded, reaching 0.02 percent in 1949–69. The rate rose again, to 0.14 percent, in 1973–82 as declines in average full-time hours accelerated among nonfarm wage and salary workers and the nonfarm self-employed, and even to a small extent among farm workers.

The third cause of changes in average hours in the sector has been a shift in the distribution of full-time workers of each sex away from farms and nonfarm self-employment, where the hours are very long, to nonfarm wage and salary employment, where the hours are shorter. I consider that otherwise similar individuals provide the same amount of labor input regardless of which of these groups they fall into, provided they work the average full-time hours of persons of their sex in that group. The effect upon average hours of shifts among groups is offset by the labor input component labeled "efficiency of an hour's work as affected by changes in hours due to specified intergroup shifts" or, for brevity, "intergroup shift offset." Not to make this adjustment would imply unrealistically that when a male farmer working the average hours of full-time male farmers becomes a nonfarm wage and salary worker working the average full-time hours of that group, his labor input drops by more than one-fourth and that he could maintain his former labor input only by working more than one-third longer than his new associates. Similarly, it would imply that when a nonfarm self-employed male makes a similar change to wage-salary status, his labor input drops by one-fifth. As with the efficiency offset index, separate indexes for the two sexes are weighted by earnings.

The 1929–82 growth rate of the intergroup shift offset index computed on a potential basis was 0.13 percent, which offset one-fifth of the drop in average hours. The rate was much the same in all the standard periods until 1973–79, when it dipped to 0.03 percent before recovering to 0.09 percent in 1979–82.

I now return to the summary index for the effect of changes in average hours upon labor input, which is the product of the indexes of average hours, the efficiency offset, and the intergroup shift offset. On a potential basis its 1929–82 growth rate was −0.31 percent (table 3-4), and its contribution to the growth rate of potential national income in nonresidential business was −0.25 percentage points (table 7-2). After 1948 the contribution of the changes in hours per worker moved steadily downward from 0.09 percentage points in 1948–53 to −0.39 percentage points in 1973–79 before returning to −0.30 points in 1979–82. Thus up to 1973–79 a shortening of hours

14. The 1929 and 1948 averages cited are adjusted to eliminate the small effect on comparability with later years of a change in 1966 in the measurement procedures used in the Current Population Survey.

was a significant factor affecting adversely the changes in the growth rate of output per person employed.

There is a counterpart in the government, households, and institutions sector to the nonresidential business sector series for the implied efficiency offset, but it is something of a statistical artifact, because its measurement must be governed by the exact way in which the BEA has measured output in this sector.[15] The contribution of shorter hours to the growth rate of potential national income in the economy as a whole was -0.25 percentage points from 1929 to 1982 (table 8-2).

Education[16]

Educational background decisively conditions both the types of work an individual is able to perform and his proficiency in any particular occupation. The distribution of American workers by highest school grade completed has shifted upward continuously and massively, and this shift has been a major growth source.

Table 3-10 provides, by sex, distributions of persons employed in nonresidential business among nine education groups. Data are on a full-time equivalent basis. From 6 percent as recently as 1948, the percentage of males who had completed four or more years of college increased to 14 percent in 1973 and 23 percent in 1983. The percentage with a completed high school education but not a completed college education changed even more, rising from 29 in 1948 to 52 in 1973 and 57 percent in 1983. The decline at the bottom of the distribution was also impressive. Those with zero to seven years of school fell from 24 percent in 1948 to 8 percent in 1973 and 4 percent in 1983.[17] In addition, as young cohorts in the employed labor force replaced those educated many years earlier, the number of days spent in school per school year completed has risen at the elementary and secondary levels. This trend resulted from an extension of the school year in rural and small-town schools to match that already prevailing in city schools, and from less absenteeism. The education of female workers has risen much like that of males.

The continuous upward shift in educational background has upgraded the skills and versatility of labor and contributed to the rise of national income.

15. See "Derivations" and *Slower Growth*, pp. 84–86, 191.

16. Besides the tables providing data on all labor input components (see footnote 8), data referring to the education of employed persons appear in tables 3-10, F-2, F-3, F-4, and F-5.

17. In these comparisons, data for 1948, which initially refer to persons 18 years of age and older, are adjusted for comparability with data for later years, which refer to persons 16 and over. They are from *Slower Growth*, p. 42.

It has enhanced the skills of individuals within what is conventionally termed an occupation, often with considerable changes in the work actually performed; it has also permitted a shift in occupational composition from occupations in which workers typically have little education and low earnings toward those in which education and earnings are higher. Education also heightens a person's awareness of job opportunities and thereby the chances that he is employed where his marginal product is greatest. A more educated work force also is better able to learn about and use the most efficient production practices.

Past studies have identified increasing education of employed persons as a major source of growth since at least 1910, and especially since about 1930. From 1929 to 1982, according to the present estimates, more education per worker was the source of 16 percent of the growth of total potential output in nonresidential business and 30 percent of the growth of potential output per person employed in that sector. Since 1970 the level of formal education of persons employed in business has risen faster than ever before.

To compute the education indexes shown in tables 3-1 and 3-2, indexes were first prepared for persons of each sex employed in nonresidential business. To obtain these indexes, the numbers in each education group were weighted by average earnings of otherwise similar individuals who differ in amount of education. Allowance was then made for changes in days per year of school. Annual changes in the indexes for the two sexes were combined by use of total earnings as weights.

On a potential basis the index for the education component of nonresidential business labor input rose at an annual rate of 0.63 percent over the whole 1929–82 period (table 3-4). Education contributed 0.51 percentage points to both the 3.14 percent growth rate of potential national income in nonresidential business (table 7-2) and the 1.68 percent growth rate of the sector's potential national income per person employed (table 7-4).

The growth rate of the education index for nonresidential business was rather stable, staying close to the 0.63 percent average rate. On a potential basis, the largest deviations were from 1941 to 1948, when the rate dipped to 0.55 percent, and from 1964 to 1979, when it rose to 0.71 percent before slipping back to 0.63 percent in 1979–82. On an actual basis the growth rate of the education index climbed to 0.74 percent in 1973–79 and 0.79 percent in 1979–82, as rising unemployment and involuntary part-time employment were concentrated in the least educated groups.

From 1948 to about 1970 a disproportionate number of the highly educated who newly entered employment had entered teaching and other jobs outside business, and the educational distribution rose less in nonresidential business than in the economy as a whole. This differential movement was subsequently reversed, and the reversal was a factor in the accelerated growth of the education index for nonresidential business after 1970. Changes in the age distribution also favored its faster rise.

Earnings differentials among education groups that were narrower after 1969 than before kept the acceleration of the index from being even greater. But the main point to be noted about earnings differentials is that they do not appear to have narrowed very much. The absence of much narrowing is an indication that percentage differences between marginal products of persons at different educational levels have not diminished much in response to the increase in education, so that raising educational levels remains a powerful way to stimulate long-term economic growth.

Because the contribution of education to growth in any period depends on the difference between the education of persons who were employed at the beginning of that period and those who were employed at the end of the period, it conveys no information about changes in the amount of education being received by current students, and its calculation requires no such information. The education of students affects future growth.

Scores on achievement tests given pupils at various grade levels and on college aptitude tests given to high school seniors indicate that for two decades students were learning progressively less at each grade level until a weak recovery began about 1982. This evidence is reinforced by the testimony of educators and of employers of recent entrants into the labor force. The Advisory Panel on the Scholastic Aptitude Test Score Decline found that, after 1970, declines in scores on that test did not result from compositional shifts in the group taking it. Test scores have not been used in calculating the education index for employed persons. In *Slower Growth* I explained that up to 1976, when the estimates presented there ended, omission of test scores from the procedure was unimportant because scores have moved in cycles, rather than following a steady trend. This pattern "assures that changes in a series for the average test scores received by employed persons when they were students would be small and grad-

ual—very muted in comparison with movements in student scores."[18] The point is still valid, although its force diminished as the period of low scores was extended.

The contribution of education to the growth rate of labor input in general government, households, and institutions cannot be isolated, and its contribution to the growth of output in the whole economy is included in unallocated labor input. Hence the contribution of education to growth in the whole economy (tables 8-1, 8-2, 8-3, and 8-4) covers only the contribution made by labor employed in the business sector. This contribution was 0.40 percentage points in 1929–82.

Unallocated Labor Input[19]

The unallocated component of labor input appears only in the tables for general government, households, and institutions and for the economy as a whole. Its contribution to the growth rate of output in the economy as a whole, which amounted to 0.16 percentage points from 1929 to 1982 on a potential basis, includes the statistical effect of intersectoral employment shifts between nonresidential business and general government, households, and institutions, in addition to the effect of compositional shifts among education, demographic, and other groups within the latter sector.[20]

Capital and Land

An increase in the nation's capital stock has provided a major source of economic growth. Over the whole 1929–82 period the increase in capital input was responsible for 0.54 percentage points, or 16.9 percent, of the 3.20 percent growth rate of total potential national income (table 8-2). The contribution was only 0.11 percentage points in 1929–48, as against 0.77 points in 1948–73, and this increase accounts for half the difference between the growth rates of output in these two periods. The contribution slipped back to 0.67 percentage points in 1973–82.

The capital that contributes to growth is divided

18. *Slower Growth*, p. 47.

19. Data for unallocated labor input appear in tables 6-1 and 6-3 as "other labor characteristics" and in tables 8-1, 8-2, 8-3, and 8-4.

20. See *Slower Growth*, pp. 106–7, supplemented by "Derivations" in the present book, for an explanation of the two components. The range from −0.02 to 0.03 percentage points spans the contribution of intersectoral shifts in 1964–73 and later periods, and the amount was sizable only in 1948–53, when it reached 0.27 percentage points on an actual basis and 0.29 points on a potential basis.

among four types in this study.[21] Two of the four, inventories and nonresidential structures and equipment, contribute to growth in the nonresidential business sector. The others, dwellings and international assets, create output in other sectors. The capital input series appropriate for analysis of actual output and potential output are the same.

Capital in Nonresidential Business[22]

Over the whole 1929–82 period total capital input in nonresidential business grew at an annual rate of 2.50 percent (table 4-7). With earnings of capital averaging 15.5 percent of national income in the sector, capital contributed 0.38 percentage points to the 3.14 percent growth rate of potential sector national income (table 7-2), some 12.1 percent of the total.

Nonresidential structures and equipment comprised 70–75 percent of the capital input in the sector during the time span covered by the estimates, and inventories 25–30 percent. Input of nonresidential structures and equipment grew at an annual rate of 2.44 percent and contributed 0.27 percentage points to the growth rate of output, while inventories grew at a 2.52 percent rate and contributed 0.11 percentage points.

Capital input has contributed importantly to past fluctuations in the rate of growth of sector national income. Lack of investment demand in the 1930s brought a negative growth rate of capital in 1929–41, and supply limitations during World War II kept its growth rate very low in 1941–48. During the postwar years capital input, like labor input, contributed to the alternation of very fast output growth in 1948–53, slower growth in 1953–64, and fast growth again in 1964–73. Unlike labor, it also contributed—although only a little—to the slackening of growth after 1973.

The growth rate of capital input in nonresidential business was only moderately less in 1973–82 than in 1948–73 (3.45 percent as opposed to 3.71 percent). The slackening was confined to inventories, whose growth rate fell from 3.71 percent to 2.05 percent. The growth rate of nonresidential structures and

equipment input rose from 3.76 percent a year in 1948–73 to 3.90 percent in 1973–82; the rate was almost the same in the 1973–79 and 1979–82 subperiods. The growth rate of structures and equipment input was about as high in 1973–82 as in the 1948–53 period of fast output growth, and was above the rate in all other standard periods before 1973 except 1964–73, when the rate reached an extraordinary 4.57 percent.

There was some difference between the behavior of the gross stock of nonresidential structures and equipment and that of the net stock (table 4-1). The growth rate of gross stock rose from 3.62 percent in 1948–73 to 3.99 percent in 1973–82, while that of net stock fell from 4.20 percent to 3.65 percent. In measuring input (or net services) of fixed capital I weight gross stock three-fourths and net stock one-fourth. Net stock is a measure of the future services stored up in capital and, so viewed, actually has no direct relevance to an investigation into contemporary changes in output. My introduction of net stock into the capital input measure is only a convenient way to make a reasonable allowance for deterioration in the contribution of capital goods to production as they age.

The contribution of capital to the growth rate of potential national income in nonresidential business fell from 0.59 percentage points in 1948–73 to 0.46 points in 1973–82. Only one-third of this reduction resulted from slower growth of capital input. The rest reflects the fact that capital comprised a smaller share of total input in the later period, so that a given percentage increase in capital input raised output by a smaller percentage than before.

Nonresidential business capital contributed less, of course, to the growth rate of potential national income in the economy as a whole than in nonresidential business. Its contribution was 0.30 percentage points in 1929–82, 0.46 points in 1948–73, and 0.36 points in 1973–82.

The Services of Dwellings[23]

The contribution of capital in the form of dwellings to national income growth is measured directly by changes in the "services of dwellings" sector's national income, except that it is necessary to eliminate the effect on the sector's national income of changes in the proportion of housing that is not occupied, which is classified as a separate growth source. From 1929 to 1982 the contribution of housing capital grew

---

21. The capital used by general government, households, and institutions is omitted because it does not contribute to the net output, as measured, that originates in these parts of the economy. It is true that business productivity may be affected by the adequacy of government services to business, but government capital is only one input into these services, which are described briefly in chapter 3.

22. Data referring to nonresidential structures and equipment and to inventories appear in tables 1-1, 4-1, 4-2, 4-4, 4-6, 4-7, 7-1, 7-2, 7-3, 7-4, 8-1, 8-2, 8-3, 8-4, and G-4.

23. Estimates for dwellings appear in tables 6-3, 6-4, 8-1, 8-2, 8-3, and 8-4.

at an annual rate of 4.52 percent and contributed 0.18 percentage points to the growth rate of potential national income in the economy as a whole. The contribution was 0.24 percentage points in both 1948–73 and 1973–82.

International Assets[24]

The increase in the net inflow of property income from abroad contributed only 0.06 percentage points to the growth rate of potential national income in the economy as a whole from 1929 to 1982. However, it was responsible for one-fourth of a percentage point, or over one-fifth, of the drop in the growth rate of potential national income from 1973–79 to 1979–82. The inflow (valued in 1972 dollars) peaked at $26 billion in 1979 before slipping to $23 billion in 1982 and $22 billion in 1983.

Saving and Investment Rates

To increase the nation's capital stock requires saving and investment, and to raise the future contribution of capital to growth requires an increase in saving and investment.

The nation's saving is necessarily equal to its investment at home and abroad when the definitions are consistent. The reason is that total income equals the value of total production, all income is either consumed or saved, and all production is either consumed or invested. This equality does not hold for individual economic units or sectors because one unit may lend to another or buy equities from it, thus transferring its ability to invest.

Gross saving and investment exceed net saving and investment by the value of capital consumption. The estimate of capital consumption used in the national income and product accounts results from an effort to measure economic depreciation; it is not based on the amount of depreciation that is deducted on tax returns. It is calculated by the perpetual inventory method, with use of an estimated actual service life for each category of capital goods and a distribution of retirements around this average; use of the straight-line formula for depreciation; and valuation at replacement cost. Table 4-3 shows gross and net saving and investment ratios for the years 1948 through 1983.

Gross private saving (gross saving by persons and corporations) is shown as a percent of GNP in table 4-3, column 1. This series has a moderate upward trend that brought the trend value from 15.6 percent

in 1948 to 17.3 percent in 1983, but the percentage has otherwise been extremely stable.[25] In the thirty-six years shown, the gross private saving percentage deviated from its trend value by an average of only 0.46 percentage points, and in only three scattered years was the deviation as much as 1 percentage point, despite large changes in many economic variables that are often thought to affect saving. From 1976 through 1983 the percentage hugged its trend line especially closely, with a mean deviation of only 0.23 percentage points. This span includes the period when radical changes were introduced in corporate and personal income tax laws in an effort to stimulate saving.[26] It should be noted that personal saving and corporate saving separately are not particularly stable. It is the fact that persons systematically save less when corporations save more that introduces stability into the private saving rate.

Government saving, representing the excess of receipts of all levels of government over their expenditures, as measured in the NIPA, must be added to gross private saving to arrive at gross national saving.[27] It is shown as a percentage of GNP in table 4-3, column 2. Government saving has been volatile, changing sign and size systematically in response to the business cycle and erratically in response to changes in budgets for other causes. Government saving introduces considerable instability, both cyclically and otherwise, in gross national saving as a percent of GNP (column 3). This percentage was lower in 1982 and 1983 than in any previous postwar year.

The upward trend in the gross private saving percentage accompanied a rise in the amount of capital consumption included in gross saving, as short-lived depreciable assets became a larger pro-

24. Estimates for international assets appear in tables 2-5, 2-6, 6-3, 8-1, 8-2, 8-3, and 8-4.

25. The computed trend line is $15.59 + 0.047t$ where t_1 is 1948. A clear upward trend in this series appeared only recently. It resulted partly from a conceptual change—the addition in the last benchmark revision of the NIPA of the net inflow from abroad of reinvested earnings of incorporated affiliates of direct investors—and partly from a July 1982 upward statistical revision of the estimates of saving in recent years.

26. It is unlikely but not inconceivable that a small rise in the saving rate induced by the incentives was offset by a cyclical decline. The absence of any cyclical movements in the gross private saving percentage throughout the postwar years argues against this possibility, but since there were such movements in the 1930s, their postwar absence shows only that it takes a really severe business downturn to affect the private saving rate. The years 1982 and 1983 were the most depressed of the postwar period (although much less than the 1930s), so that it is possible the saving rate was cyclically reduced in those years and would have been higher under prosperous conditions.

27. Capital grants received by the United States (net), a minor additional component of national saving, is ignored here. See table 4-3, footnote b.

portion of the capital stock. Net private saving, shown as a percentage of net national product in table 4-3, column 4, is free from the duplication that results from inclusion of capital consumption. It has no upward trend. Indeed, when the trend line is calculated over the same period as the gross saving trend, net private saving has a slight downward slope, with the trend value falling from 8.4 percent in 1948 to 7.6 percent in 1983.[28] However, the downward slope is entirely the result of the below-average percentages in the last four years of the period. The net private saving rate is fairly stable but, for reasons that are uncertain, less so than the gross percentage. Its mean deviation from the trend is 0.67 percentage points.

Government surplus and net national saving are shown as percentages of net national product in table 4-3, columns 5 and 6. Both were much more volatile than net private saving and dropped much more after 1979.

The percentages in column 6, which measures the net national investment rate as well as the net national saving rate, are divided between net foreign investment and net private domestic investment in columns 7 and 8. Net foreign investment, although small, was volatile even before 1979. Net private domestic investment, which consists of the change in business inventories and net investment in residential and nonresidential structures and producers' durable equipment, also fluctuated rather widely.

A great change in saving and investment patterns occurred in the 1980s. This shift is revealed by the informal table below, which shows net saving and investment as percentages of net national product.

ence was offset by moderately below-average private saving. On the investment side, net domestic investment was moderately above average, at 8.1 percent as against 7.5 percent, as is also typical approaching business cycle peaks, while net foreign investment was correspondingly below average. The changes from 1978–79 to 1980–81, a less prosperous period, were mainly cyclical in nature. The net national saving and investment percentage fell sharply, to 5.4 percent. The reduction in saving was concentrated in government saving, although net private saving fell further. The reduction in investment was in the domestic component; net foreign investment rose.

The changes in 1982–83 reflected in part a still weaker cyclical position, which further reduced government saving and domestic investment. Of longer lasting significance were the federal tax cuts, which added greatly to the federal deficit. Despite the large surpluses of state and local governments (mainly representing accumulations by pension funds), the combined deficits of all governments averaged 4.4 percent of net national product in 1982–83, a percentage that was matched in only one previous year since World War II (1975) and never even approached over any two-year period. Net foreign investment was negative, and strongly so in 1983. Net national saving and investment fell to a mere 1.9 percent of net national product.

By 1984, when the economy was in a strong expansion although still operating far below potential, the emerging pattern was clear. The net private saving rate was 8.2 percent, and the net domestic investment rate was 7.5 percent, both equal to their 1948–79 averages. But government dissaving was

	Net private saving	Government surplus	Net national saving and investment	Net foreign investment	Net private domestic investment
1948–79	8.2	−0.4	7.8	0.3	7.5
1978–79	7.3	0.4	7.7	−0.4	8.1
1980–81	6.5	−1.2	5.4	0.2	5.2
1982–83	6.4	−4.4	1.9	−0.7	2.7
1984	8.2	−3.8	4.5	−2.9	7.5

The pattern in 1978–79 had been fairly typical of the 1948–79 period. Net national saving and investment averaged 7.8 percent of net national product in 1948–79 and 7.7 percent in 1978–79. Government saving was above average in 1978–79, at 0.4 percent as against an average −0.4 percent, as was usual approaching the peak of a business cycle; the differ-

28. The computed trend line is 8.42 − 0.024*t*, where *t*₁ is 1948.

3.8 percent of net national product, thus canceling 46 percent of all net private saving. The federal government was absorbing an amount equal to a startling 65 percent of all private saving, but state and local government saving was substantially positive. As a result of government dissaving, net national saving and investment were only 4.5 percent of net national product. With national saving this small, a domestic investment rate of 7.5 percent was made possible only by a net foreign investment rate of −2.9 percent, that is, by liquidating American investments abroad and borrowing from or selling equities to foreigners at an unprecedented rate of $93 billion a year.

When federal taxes were slashed in 1981–83 by cutting rates and riddling the statutory tax base with new "preferences," a rise in the national saving rate was promised as a result. This outcome could have come from an increase in government saving if the stimulus to demand had expanded national income and hence the tax base enough to raise federal revenue more than it was reduced by the lower tax rates and the narrowing of the statutory base. Alternatively, lower taxes could have raised private saving by more than the tax reduction so as to more than offset the rise in the federal deficit. Neither alternative was plausible, and neither occurred. Rather, huge federal deficits emerged, and the private saving rate not only did not rise enough to offset the deficits, it even failed to rise above its previous average.

The enormous deficits did expand aggregate demand and help set the economy on a path of cyclical expansion that in 1983–84 rapidly narrowed the gap between actual and potential output. Moreover, the expansion took place without the reemergence of a high rate of inflation.

The moderation of price increases was partly the result of domestic influences: the presence of the largest reserve of unused productive capacity in the United States since the 1930s; the easing of the pattern of large regular wage increases as a result of the long duration of high unemployment and, perhaps, belated recognition that significant productivity gains allowing rising real wages had no longer been occurring; and a monetary policy that yielded interest rates high enough to dampen at least slightly the expansion of domestic investment. The absence of rising oil prices was also a favorable factor.

Likewise important in moderating price increases were international transactions and the effect of the federal deficit upon them. American recovery came at a time of world depression, with unemployment in other industrial countries very high and foreign producers anxious for markets. The federal deficit resulted in higher interest rates here than abroad. This interest rate differential, prospects for profit and for political stability that were perceived as especially favorable in the United States, and the loss of creditworthiness by the major borrowers among developing countries, all combined to attract an enormous inflow of foreign capital to the United States. The resulting demand for dollars yielded a

high rate of exchange for the dollar against nearly all other currencies, a situation that made it easy for foreign firms to sell in the United States and hard for American firms to sell abroad. A huge excess of imports over exports resulted and satisfied much of the rise in domestic demand. The United States thus drew on underutilized foreign resources and avoided tightness of American resources. It obtained the imports at low dollar prices, a fact that further dampened price increases for goods consumed in the United States. And the exceptionally strong foreign competition restricted the ability of American firms to raise their own prices.

By 1984 imports of goods and services (other than factor income) exceeded comparable exports by $108 billion, equal to 3.3 percent of net national product. In addition, the United States paid to foreigners $20 billion in U.S. government interest and $10 billion in net transfer payments to foreigners, together equal to an additional 0.9 percent of net national product. The sum of these net payments, after deducting a net inflow of factor income of $44 billion, or 1.3 percent of net national product, was −$94 billion, or −2.9 percent of net national product. This amount is the counterpart to our net foreign disinvestment in that year.

The huge federal deficit obviously had great immediate advantages. It reduced unemployment at home and abroad and brought actual output closer to potential output without re-igniting inflation. Its only immediate disadvantages were associated with high interest rates, which not only affected the domestic economy but also drastically raised the burden of servicing the large debts owed by a number of developing countries, and an overvalued currency that twisted the pattern of production away from that which would have prevailed under more normal conditions. Charles L. Schultze, who considered the dollar to be overvalued by 30–40 percent at the end of 1984, pointed out that this discrepancy has substantially penalized our most dynamic industries, the export industries. In the 1970s the United States had been becoming a major net exporter of capital goods, but by the end of 1984 that trend was sharply reversed; 25 percent of U.S. business investment in durable equipment now comes from abroad, and foreign markets for our high technology industries are sharply curtailed.[29]

However, the main disadvantages for the United States lie ahead. The deficit has already cut current

29. Charles L. Schultze, testimony before the U.S. Senate Committee on Finance, January 2, 1985.

investment in comparison with the outcome that could have been expected from a more usual mix of fiscal and monetary conditions that led to the same expansion of output. The fact that the curtailment is mainly in net foreign investment rather than domestic investment does not lessen the adverse effect on future national income.

A greater danger stems from the absence, as of the end of 1984, of any government plan to eliminate the federal deficit.[30] It is so large, and consequently raises the national debt so much each year, that with constant interest rates the increase in interest costs alone would require a major tax increase each year just to hold the high employment (or "structural") deficit constant, and if interest rates rise, the situation becomes much more difficult. When first the United States, and then the world, approach full utilization of resources, or—as may occur sooner—when other nations are no longer prepared to finance our domestic investment with their saving, we may be threatened with a resumption of high inflation and with interest rates that are not only unacceptable at home, but also potentially disastrous to foreign debtors with weaker economies than ours and to their creditors (including the United States). If the inflationary outcome becomes a near-term threat, the Federal Reserve Board may prefer to forestall it by using monetary policy to preserve substantial underutilization.

Domestic Investment Rate in Constant Dollars

Insofar as relative prices influence investment and saving decisions, the price relationships pertinent to such decisions are current prices, those prevailing when decisions are made. But it is net investment valued in constant dollars that contributes to growth of the real capital stock, and growth of the real capital stock that contributes to output growth. Table 4-3, column 9, shows net private domestic investment as a percent of net national product based on constant (1972) dollars, which may be compared with current dollar percentages in column 8. The two differ when the implicit price deflator for net investment differs from that of other components of net national product. The differences are irregular because the implicit price deflator for net investment (which is not published separately in the NIPA) moves erratically, a reflection of the unstable commodity composition of net domestic investment.

From 1948 to 1983 the constant-dollar percentage fell nearly 2 percentage points less than the current dollar percentage did, indicating that the relative price of investment had fallen. This movement would have been helpful to long-term capital stock growth if the price decline had been gradual and persistent. In fact, however, the changes were erratic, and the net change was concentrated at the end of the period. As recently as 1977–79 the average difference between the two percentages was almost the same as it had been in 1948–50 (or 1948–52). The relative price decline was a short-term one that helped capital stock growth only in the last short period, starting with 1979.

Land[31]

Land input is estimated not to have changed in nonresidential business and therefore not to have contributed to the growth rate of the sector's total actual or potential national income.[32] An unchanging index is not precisely correct, even though the land area of the country did not vary, because it would be desirable to adjust for any changes in the quality of agricultural, mineral, and forest land, and for transfers of land between nonresidential business and other sectors. However, agricultural, mineral, and forest land receive so little weight in the calculation of total input that no reasonable allowance for changes in quality could yield a land contribution appreciably different from zero, and there has been hardly any change in the proportion of land available to nonresidential business. Land is not shown to contribute to the growth of output in the whole economy either, because its small contribution to the growth of output in the "services of dwellings" and "international assets" sectors is included in the contributions of capital, while land does not contribute to measured growth in general government, households, and institutions.

Capital and Land per Person Employed

Over the 1929–82 period as a whole changes in the amounts of capital and land per person employed were not big enough, in view of the relatively small weight of these inputs, to make more than moderate contributions to growth rates. In nonresidential busi-

30. See Alice M. Rivlin, ed., *Economic Choices 1984* (Brookings, 1984), for a discussion of the problem and suggestions for a solution.

31. Estimates for land appear in tables 4-6, 4-7, 7-1, 7-2, 7-3, 7-4, 8-1, 8-2, 8-3, 8-4, and G-4.
32. The concept and measurement of land input are discussed in Edward F. Denison, *The Sources of Economic Growth in the United States and the Alternatives before Us* (New York: Committee for Economic Development, 1962), chap. 10 (hereafter *Sources of Growth*), and *Why Growth Rates Differ*, chap. 14.

ness, the growth rates of these inputs per person potentially employed were 0.99 percent for nonresidential structures and equipment, 1.07 percent for inventories, and −1.41 percent for land, sufficient to contribute only 0.11, 0.05, and −0.06 percentage points, respectively, to the growth rate of national income per person potentially employed (tables 3-2, 4-2, 4-6, and 7-4). In the economy as a whole, the four types of capital together contributed 0.23 percentage points to the growth rate of potential national income per person potentially employed, while land subtracted 0.05 points (table 8-4). The contributions to the growth of actual national income per person employed were a little larger (tables 7-3 and 8-3).[33]

The behavior of capital input per person potentially employed, like that of total capital input, was wholly different before and after 1948, and the contribution dropped from 1948–73 to 1973–82. In the economy as a whole capital contributed −0.12 percentage points to the growth rate of potential national income per person potentially employed in 1929–48, 0.48 points in 1948–73, and 0.26 points in 1973–82. Capital's contribution reached 21 percent of the growth rate in 1948–73, and capital accounted for almost three-fifths of the increase that took place in this growth rate from 1929–48 to 1948–73. The differences between periods are similar, although smaller, in nonresidential business. On an actual basis the contribution of capital dropped only 0.07 percentage points from 1948–73 to 1973–82 in the whole economy and 0.15 points in nonresidential business.

Total Factor Input and Output per Unit of Input[34]

Growth of national income can be broadly divided between changes in factor input (labor, capital, and land) and changes in output per unit of input. Of the growth of total potential national income over the whole period from 1929 to 1982, the increase in factor input was responsible for 63 percent and output per unit of input for 37 percent (table 8-2). Output per unit of input contributed a much larger proportion, 47 percent, to growth of potential national income in

the nonresidential business sector (table 7-2), while all growth in the three smaller sectors is attributable to factor input except for the minor effect of changes in the housing occupancy ratio. The proportion of growth contributed by output per unit of input had been larger until the last decade. In the case of potential output in the whole economy, it had been 39 percent in 1929–48 and 43 percent in 1948–73, but was only 3 percent in 1973–82. On an actual basis the contribution of output per unit of input was negative in 1973–82.

Output per unit of input has dominated the growth of national income per person employed. On a potential basis, it accounted for 75 percent of 1929–82 growth in the whole economy (calculated from table 8-4) and 87 percent in nonresidential business (calculated from table 7-4).

For nonresidential business, tables 5-1 and 5-2 show annual indexes of output per unit of input and the components of that series on actual and potential bases, while table 5-3 shows the growth rates of these indexes. The index for each determinant shows what the change in the sector's national income would have been each year if that output determinant had been the only one to change. Both actual and potential indexes are computed with actual 1972 values equal to 100. Consequently, the fact that, for example, in 1982 the index for gains from the reallocation of labor from farming on a potential basis (100.83) exceeded the index on an actual basis (100.62) by 0.2 percent means that, other things remaining unchanged, nonresidential business sector output would have been 0.2 percent higher if labor in the sector had been distributed between farm and nonfarm activities in the proportion that would have prevailed under potential conditions. Sector national income would have been 7.5 percent higher if all the determinants of output per unit of input had been at their potential values, as shown by the difference between potential and actual indexes of output per unit of input.

Components of Output per Unit of Input

Individual determinants of output per unit of input are reviewed next. They affect output only in nonresidential business (apart from the dwellings occupancy ratio). Because nonresidential business is around four-fifths of the economy, their contributions to the growth rate of national income in the whole economy, when expressed in percentage points, are about four-fifths as large as their contributions to growth in nonresidential business.

---

33. I discuss and reject a number of ways by which certain other investigators have obtained somewhat larger amounts than I do in "Accounting for Slower Economic Growth: An Update," in John W. Kendrick, ed., *International Comparisons of Productivity and Causes of the Slowdown* (American Enterprise Institute/Ballinger, 1984), pp. 10–17.

34. Data for output per unit of input and all its components except the dwellings occupancy ratio appear in tables 5-1, 5-2, 5-3, 7-1, 7-2, 7-3, 7-4, 8-1, 8-2, 8-3, and 8-4, and for output per unit of input itself, in tables 4-6 and 4-7.

Reallocation of Labor from Farming[35]

The more nearly resources are allocated to the uses in which they can contribute the most to the value of output, the larger is the output per unit of input. Mainly because shifting patterns of demand for labor have long been reducing the requirements for farm labor, while the actual transfer of labor has lagged, overallocation of labor to farming has been a chronic condition. Until recently, at least, it has been by far the biggest type of misallocation of resources among uses. As farm employment has shrunk, the fraction of total business employment thus misallocated has declined.

The gain in output per unit of input resulting from the reduction in the overallocation of labor to farming is calculated from two estimates. First, it is estimated that if labor input in the nonfarm portion of nonresidential business had been larger by 1 percent in any year, nonfarm output in the sector would have been larger by 0.8 percent, approximately the labor share of national income. Second, it is estimated that if labor input in farming had been smaller by 1 percent in any year, farm output (farm national income in 1972 prices) would have been smaller by 0.33 percent. Use of this latter percentage presumes that the reduction in labor would be concentrated on small farms with little output to the same extent as was the actual reduction of labor in farming. The shift of labor from farming raises output per unit of input in nonresidential business both because national income per person employed is far larger in nonfarm industries than in farming and because the elimination of excess labor raises productivity within farming.

The reduction of the proportion of labor misallocated to farming contributed an almost constant amount to the growth rate of potential national income in nonresidential business from 1929 to 1958. The contribution amounted to 0.34–0.36 percentage points in each of my first three standard short periods, 1929–41, 1941–48, and 1948–53, and in 1953–58. The decline in the farm percentage of nonresidential business employment was maintained at an approximately steady 0.5 percentage points a year during these three decades, despite the fact that the pool of farm employment to draw upon dropped from 24.4 percent of the sector total to 10.3 percent. The shift of labor from farming was responsible for 12 percent of the 1929–58 growth rate of total potential national income in the sector and 18 percent of the growth

rate of potential national income per person potentially employed, and thus was a major source of growth.

After 1958, the farm share of potential employment in nonresidential business continued down, reaching 3.1 percent in 1982. However, there simply was not enough surplus labor left in farming to allow the shift from farming to contribute as much as before to the growth rate of potential sector national income. The contribution dropped persistently to 0.25 percentage points in 1958–64, 0.16 points in 1964–73, 0.08 points in 1973–79, and 0.06 points in 1979–82. Over the 1929–82 period as a whole the contribution was 0.26 percentage points in nonresidential business, and 0.20 points in the whole economy.

Nonfarm Proprietors and Unpaid Family Workers[36]

Persons who are underemployed or whose labor is very wastefully utilized are also present among the nonfarm self-employed and unpaid members of their families. These individuals work in enterprises that are not only small but also highly inefficient. Little or no paid labor is hired, which holds down out-of-pocket expenses and enables an enterprise to survive when it could not do so if labor had to be paid in cash. Members of this fringe group among the self-employed contribute little to the value of production. But if hired by larger enterprises, they could contribute as much to output as other workers, and those remaining in self-employment could handle much of the work they formerly performed. Such persons are only a fraction—today, a small fraction—of the total number of self-employed and unpaid family workers engaged in nonfarm activities. However, the long-term reduction in the share of nonfarm business employment that is represented by self-employed and unpaid family workers appears to have occurred among this fringe group, rather than among those who are independent professionals; who operate more sizable establishments; who do well as craftsmen, repairmen, and the like; or who are simply unqualified for paid jobs.

The index of gains from the reallocation of labor from nonfarm self-employment, computed on a potential basis, grew at an annual rate of 0.07 percent from 1929 to 1982. This determinant was responsible for 2 percent of the growth of potential national income in the sector and 4 percent of the growth of potential national income per person potentially em-

---

35. Besides the tables indicated in footnote 34, data referring to this determinant appear in tables 3-8, 3-9, 3-10, 8-7, and H-1.

36. Besides the tables indicated in footnote 34, data referring to this determinant appear in tables 3-8, 3-9, 3-10, 8-7, and H-1.

ployed. These gains have been interrupted twice since World War II. Discharge from the armed forces of veterans anxious for the independence of being one's own boss and having access to government credit under favorable terms under the GI Bill of Rights created a huge but short-lived bulge in the number of self-employed persons immediately after the war. The second interruption was from 1976 to 1979, when self-employed and unpaid family workers increased from 9.0 percent of potential nonfarm employment in nonresidential business to 9.6 percent (calculated from tables 2-7 and 2-8). Because of these reversals the contribution to growth has fluctuated widely.

Whereas farm employment dropped in both absolute and relative terms, the number of nonfarm self-employed and unpaid family workers dropped only in a relative sense. The absolute number increased from 5.0 million in 1929 to 7.9 million in 1982. Of this 2.9 million increase, 1.5 million occurred in the six years from 1976 to 1982 and 1.1 million in the three years from 1976 to 1979, when the relative number also rose. It is possible that the 1976–79 experience calls for a change in my estimating procedures, but I have examined the demographic and industrial composition of this seemingly erratic reversal without reaching any firm conclusion as to whether it actually occurred and, if so, its significance for productivity analysis.[37]

Costs of Pollution Abatement[38]

In the last fifteen years changes in the institutional and human environment within which business must operate have adversely affected output per unit of input. I quantify the effects of three such changes, the first of which is regulatory requirements for pollution abatement. The reason that such requirements impair measured output per unit of input is that they divert labor and capital from the provision of measured output to the satisfaction of regulatory requirements, for which nothing is included in output as measured.[39]

Pollution abatement requirements did not affect the growth rate until after 1967. Although the annual amount that they have subtracted from the growth rate since then has been somewhat irregular, four periods may perhaps be distinguished. The contribution to the sector growth rate was −0.06 percentage points in 1967–69, −0.14 points in 1969–75, back to −0.06 points in 1975–78, and −0.12 points in 1978–82. In 1982 output per unit of input was 1.6 percent lower than it would have been under the conditions with respect to pollution abatement that prevailed before 1967. Table 5-4 provides a breakdown of the incremental pollution abatement costs that curtail output per unit of input.

Costs of Protecting Worker Safety and Health[40]

Costs of changes in regulations imposed upon business to protect the safety and health of workers have burdened measured output per unit of input less than pollution abatement costs. They affected the growth of output per unit of input only after 1968 and were appreciable for only a brief period. The contribution of this determinant to the sector growth rate was −0.01 percentage point in 1968–70, −0.07 points in 1970–73, −0.11 points in 1973–75, and −0.01 point in 1975–82. In 1982 the level of output per unit of input was 0.5 percent lower than it would have been under the conditions with respect to protection of safety and health that prevailed before 1968.

The estimates have three components. Together with their percentage of total incremental costs in 1982, computed from table 5-5, the components were: costs incurred for safety equipment on business motor vehicles, 31 percent; costs other than for motor vehicle equipment imposed on mining industries, mainly by special federal laws specific to mining, 42 percent; and costs other than for motor vehicle equipment imposed on other industries, mainly by the Occupational Safety and Health Act, 21 percent. Safety equipment on business motor vehicles protects the public as well as persons working for the firms that operate the vehicles.

---

37. The Current Population Survey is the primary source of data for these workers.

38. Besides the tables indicated in footnote 34, data referring to this determinant appear in table 5-4. As noted in "Derivations," Frederick J. Dreiling has updated and refined my earlier estimates, and I use his series for this determinant.

39. The article in which I introduced these series noted that my purpose in developing them "is to aid analysis of growth and productivity; it is not to judge the wisdom of government programs, which have benefits as well as costs. It must also be stressed that . . . many of the costs occasioned by pollution abatement, employee safety and health programs, and dishonesty and crime do not reduce output per unit of input and therefore are not included

in cost estimates cited. In particular, costs imposed directly upon governmental units and consumers do not have this effect. A major part of the estimating process was the division of costs between those that change output per unit of input and those that do not." See Edward F. Denison, "Effects of Selected Changes in the Institutional and Human Environment Upon Output per Unit of Input," *Survey of Current Business*, vol. 58 (January 1978), p. 22.

40. Besides the tables indicated in footnote 34, data referring to this determinant appear in table 5-5. See "Derivations" for a discussion of the changes introduced in these estimates and some recent evidence.

Costs of Dishonesty and Crime[41]

Criminal acts committed against business have increased in the United States. The increase in crime and the lessened ability to rely on the honesty of other people represent an important change in the human environment within which businesses must operate. These problems reduce measured output per unit of input in two ways. First, in an effort to limit their losses businesses may divert resources from the production of measured output to protection against criminal and dishonest acts. Second, criminal acts that nevertheless occur reduce output per unit of input. Most important, production of merchandise stolen from business before it reaches a final buyer absorbs inputs that are measured, whereas the merchandise that is stolen is not counted as output. The costs resulting from various other types of crime, such as the cost of repairing property damaged by vandalism, also reduce output per unit of input. The index measuring the effect of dishonesty and crime upon output per unit of input (tables 5-1 and 5-2) is the product of the separate indexes for costs of protection and costs of losses (table 5-6).

The index for the effect of dishonesty and crime upon output per unit of input in nonresidential business is estimated not to have changed from 1929 to 1957. Thereafter, year-to-year changes were irregular, but three periods may be distinguished: 1966–72, when the contribution to the growth rate of output per unit of input was −0.02 percentage points; 1972–76, −0.15 points; and 1976–82, −0.01 point. The latest evidence suggests that costs may have peaked in 1980. In that year output per unit of input was 1.0 percent lower than it would have been under 1957 conditions, with 20 percent of the additional loss consisting of the costs of protection and 80 percent of the cost of the losses.

Effect of Weather on Farm Output[42]

Irregular fluctuations in output per unit of input may be introduced by one-time random events that defy systematic identification and measurement. However, they result chiefly from recurrent and identifiable conditions. The first of four that are important enough to require attention is variations in weather and such natural conditions as pest infes-

tation that introduce irregular fluctuations into farm output with no commensurate effect on factor input.

The index shown for this determinant in tables 5-1 and 5-2 measures the effect of irregular fluctuations in farm output on output per unit of input in nonresidential business as a whole. As farming's share of national income declined, this index became less sensitive to fluctuations in farm output. Even so, it occasionally is still the case that fluctuations in farming importantly affect annual movements in sector output per unit of input. From 1980 to 1981 they did so by as much as 0.5 percent. Given that the series is trendless, these fluctuations usually have little effect on growth rates computed over a number of years. In my standard periods the contribution of the fluctuations was in the range of −0.02 to 0.02 percentage points except in 1979–82, when it reached 0.07 points.

Work Stoppages Due to Labor Disputes[43]

Work stoppages tend to reduce output per unit of input even though time not worked, whether in industries involved in disputes or in other industries, is excluded from labor input. Capital and land left idle are not eliminated from the input measure, and the productivity of workers remaining at work may be impaired. The range of the fluctuation in the index that measures the effect of work stoppages on output per unit of input in nonresidential business is only 0.12 percent, and this determinant has no more than a trivial effect on the growth rate in any standard period.

Length and Composition of the Year[44]

A third irregularity originates in inconsistency of data rather than real developments in the economy. The inconsistency arises from the fact that a year may consist of fifty-two weeks and a Sunday, fifty-two weeks and two work days, or anything in between. No input series is affected by differences in the length of the year because inputs are measured on a weekly average basis or the equivalent, but output is affected. The output series for nonresidential business purports to measure total output in a year. If this definition were always followed, one might be able to construct an annual series for the effects of the calendar on output per unit of input, but in fact the effect of the calendar on output per

---

41. Besides the tables indicated in footnote 34, data referring to this determinant appear in table 5-6. "Derivations" notes the loss of a source of information.

42. The tables containing data referring to this determinant are cited in footnote 34. Table 2-6 shows actual farm national income in 1982 prices.

43. The tables containing data referring to this determinant are cited in footnote 34.

44. My fullest discussion of calendar differences is in *Accounting for Growth*, pp. 67–68, 311–13.

unit of input cannot be ascertained. Differences in the calendar could cause the output per unit of input in nonresidential business to vary by as much as 1 percent from one year to the next, and these variations make comparisons of productivity changes between periods shorter than three years, at the least, hazardous unless the differences in growth rates are large. The calendar years have been classified among nine groups that are ranked starting with the group believed to be the least favorable to high measured output and ending with the group believed the most favorable. This approach makes it possible to identify the direction of bias in output over my standard periods by comparing their end years.[45] When calendar differences between end years and the lengths of the periods are both taken into account, it appears that the size of the bias cannot be important in any of these particular periods.

Fluctuations in Intensity of Demand[46]

Output per unit of input in nonresidential business fluctuates widely in response to changes in the intensity of demand for the sector's products. This situation results from the large element of overhead in inputs that prevents them from responding proportionally when production changes over the course of the business cycle. Instead, the intensity with which inputs are used fluctuates. The fluctuations are complex and irregular, and the irregularity is greatly intensified by the tendency for changes in employment to lag behind changes in output.

In the typical business cycle output per unit of input is highest, relative to its trend, during the phase of the cyle in which output is expanding rapidly—unless the level of output is still far below potential. Output per unit of input drops when the expansion of total output slackens with the approach of the business cycle peak; on some occasions materials shortages may contribute to a low rate of utilization. Output per unit of input remains low until the trough of the next recession approaches, and then it turns up. Each cycle nevertheless has its own characteristics. Moreover, the intensity of utilization is much higher at the peak or trough of some cycles than of others. It has been persistently low since 1969.

45. Only the 1929–41 and 1973–79 growth rates were unaffected. The growth rates for 1929–82, 1929–48, 1973–82, 1941–48, 1953–64, and 1979–82 tend to be overstated because of calendar differences while those for 1948–73, 1948–53, and 1964–73 are understated. Table 5-7 shows the ranking of years.
46. Besides the tables indicated in footnote 34, data referring to this determinant appear in tables 2-4, I-1, I-2, I-3, I-5, and I-8.

Table 5-1 provides an index of the effect on output per unit of input in nonresidential business of changes in the intensity of the utilization of employed resources that result from fluctuations in the pressure of demand. The index plays an important part in the derivation of the series for potential output, and its construction is described in "Derivations." The index fluctuates widely during the years covered by the study, ranging from 96.29 in 1974 to 106.56 in 1941, a difference of nearly 11 percent. Changes in the intensity of utilization not only dominate year-to-year productivity changes, but also have an important effect on growth rates over a number of years, including my standard periods. This statement refers to the growth of output and productivity measured on an actual basis. Potential output is unaffected because, in accordance with its definition, it is measured with intensity of use, as affected by demand pressures, at a constant rate. Changes in intensity of use are responsible for most of the difference between the growth rates of actual and potential output per unit of input in the postwar standard periods.

Occupancy Ratio for Dwellings[47]

The output of the "services of dwellings" sector is determined not only by the stock of housing, but also by the proportion of the housing stock that is used. Vacation and other homes reserved for the use of their owners or renters count as in use because their rental value is included in output in the NIPA. Table 6-4 shows an index of the effect of changes in the occupancy ratio upon national income originating in the housing sector. The index starts from its lowest point (among the years covered in this study) in 1929, when vacancies were numerous, then rises to its highest point in 1947, from which it falls quickly until 1951, and then falls more slowly to a low in 1965. The index then rises slowly, with an interruption in only one year, until 1978. Since then it has moved but little. Because the swings in the index are long and gradual and in any year have little or no relationship to the business cycle position in that year, housing vacancies are not considered to introduce a difference between actual and potential national income. The change in the dwellings occupancy ratio contributed 0.17 percentage points to the growth rate of output in the services of dwellings sector over the whole 1929–82 period, but this movement amounted

47. Data referring to this determinant appear in tables 6-3, 6-4, 8-1, 8-2, 8-3, and 8-4.

to only 0.01 percentage point in the economy as a whole.

The Semiresidual[48]

An index measuring the effect on output per unit of input in nonresidential business of economies of scale, advances in knowledge, and all other determinants that have not yet been measured is shown in column 10 of tables 5-1 and 5-2. This index grew rather steadily from 1948 to 1973 at a rate averaging 1.80 percent a year, up from 0.50 percent in 1929–41 and 1.57 percent in 1941–48. The rate fell to a mere 0.20 percent in 1973–82. The reason the semiresidual is shown separately is that it is particularly difficult to make a further division.

Economies of Scale Associated with Growth of the National Market[49]

Growth of an economy automatically means growth in the average size of the local, regional, and national markets for end products that business serves. Growth of markets brings opportunities for greater specialization—both among and within industries, firms, and establishments—and opportunities for establishments and firms within the economy to become larger without impairing the competition that stimulates efficiency. Larger production runs for individual products become possible, as do larger transactions in buying, selling, and shipping in almost all industries, including wholesale and retail trade. Larger regional and local markets permit greater geographic specialization and less transporting of products. The opportunities for greater specialization, bigger units, longer runs, and larger transactions provide a clear reason to expect increasing returns in the production and distribution of many products, and examples of increasing returns are plentiful.

My estimates assume that an increase in any other determinant of output that would have sufficed to raise nonresidential business national income by 1.0 percent under constant returns to scale actually increased it by 1.125 percent: that is, economies of scale amounted to 12.5 percent, or one-eighth. This assumption meant that the cost reductions resulting from economies of scale associated with the growth of the national market were credited with being the source of one-ninth of the growth rate of sector output. This fraction is assumed not to have declined

as markets and the scale of output grew because knowledge of technology and business organization develops and adapts to the new situation that exists with enlarged markets, and opportunities for scale economies are constantly replenished.[50]

Economies of scale, in the sense used here, are related to the size of markets that business is organized to serve. (The so-called short-run economies of scale that are associated with fluctuations in output are measured in the indexes for the effects of fluctuations in the intensity of utilization.) Clearly, actual output is not an appropriate series on which to base gains from economies of scale, but when there has been an extended period of underutilization, neither is potential output. The output series used, a compromise, is shown in table J-1 and described in "Derivations."

Gains from economies of scale contributed an estimated 0.34 percentage points to the growth rate of potential national income in nonresidential business over the whole 1929–82 period, or nearly 11 percent of the growth rate. The amount was as much as 0.50 percentage points, or close to it, in 1941–48, 1948–53, and 1964–73, and as little as 0.13–0.16 percentage points in 1929–41 and 1979–82. Economies of scale contribute less to the growth rate in the whole economy than in nonresidential business because they do not affect measured output in other sectors. Over the whole 1929–82 period their contribution was 0.27 percentage points, or 8.4 percent of the growth rate of potential national income.

The rate of growth of the national market, which depends on all output determinants, determines the contribution that economies of scale make to the growth rate when obstacles to their realization do not change. That concept is what I attempt to measure. Obstacles to full realization of possible economies of scale, such as international trade barriers or certain types of monopolistic actions, may change, but these obstacles are considered separate determinants of output.

48. Data referring to the semiresidual appear in tables 5-1, 5-2, 5-3, I-3, and I-4.

49. Besides the tables indicated in footnote 34, data referring to this determinant appear in table J-1.

50. Edwin Mansfield provides additional new evidence of this process in his finding that process innovations in the chemical, petroleum, and steel industries resulted in increases in the minimum efficient scale of plant far more often than in decreases. See Edwin Mansfield, "Technological Change and Market Structure: An Empirical Study," *American Economic Review*, vol. 73 (May 1983, *Papers and Proceedings, 1982*), pp. 205–9. According to Ralph Landau, in the case of the Hall process in the aluminum industry the learning curve (which he relates both to learning how to do things better as the total number of pounds or units produced increases, and to the scale of production) has repeatedly been descended with each improvement of the process. See Ralph Landau, "Process Innovation" [Perkin Medal Address], *Chemistry and Industry*, no. 9 (May 2, 1981), pp. 321–27.

Advances in Knowledge and Miscellaneous Determinants[51]

Advancing knowledge of ways to produce at low cost is the biggest and most basic reason for the persistent long-term growth of output per unit of input. The term "advances in knowledge" covers both technological knowledge and managerial and organizational knowledge. It includes knowledge originating in this country and abroad, and knowledge obtained in any way: by organized research, by individual research workers, and by simple observation and experience.

The term must, however, be limited in a study of the sources of growth of any output series to those advances in knowledge that allow the same amount of *measured* output to be obtained with less input. This limitation automatically excludes knowledge applied outside the business sector. It also excludes new knowledge that leads to "unmeasured" quality change in the final products of the business sector. The introduction of new and improved products for final sale from the business sector to consumers and government provides the buyer with a greater range of choice or enables him to meet his needs better with the same use of resources, but it does not in general contribute to growth as measured; rather, it results in unmeasured quality change. Hence advances in knowledge that permit business to supply households and government with final products that are different from those previously available are excluded.

Organized R&D conducted in the United States of the type covered by the National Science Foundation series for R&D expenditures contributed an estimated 0.2 percentage points, or, at most, 0.3 points to the growth rate of measured output in nonresidential business during the postwar period.[52]

To obtain such estimates, the dollar value of the contribution of R&D to yearly growth is calculated by multiplying the annual cost of R&D expenditures of types that, if successful, will raise measured output per unit of input by a social rate of return on such R&D expenditures (estimated to be extremely high) that is based on sample studies (mainly, the admirable work of Edwin Mansfield and his collaborators). Sometimes a deduction is made for estimated obsolescence on knowledge acquired from previous R&D.[53] Unfortunately, there is no way to estimate directly the contribution of advances in knowledge derived from any other source, or all other sources, to the growth rate of output per unit of input in nonresidential business.

The combined contribution of changes in all determinants of output that were not directly measured on an annual basis, including advances in knowledge and a group of miscellaneous determinants, is obtained by removing from the growth rate of output the effects of changes in all determinants that were so measured. Table 5-1, column 12, shows an index constructed in this way. From 1948 to 1973 it grew at an annual rate of 1.38 percent (table 5-3).

---

51. Besides the tables indicated in footnote 34, data relating to this determinant appear in table 4-4.

52. For a discussion of these estimates see *Slower Growth,* pp. 123–26; Zvi Griliches, "R&D and the Productivity Slowdown," and Edward F. Denison, "Comment," both in *American Economic Review,* vol. 70 (May 1980, *Papers and Proceedings, 1979*), pp. 343–48, 354–55; Barry P. Bosworth, *Tax Incentives and Economic Growth* (Brookings, 1984), pp. 32–33; and citations in these sources. As I explain later (in chapter 3), a higher estimate by John W. Kendrick is not comparable, nor pertinent to an explanation of changes in any existing output series, because Kendrick is really estimating what R&D would have contributed to an imaginary output series that would be obtained if the rise in output could somehow capture the welfare benefits from new and improved final products. Kendrick has implicitly recognized this situation by noting that the part of R&D "that results in cost reduction increases productivity and the part that results in new and improved consumer goods increases satisfaction. However, . . . real product and productivity estimates are generally considered to understate growth to the extent that there have been net

improvements in the quality of goods and services." See John W. Kendrick, *The Formation and Stocks of Total Capital* (New York: National Bureau of Economic Research, 1976), pp. 9–10. To obtain the contribution of R&D to growth of measured output, either R&D that does not contribute to measured productivity must be excluded or, if such R&D is counted, the rate of return must be lowered by including it with a zero rate of return.

53. The estimates assume, I believe correctly, that but little knowledge that raises measured output results from the spinoff of findings of military research to commercial applications. Richard R. Nelson finds that whatever spinoff may once have occurred, it dwindled away decades ago as military hardware became more specialized and distinct from its civilian counterparts (as in the case of the airplane) or became concentrated in areas without civilian counterparts. See Richard R. Nelson, "Policies in Support of High Technology Industries," Working Paper 1011 (Institution for Social and Policy Studies, Yale University, July 1984). David M. Levy and Nestor E. Terleckyj infer from correlation analysis that federally financed R&D has an effect on commercial output but that it does so by stimulating government contractors to increase their private expenditures on R&D in order to adapt their findings to commercial products. See David M. Levy and Nestor E. Terleckyj, "Effects of Government R&D on Private R&D Investment and Productivity: A Macroeconomic Analysis," paper presented to the Southern Economic Association, Atlanta, November 11, 1982. Edwin Mansfield reached a similar conclusion based on a questionnaire survey ("Engineering Employment, Federal Funding, and Company-financed R&D Expenditures," paper presented to the American Economic Association, New York, December 1982) while Frank R. Lichtenberg reached the opposite conclusion ("The Relationship Between Federal Contract R&D and Company R&D," *American Economic Review,* vol. 74 [May 1984, *Papers and Proceedings, 1983*] pp. 73–78). Because all private expenditures are counted, when appropriate, in computing the estimate of the contribution of R&D to the growth rate that is cited in the text, the estimate includes any positive or negative effect of government expenditures on private R&D.

In the past I have interpreted the movement of this index from 1948 to 1973 (but not thereafter) as an acceptable approximation of the contribution made to growth by the incorporation of new knowledge into the process of production. Because the effects of so many determinants were measured, this series is far more refined than the indexes of output per hour worked and unit of capital that have often been identified as measures of "technical progress." However, my interpretation was based on more than improvement upon precedent. It was supported by the following considerations.

First, and most important, the index displayed the stable growth that an index measuring the contribution of advances in knowledge would be expected to show in the world's most advanced, largest, and most diversified economy. From 1948 to 1973 it rose every year. Moreover, it did so at a rather steady rate. In the three shorter periods in this time span its growth rates were 1.33 percent, 1.34 percent, and 1.46 percent. Irregularities in the size of the annual increases were scarcely greater than one might have expected from calendar differences alone, even though the series picks up the effect of errors in the output measure as well as certain errors in the indexes for other output determinants.

A second consideration was that similar residual estimates for other countries revealed a pattern that appeared reasonable for the contribution of knowledge.[54] In brief, despite large differences in the growth rates of output, the residuals were fairly similar in the United States and other advanced Western countries and moderately higher in Japan—a pattern that conformed to the accepted belief that in Japan technology was moving up toward the much higher levels prevailing in the West. The fact that the growth rate of the index had increased from earlier periods in the United States itself was also in accord with usual beliefs about the pace of new knowledge.

Finally, although I had not attempted annual estimates for the miscellaneous determinants that may affect the residual index, I had attempted to quantify the contribution of some of them over longer periods and to judge the possible magnitude of others.[55] My conclusion was that the effects of the miscellaneous determinants probably were small and

offsetting. Confidence in this conclusion, as applied to 1948–73, is weakened by experience after 1973, when miscellaneous determinants apparently exerted a large negative effect on growth. Although there are reasons why miscellaneous determinants should have changed more after 1973 than before, it is not clear why their effect was so large. Despite this later experience, I still consider that the 1.38 percent growth rate of the residual provides a reasonable estimate of the contribution of advances in knowledge in 1948–73.

The growth rate of the residual is also, I believe, an acceptable estimate of the contribution of advances in knowledge in 1941–48. It was 1.11 percent. Interpretation of the 0.34 percent growth rate in 1929–41 is more dubious. In a previous examination of the period I concluded that restrictive practices introduced during the Depression that affected the miscellaneous determinants restrained the growth of output per unit of input, but probably were not responsible for much more than one-tenth of a percentage point of the difference between the 1929–41 and 1948–69 growth rates.[56] Advances in knowledge evidently contributed much less to growth in 1929–41 than in 1948–73.

The behavior of the residual series since 1973 has been altogether different from anything that has gone before (tables 5-1 and 5-3). Its growth rate dropped by 1 full percentage point, or 72 percent, from 1948–73 to 1973–78, and by an additional full percentage point from 1973–78 to 1978–82. In 1973–78 the growth rate was about as low as it had been in 1929–41, and thereafter it was actually negative by a substantial amount, −0.66 percent, in 1978–82 and was probably little different in 1978–83. The peak in the index to date was reached in 1978. The decline in the growth rate after 1973 was abrupt, with no hint of slackening through 1973 and a sudden decline thereafter. Moreover, since 1973 the index has behaved erratically, rising in four years and falling in five.

It is not plausible that an index measuring the contribution of advances in knowledge would have behaved this way. I can only conclude that some of the miscellaneous determinants of output were responsible for the collapse in the growth rate of the residual and its erratic movement. I offer this opinion

54. Edward F. Denison, "A Cross-Country View of the Contribution of Knowledge to Economic Growth," published in Russian translation in T. S. Khachaturov, ed., *The Soviet-American Symposium of Economics* (Moscow, 1978), pp. 39–46.

55. Examples of such estimates are scattered throughout my writings. See Denison, *Sources of Growth,* chaps. 15–20; *Why Growth Rates Differ,* chaps. 3, 9, 17 (part 3), 18, parts of chaps.

12, 20, 21, and appendixes M, N; *Accounting for Growth,* pp. 76–79; *Slower Growth,* pp. 81–83 and chap. 9; and "Accounting for Slower Economic Growth: An Update," pp. 21–37.

56. *Accounting for Growth,* pp. 81–82. An alternative way of measuring real output—using current price weights for each decade instead of the same weights for all periods—would also narrow the differences between periods.

even though, as the next chapter indicates, the evidence is insufficient to establish conclusively which of the many developments suspected of being the culprits responsible for the collapse were really to blame.

This conclusion leaves no way to measure what actually happened to the contribution of advances in knowledge after 1973. It is not unlikely that the contribution was reduced. The period from World War II to 1973 was one in which, it appears, progress in all types of knowledge was exceptionally fast by historical standards. A gradual falling back to longer term rates would not have been surprising. However, there is no certainty that such a decline occurred.

In the following section I summarize estimates of the sources of growth of output over the 1929–82 period as a whole. Solely for this purpose I assume (reasonably) that the residual series measures the contribution of advances in knowledge from 1941 to 1973; and (as guesses) that the 0.34 percent growth rate of the residual from 1929 to 1941 consisted of a 0.45 percent rate for advances in knowledge and a −0.11 percent rate for miscellaneous determinants, while the −0.07 percent growth rate of the residual from 1973 to 1982 consisted of a 1.00 percent growth rate for advances in knowledge and a −1.07 percent growth rate for miscellaneous determinants. This procedure results in an estimate that advances in knowledge contributed 1.07 percentage points to the 1929–82 growth rate of total potential national income in nonresidential business, while miscella-

neous determinants subtracted 0.21 points. Neither source affects growth of measured output in the other sectors, and so these sources contributed smaller amounts to the growth rate of potential national income in the whole economy: advances in knowledge, 0.84 percentage points, and miscellaneous determinants, −0.16 points. Reasonable variations in the numbers used for 1929–41 and 1973–82 would not greatly change these results.

Sources of Long-Term Growth

Detailed estimates of the contributions that the output determinants made to the growth rates of various output series during each of the eleven standard periods are shown in tables 7-1 to 7-4 and 8-1 to 8-4. These sources-of-growth tables are provided for four measures of total national income and four of national income per person employed, as well as for output per unit of input, a subtotal given in the tables. The tables show the number of percentage points contributed to the growth rate.

The tabulation below condenses growth sources into ten groups and shows the percentage of the growth rate of each of the eight output series contributed by each group of determinants over the fifty-three years from 1929 to 1982. This tabulation identifies the sources of growth in the United States over the longest period presently possible. However, these distributions should not be regarded as "normal" or "typical" patterns. The data in this study

	Contributions to 1929–82 growth rates							
	Potential national income				Actual national income			
	Total		Per person employed		Total		Per person employed	
	Whole economy (1)	Nonresidential business (2)	Whole economy (3)	Nonresidential business (4)	Whole economy (5)	Nonresidential business (6)	Whole economy (7)	Nonresidential business (8)
Growth rate	3.2	3.1	1.6	1.7	2.9	2.8	1.5	1.6
Percent of growth rate								
All sources	100	100	100	100	100	100	100	100
Labor input except education	34	25	−13	−23	32	20	−12	−25
Education per worker	13	16	26	30	14	19	27	34
Capital	17	12	15	10	19	14	20	13
Advances in knowledge	26	34	54	64	28	39	55	68
Improved resource allocation	8	11	16	19	8	11	16	18
Economies of scale	8	11	17	20	9	12	18	22
Changes in legal and human environment	−1	−2	−3	−4	−1	−2	−3	−4
Land	0	0	−3	−4	0	0	−3	−3
Irregular factors	0	0	0	0	−3	−5	−7	−8
Other determinants	−5	−7	−10	−13	−5	−8	−10	−13

show that patterns have changed from period to period, and other studies show that they have differed widely among countries.[57]

The greatest interest attaches to the estimates for potential output shown in the first four columns. The first column of the tabulation analyzes the growth of potential national income in the whole economy. By the classification adopted, six groups of sources made positive contributions to this growth rate. The largest contribution, 34 percent of the growth rate, is identified in the table as coming from the increase in "labor input except education." It represents the increase in the amount of work done in our economy, when account is taken of the number, working hours, and characteristics of workers (except their education) and of the effect of changes in the hours of work upon the work done in an hour. Second largest, at 26 percent, is the incorporation into the productive process of advances in knowledge of how to produce at low cost. Third, at 17 percent, is the increase in the services provided by four types of capital. Fourth, at 13 percent, is the increase in the level of education of persons employed in the nonresidential business sector. (If the two components of labor input are combined, they account for nearly half—47 percent—of the growth rate.) Fifth and sixth, at 8 percent each, are gains from economies of scale and the reduction in the overallocation of labor to farming and to nonfarm self-employment. Land and irregular factors neither added to nor subtracted from this growth rate. Three changes in the legal and human environment subtracted an amount equal to 1 percent, and other determinants an amount equal to 5 percent, of the growth rate. The latter consists of the amount allocated to miscellaneous determinants in the preceding section, with a slight offset from the inclusion of the dwellings occupancy ratio.

The second column analyzes the growth of potential output in the nonresidential business sector alone. When the other three sectors are eliminated, the contributions of labor input and of capital are reduced and the contributions (positive or negative) of the other sources are increased. The reason is that all growth in the government, households, and institutions sector is ascribable to labor input except education, and practically all growth in the services of dwellings and international assets sectors is ascribable to capital. Advances in knowledge were much the largest source of growth in nonresidential business, followed by labor input except education.

The third column of the tabulation analyzes the growth of potential output per person potentially employed in the whole economy. To an important extent this growth rate was the net result of offsetting positive and negative influences. Five of the ten groups of determinants contributed an amount equal to 128 percent of the growth rate, one (irregular factors) did not affect it, and four subtracted an amount equal to 28 percent.[58] When expressed in percentage points, the contributions of education per worker, advances in knowledge, improved resource allocation, economies of scale, changes in legal and human environment, irregular factors, and "other determinants" are all practically the same as their contributions to the growth rate of total potential output in the whole economy, but when expressed as percentages of the growth rate, they are about twice as large. The contribution of advances in knowledge equaled 54 percent of this growth rate. On a per person employed basis, labor input except education declined and made a negative contribution equal to 13 percent of the growth rate because of declining average hours (including the effect of an increase in part-time employment) and the change in the demographic composition of hours worked. Land per person potentially employed also declined and subtracted an amount equal to 3 percent of the growth rate.

The fourth column refers to potential national income per person potentially employed in nonresidential business. The contribution of capital was a smaller percentage of the growth rate than in the whole economy, where it includes dwellings and international assets, but the positive or negative contributions of all other determinants were larger and the importance of offsets correspondingly greater. Advances in knowledge alone contributed an amount equal to 64 percent of the growth rate, education per worker 30 percent. In all, five groups contributed an amount equal to 143 percent of this growth rate, while four subtracted an amount equal to 43 percent.

Columns 5 through 8 of the informal tabulation provide estimates for the actual output series that are the counterparts of the potential output series just reviewed. The contributions of many determinants are the same on an actual as on a potential basis when expressed in percentage points, but differ when expressed as percentages of the growth rate because the growth rates are different. When contributions expressed in percentage points differ, the

57. See Denison and Chung, *How Japan's Economy Grew So Fast*, pp. 39–45.

58. There were also offsetting pluses and minuses within the "labor input except education" group and also, no doubt, among the "other determinants."

only reason is that the positions of 1929 and 1982 with respect to the business cycle and productivity cycle were different. Irregular factors make a negative contribution to growth rates on an actual basis because the index for the effect on output per unit of input in nonresidential business of changes in the intensity of utilization of employed resources resulting from fluctuations in intensity of demand was 7 percent lower in 1982 than in 1929.

Contributions to the series computed on a potential basis are not affected by the cyclical positions of end years, but even they may be somewhat affected by the cyclical pattern—and international events—of the past. However, the effect is rarely known. For example, would the sizes of the capital stock and potential employment in 1982 have been bigger if the Depression and World War II had not cut net capital formation and birth rates in 1930–46? Or were capital formation and population growth in the postwar years larger than they would otherwise have been so that the deficiency was eliminated? The reader may suppose that the percentage of growth contributed by capital is reduced by inclusion of the period's last three years, 1980–82, in which business activity was weak, but in fact all the percentages for capital in the informal tabulation were the same or lower in 1929–79 than in 1929–82.

The following chapter examines changes in the sources of growth after 1973. Readers are encouraged to look at the estimates for other periods shown in the tables, which have been discussed in my previous books.

CHAPTER THREE

The Slowdown in Growth

The growth rates of all my major measures of output and productivity dropped sharply from the 1948–73 long period to the incomplete 1973–82 long period. The amounts by which they dropped are shown in the first column of the informal tabulation below. The growth rate of total potential national income in the whole economy fell by 1.28 percentage points, or from 3.89 percent to 2.61 percent. The declines in most series were bigger, ranging up to 2.71 percentage points in the case of actual national income per person employed in nonresidential business.

The remaining columns of the table show the declines in growth rates that occurred in each of the two most recent short periods. The declines from 1973–79 to 1979–82 were not as big as those from 1964–73 to 1973–79, except in the two series that measure total actual output, but all were large nevertheless. In all series the total decline from 1964–73 to 1979–82, the sum of the last two columns, exceeded the decline from 1948–73 to 1973–82. It was two or two-and-a-half times as large in the four series that measure total output, because the 1964–73 growth rates were much above the 1948–73 rates, while the 1979–82 rates were much below the 1973–82 rates. The growth rates of all series were lower in 1979–82 than in 1973–82.

Determinants Responsible for the Declines in Growth Rates

This section summarizes the sources of some of these declines in growth rates. Advances in knowledge and miscellaneous determinants are treated here as a single source; they are examined in detail in the following sections.

Potential Output, Total and per Person Employed: Declines, 1948–73 to 1973–82

The output determinants responsible for the decline from 1948–73 to 1973–82 in the growth rate of total potential output in the whole economy are shown in the first column of the informal table on the following page. The most detailed classification of

	Change in growth rate (percentage points)		
	1948–73 to 1973–82	1964–73 to 1973–79	1973–79 to 1979–82
Whole economy			
Potential output—total	−1.28	−1.26	−1.19
Per person employed	−2.03	−1.49	−0.77
Per hour	−2.00	−1.49	−0.90
Per unit of input	−1.74	−1.32	−0.80
Residual productivity	−1.14	−0.92	−0.80
Actual output—total	−2.15	−1.31	−3.15
Per person employed	−2.10	−1.23	−0.90
Per hour	−1.92	−1.27	−0.70
Per unit of input	−1.80	−1.18	−1.25
Residual productivity	−1.14	−0.92	−0.80
Nonresidential business			
Potential output—total	−1.16	−1.50	−1.08
Per person employed	−2.59	−2.05	−0.82
Per hour	−2.45	−2.00	−0.90
Per unit of input	−2.05	−1.76	−1.00
Residual productivity	−1.47	−1.18	−1.03
Actual output—total	−2.32	−1.55	−3.68
Per person employed	−2.71	−1.74	−1.01
Per hour	−2.45	−1.73	−0.77
Per unit of input	−2.35	−1.56	−1.62
Residual productivity	−1.47	−1.18	−1.03

	Potential national income in the whole economy (percentage points)	
	Total	Per person potentially employed
Growth rate, 1948–73	**3.89**	**2.26**
Plus increased contributions in 1973–82	**0.69**	**0.07**
Employment	0.62	. . .
Education	0.04	0.04
Dwellings occupancy ratio	0.02	0.02
Weather in farming	0.01	0.01
Less reduced contributions in 1973–82	**1.97**	**2.10**
Hours	0.09	0.09
Age-sex composition	0.09	0.09
Unallocated labor input	0.08	0.08
Inventories	0.08	0.08
Nonresidential structures and equipment	0.02	0.08
Dwellings	. . .	0.05
International assets	. . .	0.01
Land	. . .	0.02
Reallocation from farming	0.15	0.15
Reallocation from nonfarm self-employment	0.08	0.08
Pollution abatement	0.07	0.07
Worker safety and health	0.02	0.02
Dishonesty and crime	0.04	0.04
Economies of scale	0.11	0.11
Residual productivity	1.14	1.13
Equals growth rate, 1973–82	**2.61**	**0.23**

growth sources is used, except that the effect of changes in working hours is handled as a single source. Changes in the contributions of four determinants were favorable to a higher growth rate in the later period. By themselves they would have raised the growth rate by 0.69 percentage points from its level of 3.89 percent in 1948–73, with employment responsible for nine-tenths of this change. However, twelve determinants subtracted 1.97 percentage points. Of this amount, three components of labor input subtracted 0.26 percentage points; two components of capital input, 0.10 points; two components of resource reallocation, 0.23 points; three components of the human and institutional environment, 0.13 points; and economies of scale, 0.11 points. The 0.83 percentage points ascribable to these eleven determinants, whose contributions were independently estimated, were equal to 65 percent of the decline in the growth rate and 45 percent of the decline in the contribution of the determinants whose contributions declined. The rest of the latter total represents the decline in the contribution of residual productivity, which measures the contribution of advances in knowledge and miscellaneous determinants.

The second column of the same table reconciles the 1948–73 and 1973–82 growth rates of potential national income per person potentially employed in the whole economy. Most entries are the same as for total potential output. However, employment disappears as a growth source. The contribution of the other three determinants whose contributions increased in the second period rose by only 0.07 percentage points. Capital and land components now refer to input per person potentially employed. Their contributions to potential output per person employed fell more than their contributions to total potential output because the growth of potential employment accelerated in the second period. In all, the contributions of fifteen determinants dropped by 2.10 percentage points, including a 1.13 point drop in the growth of residual productivity. The contributions of three components of labor input dropped 0.26 percentage points; of four components of capital input, 0.22 points; of land, 0.02 points; of two components of resource reallocation, 0.23 points; of three components of the legal and human environment, 0.13 points; and of economies of scale, 0.11 points. These fourteen determinants whose contributions were independently estimated were responsible for

48 percent of the decline in the growth rate and 46 percent of the decline attributed to the determinants, including residual productivity, whose contributions declined. These determinants by themselves would have cut the growth rate by 43 percent from 1948–73 to 1973–82.

Potential Output per Person Employed: Declines, 1964–73 to 1973–79 and 1973–79 to 1979–82

The next informal table analyzes the declines that occurred in the same series—potential national in-

amount each period, changes in the age-sex composition of hours worked tended to raise the growth rate slightly in 1973–79 and appreciably in 1979–82. Although the familiar view that changes in demographic composition contributed to the growth slowdown is correct if one compares the long periods, as was done earlier, the opposite is the case if one examines the growth slowdown since 1964–73.

The second group of determinants consists of nine that were working toward an increase in the growth rate in the second period after contributing to the decline in the first (or, in three cases, not affecting the change in the rate in the first). This group includes

	Changes in contributions to growth rate of potential national income per person potentially employed, whole economy (percentage points)	
	Change, 1964–73 to 1973–79	Change, 1973–79 to 1979–82
All sources	**−1.49**	**−0.77**
Contributions that increased in both periods	**0.02**	**0.16**
Age-sex composition	0.02	0.16
Contributions that decreased or were constant, then increased	**−0.35**	**0.43**
Hours	−0.07	0.09
Nonresidential structures and equipment	−0.09	0.04
Dwellings	−0.01	0.07
Land	0.00	0.02
Reallocation from nonfarm self-employment	−0.11	0.06
Worker safety and health	−0.02	0.04
Dishonesty and crime	−0.05	0.05
Weather in farming	0.00	0.05
Labor disputes	0.00	0.01
Contributions that decreased, then decreased again or were constant (except residual)	**−0.35**	**−0.23**
Unallocated labor input	−0.05	0.00
Inventories	−0.06	−0.05
Reallocation from farming	−0.07	−0.01
Pollution abatement	−0.04	−0.01
Economies of scale	−0.13	−0.16
Contributions that increased, then decreased	**0.10**	**−0.33**
Education	0.03	−0.06
International assets	0.05	−0.24
Dwellings occupancy ratio	0.02	−0.03
Residual productivity	**−0.91**	**−0.80**

come per person potentially employed in the whole economy—from 1964–73 to 1973–79 (1.49 percentage points) and from 1973–79 to 1979–82 (0.77 points). This table has some surprising features.

The first group of determinants in the table, those making positive contributions to the change in the growth rate in both periods, contains only age-sex composition. By subtracting a progressively smaller

working hours, both components of fixed capital input, land, reallocation from nonfarm self-employment, two changes in the legal and human environment, and two irregular factors. Together they contributed 0.35 percentage points to the slowdown in 1973–79 and 0.43 points toward an increase in 1979–82. As a group they actually contributed even more to the growth rate in 1979–82 than in 1964–73.

A third group of five determinants made negative contributions to the change in the growth rate in both periods or, in one case, a negative contribution in the first period and no contribution in the second. Three of the five, however, contributed only a combined 0.02 percentage points to the decline in the growth rate in the second period; these are unallocated labor input, reallocation from farming, and pollution abatement. If these three determinants are combined with the ten in the first two groups, thirteen determinants made positive contributions, no contribution, or a trivial negative contribution to the change in the growth rate from 1973–79 to 1979–82 after making negative contributions, no contribution, or a trivial positive contribution to the change from 1964–73 to 1973–79. Together they contributed 0.49 percentage points to the decline in the growth rate in 1973–79 and 0.57 percentage points toward an increase in 1979–82. Among these determinants are some that various optimists have identified as among those they expect to restore a high future growth rate of productivity. Hence, it is worthy of note that these determinants had already moved toward a sharp recovery of the growth rate by 1979–82, but the growth rate of productivity nevertheless tumbled for a second time in this period.[1]

1. John W. Kendrick, who argued that "the 1970s slump in productivity was over" and "we can look forward to relatively strong economic growth through the 1980s," is especially optimistic. See John W. Kendrick, "Productivity Gains Will Continue," *Wall Street Journal,* August 29, 1984, and "Productivity and Cost Prospects for 1984–85," *AEI Economist* (April 1984), pp. 1–9. Kendrick relies on the following favorable developments: "passing of the 'baby boom' generation into the experienced labor force"; a lessened drag from compliance with government regulations; the rise in total R&D expenditures as a percentage of GNP since 1977; embodiment of more new technology as a result of an expected boom in investment; more favorable labor-management relations and increased use of quality circles; the decline in energy prices since 1981; and deceleration in the general rate of inflation.

Projections are unusually hazardous at this time, and I shall offer none myself, but I will note that the developments cited by Kendrick need not be decisive. Any improvement in the growth rate that they provide may not be large and could easily be offset by other developments. Changes in demography and costs of regulation had already turned more favorable by 1979–82. My discussions in this book indicate that organized R&D, embodiment, and even energy have not contributed large amounts to the changes in growth rates and that the effects of quality circles and the like on productivity are uncertain. As for inflation, to which I frequently refer, both the amount by which inflation at a given unemployment rate has actually improved and the importance of inflation as a determinant of productivity on a potential basis are problematical. Apart from any effect on potential output, conquering inflation other than by underutilization of resources would permit the elimination or even temporary reversal of the gap between actual and potential productivity. In 1982, when potential output per hour exceeded actual output per hour by 3.2 percent in nonresidential business and 2.0 percent in the whole economy (tables 2-7 and 2-8), scope for such a gain was appreciable, but most of the

The fourth group, consisting of three determinants, helped to moderate the drop in the growth rate in the first period but contributed to the drop in the second. Education and the dwellings occupancy ratio are in this group, but it is dominated by earnings from international assets, which contributed 0.24 percentage points to the growth rate decline in the second period, equal to nearly one-third of the total decline.

Finally, residual productivity contributed 0.91 percentage points to the first drop in the growth rate and nearly as much, 0.80 points, to the second.

The data may also be grouped in another way. In the first period, when the growth rate dropped 1.49 percentage points, the contributions of four determinants rose by a total of 0.12 percentage points, while those of twelve fell by 1.62 points, of which 0.70 points were contributed by separately estimated determinants and 0.91 points by residual productivity. In the second period the growth rate dropped by 0.77 points. The contribution of nine determinants rose by 0.59 percentage points, while the contribution of eight fell by 1.35 points, of which 0.55 points were contributed by separately estimated determinants and 0.80 points by residual productivity.

Potential and Actual Output per Person Employed in Nonresidential Business: Declines, 1948–73 to 1973–82

There is considerable interest in productivity changes in nonresidential business because that sector is more homogeneous than the economy as a whole. The growth rate of potential national income per person potentially employed in nonresidential business fell from 2.59 percent in 1948–73 to 0.00 percent in 1973–82. The first column of the next informal table shows the changes in the contributions of its determinants. It differs from the corresponding column in the table for the whole economy mainly in that the growth determinants not present in nonresidential business disappear and the positive or negative contributions of determinants present only in nonresidential business are bigger. The contributions of only two determinants increased, by a total of 0.08 percentage points, from 1948–73 to 1973–82, while

gap appears to have been eliminated subsequently by the cyclical rise in actual productivity in 1983–84.

Peter K. Clark, writing in 1984, like me found neither recent improvement in the cyclically adjusted productivity growth rate nor reason confidently to expect improvement. However, his technique, unlike mine, did not yield a decline in this rate from 1973–79 to 1979–82. (Peter K. Clark, "Productivity and Profits in the 1980s: Are They Really Improving?" *BPEA, 1:1984,* pp. 133–67.)

	National income per person employed in nonresidential business (percentage points)	
	Potential	*Actual*
Growth rate, 1948–73	**2.59**	**2.45**
Plus increased contributions in 1973–82	**0.08**	**0.13**
Education	0.05	0.10
Weather in farming	0.03	0.03
Less reduced contributions in 1973–82	**2.67**	**2.84**
Hours	0.14	0.27
Age-sex composition	0.12	0.02
Inventories	0.12	0.09
Nonresidential structures and equipment	0.17	0.06
Land	0.04	0.02
Reallocation from farming	0.18	0.19
Reallocation from nonfarm self-employment	0.11	0.17
Pollution abatement	0.10	0.10
Worker safety and health	0.02	0.02
Dishonesty and crime	0.05	0.05
Economies of scale	0.15	0.15
Intensity of demand	. . .	0.23
Residual productivity	1.47	1.47
Equals growth rate, 1973–82	**0.00**	**−0.26**

the contributions of eleven separately estimated determinants declined, by a total of 1.20 percentage points, and the contribution of residual productivity also dropped, by 1.47 points.

No growth rates of actual output have yet been examined in this chapter. The second column of the informal table just discussed shows the determinants responsible for the drop of 2.71 percentage points from 1948–73 to 1973–82 in the growth rate of actual output per person employed in nonresidential business. Series similar to this one (although sometimes differing by referring to a slightly different sector, to output per hour instead of per person, to GNP instead of national income, or to a different time period) have been the focus of most studies of the productivity slowdown by other investigators.

Although the increase in the contribution of the only two determinants, education and the weather with respect to farming, that contributed more after 1973 than before was greater on an actual than on a potential basis, it amounted to only 0.13 percentage points. Twelve determinants that were separately estimated contributed 1.37 percentage points to the decline in this growth rate, an amount equal to 51 percent of the total decline and 48 percent of the decline in the contribution of the determinants contributing to the decline. This contribution was sufficient in itself to have cut the 1948–73 growth rate by some 53 percent. Of these 1.37 percentage points,

two labor input components (mainly hours) contributed 0.29 points; two capital input components, 0.15 points; land input, 0.02 points; two types of reallocation, 0.36 points; changes in three aspects of the institutional and human environment, 0.17 points; economies of scale, 0.15 points; and changes in the intensity of utilization of employed resources resulting from fluctuations in the intensity of demand, 0.23 points. Residual productivity was responsible for the remaining 1.47 percentage points of the growth rate decline.

Potential Output per Person Employed in Nonresidential Business: Declines, 1964–73 to 1973–79 and 1973–79 to 1979–82

The next informal table shows the contributions of the determinants to the 2.05 percentage point decline from 1964–73 to 1973–79, and to the 0.82 percentage point decline from 1973–79 to 1979–82, in the growth rate of potential national income per person potentially employed in nonresidential business. The pattern is similar to that described earlier for the corresponding series in the economy as a whole. In particular, it should be observed that eleven determinants, those in the first two groups in the table plus reallocation from farming and pollution abatement, after contributing a combined 0.62 percentage points to the drop in the growth rate in the first period, contributed 0.59 percentage points to-

	Changes in contributions to growth rate of potential national income per person potentially employed, nonresidential business *(percentage points)*	
	Change, 1964–73 to 1973–79	Change, 1973–79 to 1979–82
All sources	**−2.05**	**−0.82**
Contributions that increased in both periods	**0.03**	**0.21**
Age-sex composition	0.03	0.21
Contributions that decreased or were constant, then increased	**−0.51**	**0.41**
Hours	−0.08	0.09
Nonresidential structures and equipment	−0.16	0.03
Land	−0.02	0.02
Reallocation from nonfarm self-employment	−0.16	0.09
Worker safety and health	−0.03	0.05
Dishonesty and crime	−0.06	0.05
Weather in farming	0.00	0.07
Labor disputes	0.00	0.01
Contributions that decreased in both periods (except residual)	**−0.38**	**−0.32**
Inventories	−0.08	−0.08
Reallocation from farming	−0.08	−0.02
Pollution abatement	−0.06	−0.01
Economies of scale	−0.16	−0.21
Contributions that increased, then decreased	**0.01**	**−0.07**
Education	0.01	−0.07
Residual productivity	**−1.20**	**−1.05**

ward an increase in the second period.[2] Despite these favorable movements, the growth rate dropped by 0.82 percentage points.

Actual Output per Person Employed in Nonresidential Business: Declines, 1964–73 to 1973–79 and 1973–79 to 1979–82

The next informal table provides a similar analysis of the recent short-period declines in the growth rate of actual national income per person employed in nonresidential business. Although actual series have been used in most analyses of the productivity slowdown, their sensitivity to the exact time period used and the difficulty of discerning underlying trends from them make them less appropriate than potential series for such analyses, and they do not provide a convenient starting point to appraise the future. Several entries in this table differ markedly from those on a potential basis.

Almost all determinants contributed to the 1.74

2. The combined contribution of these determinants to the growth rate, as distinguished from the change in the contribution, was negative throughout: −0.33 percentage points in 1964–73, −0.95 points in 1973–79, and −0.36 points in 1979–82. See table 7-4.

percentage point reduction in this growth rate in the first period. Offsets totaling 0.32 percentage points were provided only by age-sex composition and education of labor and by the effect of demand on the intensity of utilization of employed resources. In contrast, in the second period the contributions of eight determinants (all those in the first two groups shown in the table) increased by a total of 1.04 percentage points. The largest increases were 0.43 percentage points in the contribution of age-sex composition (which rose from −0.34 points to 0.09 points) and 0.28 points in the contribution of nonresidential structures and equipment per person employed. The contributions of the remaining determinants subtracted 2.05 percentage points, of which hours were responsible for 0.24 points, reallocations from farming and nonfarm self-employment for 0.14 points, pollution abatement for 0.01 point, economies of scale for 0.21 points, the effect of demand on intensity of utilization for 0.42 points, and residual productivity for 1.03 points.

Three Generalizations

The reader can readily examine the changes in contributions to growth rates of other series and in

	Changes in contributions to growth rate of actual national income per person employed, nonresidential business (percentage points)	
	Change, 1964–73 to 1973–79	Change, 1973–79 to 1979–82
All sources	**−1.74**	**−1.01**
Contributions that increased in both periods	**0.11**	**0.47**
Age-sex composition	0.06	0.43
Education	0.05	0.04
Contributions that decreased or were constant, then increased	**−0.23**	**0.57**
Nonresidential structures and equipment	−0.13	0.28
Land	0.00	0.10
Worker safety and health	−0.03	0.05
Dishonesty and crime	−0.06	0.05
Weather in farming	−0.01	0.08
Labor disputes	0.00	0.01
Contributions that decreased, then decreased again or were constant (except residual)	**−0.65**	**−0.60**
Hours	−0.10	−0.24
Inventories	−0.07	0.00
Reallocation from farming	−0.09	−0.06
Reallocation from nonfarm self-employment	−0.18	−0.08
Pollution abatement	−0.06	−0.01
Economies of scale	−0.15	−0.21
Contributions that increased, then decreased	**0.21**	**−0.42**
Intensity of demand	0.21	−0.42
Residual productivity	**−1.18**	**−1.03**

other periods.[3] However, the main changes that have occurred since 1973 have already been identified. A few generalizations are worth recapitulating.

First, almost all sources contributed to the declines in growth rates measured from 1948–73 to 1973–82 or from 1964–73 to 1973–79. Employment was a major exception in the case of the series measuring total output. Other exceptions were education and, for changes in actual series from 1964–73 to 1973–79 only, demand-related fluctuations in intensity of utilization. No single separately estimated determinant dominated the declines.

Second, the declines in growth rates from 1973–79 to 1979–82 took place in the face of the fact that

3. The contributions themselves are shown in tables 7-1 through 7-4 and 8-1 through 8-4 for all the series for total output, output per person employed, and output per unit of input that are listed at the beginning of this chapter. Sources of growth tables for output per hour can be approximated from the corresponding tables for output per person employed by deleting the entry for "average hours" (not "hours") under labor input. (The growth rate will exceed the contribution of the remaining sources by an amount equal to about one-fourth of the contribution of average hours, which is always less than 0.2 percentage points.) Use of the same contributions for capital and land as in the tables for output per person implies, reasonably, that the needs for these inputs are more closely related to the number of persons employed than to the total hours worked.

the changes in a large number of determinants were favorable to an increase. The declines were possible because the contributions of some determinants that declined in 1973–79 did so again in 1979–82, while the contributions of some that had increased in the first period decreased in the second. Employment was among the latter group in the case of all the series for total output, but was especially important for those on an actual basis; demand-related intensity of utilization was important for all actual series; and international assets were important in the case of all series for the economy as a whole.

Third, residual productivity contributed very importantly to the declines in all the series from 1948–73 to 1973–82, from 1964–73 to 1973–79, and from 1973–79 to 1979–82.

The Decline in Growth of Residual Productivity

It is time to look more closely at residual productivity in nonresidential business. This series rose quite steadily from 1948 to 1973. Its growth rate displayed no tendency to decline; indeed, it was a little higher in 1964–73 than in the 1948–73 period as a whole. The sudden drops in its growth rate and the growth rates of potential national income and productivity all began unequivocally with their 1973–74 changes. Although the timing of the second drop in the growth rate of potential national income is equally clear and dictates the use of 1979 to divide the latest short periods, for the residual the division could be placed at 1978 with slightly better justification.[4]

This section explores the causes of the decline of 1.47 percentage points in the growth rate of the residual index in nonresidential business from 1948–73 to 1973–82. This decline cut the growth rates of all series for nonresidential business output shown in the informal tabulation on page 33 by about the same amount, and the growth rates of all series for the economy as a whole by about 1.14 percentage points. That the total decline from 1948–73 to 1979–82 was larger and occurred in two stages should be borne in mind, but it generally is fruitless to devote attention to the causes of the separate declines. I do so only in examining energy use.

Components of the Series

The residual index is an estimate of the contribution of advances in knowledge and miscellaneous determinants to the growth rate of national income in nonresidential business.

The contribution of advances in knowledge is the gain in measured output that results from the incorporation into production of new knowledge of any type—managerial and organizational as well as technological—regardless of the source of that knowledge, the way it is transmitted to those who can make use of it, or the way it is incorporated into production. In principle, one can distinguish between advances in knowledge as such and changes in the gap that exists between actual average practice and the best practice because of lags in the application of new knowledge.

The miscellaneous determinants fall into seven main groups:

1. Changes in the personal characteristics of workers that are not measured in labor input, such as effort exerted, experience on the present job (as distinguished from total experience), health, and training other than formal education.

2. Changes in the extent to which the allocation of inputs departs from that which would maximize national income, except for overallocation of labor to farming and nonfarm self-employment.

3. Changes in the amount by which output obtained with the average production technique actually used falls below what it would be if the best technique were used, because of changes in obstacles imposed (usually by government or labor union regulation) on efficient utilization of resources in the use to which they are put.

4. Changes in the costs of business services to government, such as collecting taxes or filing statistical reports.

5. Changes in the adequacy of government services to business, such as police protection, law courts, and roads for business use.

6. Changes in aspects of the legal and human environment within which business must operate, other than the effects I have measured (which pertain to regulatory requirements for pollution abatement and worker safety and health, and to dishonesty and crime).

7. Changes in productive efficiency that take place independently of changes in any of the other determinants identified. Efficiency, so defined, rather clearly differs among countries, and I surmise that it may vary over time within a country. One plausible explanation is that the efficiency actually achieved is affected by the strength of competitive pressures upon firms to minimize costs. Another explanation, not unrelated, stresses the quality of management.

I now examine some developments that, it is plausible to believe, may have (1) occurred and (2) if they did, contributed appreciably to the decline in the growth rate of the residual. I group them in five categories: technological knowledge; managerial knowledge and performance; work effort; misallocation of resources; and energy use. The reader should recognize that many developments that affected output per hour and even output per unit of input are not pertinent to this discussion because they did so by affecting output determinants whose effects were eliminated before arriving at the residual.

Technological Knowledge

Did incorporation of new technological knowledge into production contribute less to the growth rate of the residual after 1973 than before and, if so, how much less? Edwin Mansfield is as informed and judicious an observer of this scene as can be found. His view is that it is uncertain whether a slackening of technological advance contributed at all to the productivity slowdown but that it probably did although there is no strong evidence that its contribu-

---

4. The 1978–79 change in the residual was −0.23 percent, a little closer to the −0.75 percent growth rate of 1979–82 than to the 0.38 percent rate of 1973–78.

tion was very large.[5] It would be foolhardy for me to take a firmer position than Mansfield, and I shall not do so. Some considerations bearing on the question are worth pointing out, however. Expenditures for R&D in the United States will be examined first.

DOMESTIC R&D. Expenditures for industry-financed R&D, valued in constant (1972) prices, increased rapidly until 1969. From 1960 to 1969 the annual rate of increase was 6.5 percent. These expenditures then grew more slowly but still continuously—at an average annual rate of 2.6 or 2.0 percent from 1969 to 1979, depending on the choice of price series for deflation.[6] Expenditures for R&D by universities and other nonprofit organizations, which are relatively small, also increased. If the knowledge obtained per constant dollar of industry-financed, or industry and nonprofit organization-financed, R&D could raise output per unit of input as much as before, then the contribution of R&D to the growth rate of the residual would have increased continuously rather than fallen, although the rate of increase would have slowed. This conclusion would follow no matter what the time lag might be between R&D expenditures and their effect on productivity, which F. M. Scherer

says is at least several years.[7] Government-financed R&D fell from a 1967 peak until 1974 before beginning to recover, and total R&D expenditures including those of the government were essentially flat from 1966 to 1976 before resuming their rise. However, because the fruit of successful government-financed R&D is unmeasured quality change (see page 28), there is little reason to believe that such R&D affects the measured output per unit of input of business by any appreciable amount and no justification for counting it as having had as much effect as industry-financed R&D.

Has the yield of industry-financed R&D, defined as increased output per unit of input obtained from each constant dollar of industry-financed R&D expenditures, declined since, say, the 1960s? Mansfield and his associates give some possible reasons that it might have done so.[8] First, there may have been diminishing returns as more and more money was invested in R&D. Second, in some industries increased regulatory requirements delayed the use of new technology. Third, firms have come to view R&D as an activity that can and should be managed in more detail than was earlier thought to be optimal, and, notes Mansfield, "although there is general agreement that a greater emphasis on detailed management was justified, many observers wonder whether the pendulum may have swung too far." Fourth, the proportion of young engineers in industry's R&D engineering labor force has declined "with possible negative effects on the fate of innovation." Fifth, changes in the composition of R&D may have been adverse.[9]

The effect of R&D on future productivity is usually evaluated by reference to rates of return on R&D expenditures. Unfortunately, direct evidence on the

5. Thus, Mansfield and his colleagues state that "many of the available bits and scraps of data point to a slackening in the pace of innovation in the United States. But the data are so crude and incomplete that it would be foolish to put much weight on them. . . . We think that in some important industries, such as pharmaceuticals, there may well have been a fall in the rate of innovation. . . . [But] there is little evidence of such a slackening in other important industries. . . . It would be a mistake, in our opinion, to regard . . . statistics [that suggest a slackening, such as productivity change, number of patents, and number of major innovations] as reasonably reliable measures [of innovation], even though we tend to agree that there may have been some reduction in the overall rate of innovation." And again, "even though available measures of the rate of innovation are very crude at best, the fact that some of them seem to indicate a slowdown in the rate of innovation, at least in some important sectors of the economy, is cause for concern." However, as noted below, Mansfield views as substantially too big an estimate by Kendrick that slower growth of R&D-derived knowledge was responsible for one-fourth of the deceleration from 1948–66 to 1973–78 in the growth of output per hour. See Edwin Mansfield, Anthony Romeo, Mark Schwartz, David Teece, Samuel Wagner, and Peter Brach, *Technology Transfer, Productivity, and Economic Policy* (Norton, 1982), pp. 219–21, 231. The quotes have been rearranged.

6. The 2.6 percent rate is based on the use of the implicit deflator for GNP, which has been the National Science Foundation practice in the absence of a specially designed index. The original National Science Foundation data are from *Science Indicators 1980* (National Science Board, 1981). Edwin Mansfield, Anthony Romeo, and Lorne Switzer developed a Laspeyres index for inputs into R&D in eight industries and found that from 1969 to 1979 the growth rate of real R&D expenditures in these industries was reduced from 0.7 percent to 0.1 percent when this price index was substituted for the GNP deflator, or a reduction of 0.6 percentage points. See "R&D Price Indexes and Real R&D Expenditures in the United States," *Research Policy*, vol. 12 (1983), pp. 105–12.

7. David Ravenscroft and F. M. Scherer found in a correlation analysis that the best fitting lag between firms' R&D expenditures and their profitability is binomial in shape, with peak profits accruing four to six years after the R&D spending. See F. M. Scherer, "Inter-Industry Technology Flows and Productivity Growth," *Review of Economics and Statistics*, vol. 64 (November 1982), p. 629, and "R&D and Declining Productivity Growth," *American Economic Review*, vol. 73 (May 1983, *Papers and Proceedings, 1982*), p. 215.

8. Mansfield and others, *Technology Transfer, Productivity, and Economic Policy*, pp. 117–31, 221–22.

9. Ibid., pp. 126–30. A study of 119 firms showed the proportions of R&D they devoted to basic research, relatively risky projects, and wholly new products and processes (as distinguished from improvements) all declined from 1967 to 1977. So did the proportion devoted to long-term research when the investigators excluded industries (such as drugs) whose firms stated that regulatory changes resulted in a significant lengthening of projects. Mansfield finds a positive correlation between productivity increase and both basic research and (when the amounts of basic and applied research are both held constant) the proportion of research that is long term.

changes in such rates is hard to come by. Mansfield reports, although cautiously, that studies of the 1970s show the "marginal rate of return from R&D investment was not as high as in earlier years."[10] His evidence consists of a study of one large firm that showed its private rate of return to be lower during the late 1960s and early 1970s than during the early 1960s; regression results for chemical and petroleum firms indicating that their private rate of return was lower in 1960–76 as a whole than in the early 1960s; opinions expressed by many R&D managers in these industries; and additional regression studies.[11] A regression study by Scherer, on the other hand, finds "there is no clear indication that the productivity slump of the 1970s resulted from a decrease in the marginal productivity of R&D," and Zvi Griliches concludes from studies at the National Bureau of Economic Research that "there is no strong evidence for a decline in the 'fecundity' of R&D in the estimated elasticities or rates of return. If anything, the scattered evidence points in the opposite direction."[12]

Kendrick assumed a decline in the social rate of return from 50 percent in 1948–66 to 45 percent in 1966–73 and 40 percent in 1973–78; these figures imply a decline of 17.7 percent from 1948–73 to 1973–78.[13] If, as I suggested in chapter 2, organized R&D

in the United States contributed 0.2 percentage points to the growth rate of the residual in 1948–73, if the amount of R&D had been unchanged, and if the increase in residual productivity in future years from each constant dollar of expenditure had dropped by 17.7 percent, then the growth rate of the residual would have been reduced by 0.04 percentage points. (The timing of the drop, however, is unclear.) In fact, the average annual amount of relevant R&D was much higher after 1967 or 1973 than in 1948–66, and the contribution may not have dropped at all.[14]

FOREIGN R&D. Foreign R&D is a second source of advances in technological knowledge in the United States. The cost of transferring technology, although substantial, is much less than the cost of original R&D. The contribution of foreign R&D to growth of the residual in 1948–73 is unknown, but it was certainly smaller than that of domestic R&D, probably less than 0.1 percentage point.

The volume of civilian R&D expenditures has continued to increase in foreign industrial countries, although much less rapidly than before 1967. Two additional considerations mentioned by Mansfield make it likely that the contribution of foreign R&D also increased.[15] First, Manfield reports that in many important industries international companies have been carrying on increasing shares of their R&D abroad and that, in addition, a greatly increased number of companies has achieved efficient integra-

10. Edwin Mansfield, "How Research Pays Off in Productivity," *EPRI Journal*, vol. 4 (October 1979), p. 25.

11. Ibid; and Mansfield and others, *Technology Transfer, Productivity, and Economic Policy*, pp. 116, 125, 221. Private rates of return provide evidence about changes in the social rate of return relevant to an analysis of the change in residual productivity only if it can be assumed that the algebraic excess of the social rate over the private rate did not increase. The social rate of return clearly is above the private rate for R&D whose use raises measured output per unit of input. For R&D that leads to new or improved final products, however, the reverse is true: the private rate is positive while the social rate relevant to analysis of changes in residual productivity is zero, because measured output is unaffected by the change in the economy's product composition to which the research leads.

12. Scherer, "Inter-Industry Technology Flows and Productivity Growth," p. 634; and Zvi Griliches, "Productivity and Technical Change," *N.B.E.R. Reporter* (Spring 1983), p. 3.

13. John W. Kendrick, "Productivity Trends and the Recent Slowdown: Historical Perspective, Causal Factors, and Policy Options," in *Contemporary Economic Problems 1979* (Washington, D.C.: American Enterprise Institute for Public Policy Research, 1979). The 50 percent figure is justified as follows: "Relevant studies summarized in a recent National Science Foundation colloquium suggest that, for the earlier period, private before-tax rates of return average around 25 percent and social rates at least twice as much" (p. 38). The rate of return is assumed to have dropped from 1948–66 to 1966–73 by the same percentage—10—as did the much lower rate of return on total capital in "high level years," and then to have experienced a second decline of the same size to 1973–78. Despite the weak basis for Kendrick's rates, I would not quarrel with them as plausible guesses if they referred to R&D of types whose effects are captured by output measures. They are far too high to refer to all R&D. See note 14.

14. Kendrick estimated the drop at 0.21 percentage points, from 0.81 in 1948–73 (based on 0.85 in 1948–66 and 0.71 in 1966–73) to 0.6 in 1973–78. (Kendrick, "Productivity Trends and the Recent Slowdown.") His relatively large figure results in part from his overestimation (as I view it) of the contribution in 1948–73 as a result of combining a rate of return appropriate for R&D that raises measured output with changes in a stock of knowledge that includes knowledge that does not raise measured output (as noted in chapter 2, note 52). He further overestimates the drop in the contribution because the growth rate of this overly inclusive stock drops more than that of the stock that raises measured output and because he deducts obsolescence based on time rather than on the creation of new knowledge that would displace old knowledge. Mansfield and his associates (*Technology Transfer, Productivity, and Economic Policy*, pp. 220–21), Barry P. Bosworth (*Tax Incentives and Economic Growth* [Brookings, 1984], p. 33), and I (*Slower Growth*, p. 125) are among those who have indicated that Kendrick overestimates the decline in the contribution of R&D.

A conclusion by Scherer must be read carefully. He reports that as of 1978 the "productivity growth shortfall attributable to lower R&D is estimated to be on the order of 0.20 to 0.28 percentage points per year" or, if a different sample is used to obtain elasticities, 0.39 percentage points. However, he is comparing the contribution made by R&D as of 1978 not with that in an earlier period, but with what the contribution would have been in 1978 if R&D spending had continued to increase until 1978 at the growth rate it achieved in the 1960s, a wholly different matter. See "R & D and Declining Productivity Growth," p. 216.

15. Mansfield and others, *Technology Transfer, Productivity, and Economic Policy*, pp. 209–10, 232.

tion of their R&D in different countries. R&D by international companies comprises an important part of foreign R&D; in the early 1970s about one-half of the industrial R&D performed in Canada and one-seventh of that in the United Kingdom and West Germany was done by U.S.-based firms. Second, the reduction of the American technological lead over Western Europe and Japan should have made the findings of research by firms native to those countries more valuable to the United States.

OTHER SOURCES OF TECHNOLOGICAL KNOWLEDGE. There is no usable information concerning the size of the contribution made to the growth rate of the residual in 1948–73 by advances in technological knowledge that did not stem from organized domestic or foreign R&D (although I believe this contribution probably was much larger than that of organized R&D) or the direction or size of any change in this contribution.

LAGS IN USING NEW TECHNOLOGY. The incorporation of new technological knowledge into production can be affected by a change in the lag of average technology behind the latest technology. Mechanisms for transmitting knowledge between firms and countries, which include publications, meetings, movement of people (which Mansfield considers particularly important), education, and special programs for dissemination of research findings certainly have not deteriorated and presumably have improved.[16] Mansfield and his associates found, with respect to the transmission of new technology from the initiator to other firms and to other countries, that firms and countries (such as the United States) that spend relatively large amounts on R&D have relatively short imitation lags, a finding that restricts the scope for reductions in the lag to raise productivity. For a sample of companies they also found that among technologies that were transferred to subsidiaries in developed countries the proportion that was less than five years old rose from 27 percent in 1960–68 to 75 percent in 1969–78, while there was no

change in the newness of technologies transferred through channels other than subsidiaries.[17]

Some advances in technological knowledge consist of improvements in equipment or structures, while the use of some other advances, such as improved raw materials or procedures, may require modification of equipment or structures. Consequently, a group of workers equipped with the latest fixed capital is likely to have higher output per worker than an otherwise similar group working with antiquated capital. From this observation some analysts have jumped to the wholly wrong conclusion that, on an economywide basis, changes in the average age of fixed capital goods have had a major effect on the lag of average practice behind the best practice known. They have invented "vintage" models to incorporate the supposed effect of changes in average age upon output per unit of input. I next indicate what the maximum effect could have been if such models were tenable, and then state why they are not.

The ratio of the net stock of nonresidential structures and equipment to the gross stock (shown in table 4-1, column 5) measures the percent of the value of such capital when it was new that still remains. Hence the ratio provides a measure of the newness of the stock. This ratio is not affected by changes in the distribution of the stock among types of capital with different service lives (an essential feature that a composite measure of average age lacks). The stock was becoming younger from 1948 until 1970, and after 1973 it was becoming older. Table 4-4 provides a simple calculation, updated from *Slower Growth*, of the largest possible effect that one can obtain from a vintage model. It assumes that the use of every advance in both technological and managerial knowledge requires the replacement of structures and equipment. It also assumes that the rate of advance in knowledge continued unabated after 1973. This extreme model indicates that the change in the age of capital contributed 0.10 percentage points to the growth rate of output in nonresidential business in 1948–73 and −0.06 points in 1973–82, and thus was responsible for 0.16 percentage points, or one-eighth, of the decline in the growth rate of the residual.[18] But in fact there was no such

16. The only contrary statement I recall appears in the report of the Coordinating Committee of the National Technological Cooperation Conference, which refers to the "relationship between falling productivity in the United States and our increasing failure to disseminate technical discoveries from laboratories and research centers to commercial and industrial users." However, although the report is devoted to what it regards as the unsatisfactory state of technology diffusion, it contains no other mention of nor support for a finding that the failure was "increasing." See *A Call for National Technological Cooperation*, Report of the First National Technological Cooperation Conference (Livermore, Calif.: The Engineering Foundation with the University of California and the Lawrence Livermore National Laboratory, 1980).

17. Mansfield and others, *Technology Transfer, Productivity, and Economic Policy*, pp. 29, 35, 209.

18. The explanation of table 4-4 may be illustrated by the data for the 1948–73 period. The ratio of net to gross rose by 0.077 points (or 7.7 percent of the average service life) from 1948 to 1973 (row 1). Since the average service life is estimated at twenty-four years, this increase implies a reduction of 1.84 years in average age when the effect of mix changes is excluded (row 2),

effect. Vintage models are indefensible, quite apart from assumptions about embodiment. The reason (in brief) is as follows.[19]

During any span of time different types of capital goods undergo very different amounts of quality improvement. The greater the quality improvement in new goods of any type, the greater the obsolescence of existing capital goods for which the new goods are a substitute. Other things being equal, the rate of return on replacement investment, and hence the incentive to invest, is highest for types of capital goods that have experienced the most obsolescence. Any substantial gross investment in a period permits investment opportunities created by sizable quality improvements in new capital goods to be grasped. It is only the less profitable investments, involving replacement of capital goods for which quality change has been small, that are sensitive to variations in the amount of gross investment on which changes in average age depend. Thus, the capital goods that will be bought at one level of investment but not at a lower level are unlikely to include capital goods embodying large improvements in quality. Similarly, the advantage of improvements will be greater in some uses than others even for the same type of goods, and new acquisitions will be used first where the gains are greatest. The gain in the average quality of the capital stock that vintage models imagine to be derived from additional new investment is not realized because a shortening in average age automatically is largely offset by a reduction in the average amount of quality improvement incorporated in new capital.

I have pointed out elsewhere that this reasoning does not apply when investment is eliminated by the fiat of regulating authorities rather than because it appears insufficiently profitable. If the investment that is blocked departs at all from the average rate of technological improvement, it is likely to incorporate an above-average amount. This is because regulators are likely to be more cautious, and public interest groups most vociferous in their opposition, when major changes, such as the use of nuclear energy, are proposed.[20] Delay of new projects by regulation

may have been responsible for a few hundredths of a percentage point of the slowdown in the growth rate of residual productivity.[21]

Managerial Knowledge and Managerial Performance

If, as I have suggested, the contribution of advances in knowledge was about the same as the 1.4 percent growth rate of residual productivity in 1948–73, and if organized R&D at home and abroad contributed about 0.3 percentage points, then 1.1 points remain to be divided between advances in technological knowledge from other sources and advances in managerial and organizational knowledge. I cannot make this division, but it seems probable that the advance in managerial and organizational knowledge was a large source of growth in 1948–73.

A sizable body of informed opinion holds that performance of American management, as it relates to productivity, has deteriorated badly since then. When, as now, there is controversy as to whether innovations represent progress or retrogression, it becomes impractical to distinguish between advances in managerial knowledge and changes in managerial performance relative to the best practice. But it is plausible if not demonstrable that, one way or the other, much of the decline in the growth of residual productivity is traceable to management. Three separate perspectives, all pointing to this conclusion, may be distinguished.

One stresses the diversion of the attention of top-level managers away from the efficient production and distribution of goods and services.[22] Profitability of a business is now affected far more than it was before the 1970s by its responses to rapid changes in government regulations and tax codes. Failure to learn of and conform to regulations can have serious legal consequences, including criminal penalties. Failure to find the cheapest way to conform can be expensive. Failure to learn of proposals for new laws or regulations and to participate in hearings and to use other channels to help shape their final form can bring permanently higher costs or loss of markets, as can failure to foresee changes in laws and regulations and to take timely action in advance to minimize losses or maximize gains from the changes. Not only are laws and regulations actually proposed or made effective pertinent; one must anticipate possible

---

and an average annual reduction of 0.07 years (row 3). If the advance in knowledge raised output 1.4 percent a year, the assumption of the model that all progress is embodied means that a reduction of one year in average age would raise output by 1.4 percent; hence, an annual reduction of 0.07 years would raise output by 0.10 percent a year (row 4).

19. For fuller discussions see *Why Growth Rates Differ,* pp. 144–50, and citations given there.

20. Edward F. Denison, "Research Concerning the Effect of Regulation on Productivity," in John D. Hogan, ed., *Dimensions of Productivity Research,* vol. 2 (Houston, Texas: American Productivity Center, 1980), pp. 1024–25.

21. Because such retardation is a consequence of regulation and can be changed only by regulation, its effect is properly classified under the third group of miscellaneous determinants (p. 40) rather than under advances in knowledge.

22. The main points are described in more detail and annotated in *Slower Growth,* pp. 129–30.

future proposals. Under these conditions it is not surprising that top management, department heads, and other business people of great talent devote more and more of their time to their firm's interaction with government and correspondingly less time to its interaction with competitors, customers, and suppliers, and to its internal operations.

Problems stemming from inflation, unprecedented interest rates and unusual relationships among long- and short-term rates, fluctuations in exchange rates, and the volatility of aggregate output have also contributed to a situation in which profits and survival seem to depend less on efficiency in production and marketing than on success in dealing with financial markets and government. Such rearrangements of emphasis among the activities needed for a business to prosper also affect the type of person who emerges at the top of the corporate hierarchy and the relative influence of its other members. More stress is placed on knowledge of the law, the legislative process, and public relations and less on production, sales, and internal management. All these factors could hardly have failed to impair productivity.

Additionally, and in the minds of many businessmen crucially, values of securities have fallen far below the values of corporate assets, seemingly making it cheaper to buy firms than things.[23] When this attitude is combined with the perceived emphasis of the stock market on the latest reported quarterly profits, management feels compelled to maximize immediate reported profits, sacrificing the firm's long-term welfare by foregoing investment, research, or product development that has a long payoff period. This strategy is considered necessary to avoid management changes and to hold off unwanted corporate takeovers.

This description does not necessarily imply that business management has become inefficient, although this possibility is not ruled out. It need only imply that the American government and economy have been providing a new system of rewards to management (and, for the most part, to stockholders as well) that at least partially replaces efficiency in production and distribution as the keys to success.

The second perspective is typified by a much-quoted article by Robert H. Hayes and William J. Abernathy of the Harvard School of Business Administration. Although they cited some of the same characteristics of management and managers as those espousing the first perspective, they did not consider government and the economic environment the main culprits. Rather, they placed primary blame on doctrines that have become accepted as standards for state-of-the-art management, and which executives of most leading corporations have now adopted. Practices stemming from these doctrines, they indicated, not only are responsible for much of the productivity slowdown but also are bad for company profits. The article is short and understandable, and I recommend it to the reader. The following quotes suggest some of its main points.

Our experience suggests that, to an unprecedented degree, success in most industries today requires an organizational commitment to compete in the marketplace on technological grounds—that is, to compete over the long run by offering superior products. Yet, guided by what they took to be the newest and best principles of management, American managers have increasingly directed their attention elsewhere. These new principles, despite their sophistication and widespread usefulness, encourage a preference for [1] analytic detachment rather than the insight that comes from "hands on" experience and [2] short-term cost reduction rather than long-term development of technological competitiveness. It is this managerial gospel, we feel, that has played a major role in undermining the vigor of American industry.

American management, especially in the two decades after World War II, was universally admired for its strikingly effective performance. But times change. An approach shaped and refined during stable decades may be ill suited to a world characterized by rapid and unpredictable change, scarce energy, global competition for markets, and a constant need for innovation. This is the world of the 1980s and, probably, the rest of this century.[24]

The conclusion is painful but must be faced. Responsibility for [American] competitive listlessness belongs not just to a set of external conditions but also to the attitudes, preoccupations, and practices of American managers. By their preference for servicing existing markets rather than creating new ones and by their devotion to short-term returns and "management by the numbers," many of them have effectively forsworn long-term technological superiority as a competitive weapon. In consequence, they have abdicated their strategic responsibilities.[25]

As more companies decentralize their organizational structures, they tend to fix on profit centers as the primary

23. Robert H. Hayes and David A. Garvin state that in actuality "the bargain basement character of [corporate acquisitions] is an illusion resulting from attention to the wrong set of figures." Acquisition prices in actual acquisitions have been far above the previous market values of acquired companies and not below replacement costs, they state. They also state that many American managers "are so firmly convinced that the grass is greener in almost any industry other than their own that they are far less tough minded in evaluating acquisition candidates than . . . internal investment proposals." See "Managing as if Tomorrow Mattered," *Harvard Business Review*, vol. 60 (May–June 1982), pp. 72–73, 77.

24. Robert H. Hayes and William J. Abernathy, "Managing Our Way to Economic Decline," *Harvard Business Review*, vol. 58 (July–August 1980), p. 68.

25. Ibid., p. 70.

unit of management responsibility. This development necessitates, in turn, greater dependence on short-term financial measurements . . . for evaluating the performance of individual managers and management groups. . . . The predictable result of relying too heavily on short-term financial measures—a sort of managerial remote control—is an environment in which no one feels he or she can afford a failure or even a momentary dip in the bottom line.[26]

Consider [the effect of the new principles] on three major kinds of choices regularly faced by corporate managers: the decision between imitative and innovative product design [too much is imitative], the decision to integrate backward [it is done too frequently], and the decision to invest in process development [it is done too rarely].[27]

What has developed . . . is a preoccupation with a false and shallow concept of the professional manager, a "pseudo-professional" really—an individual having no special expertise in any particular industry or technology who nevertheless can step into an unfamiliar company and run it successfully through strict application of financial controls, portfolio concepts, and a market-driven strategy.

In recent years, this idealization of pseudo-professionalism has taken on something of the quality of a corporate religion. Its first doctrine . . . is that neither industry experience nor hands-on technological expertise counts for very much. . . . It encourages the faithful to make decisions about technological matters simply as if they were adjuncts to finance or marketing decisions.[28]

More disturbing still, true believers [insist] that as issues rise up the managerial hierarchy for decision they be progressively distilled into easily quantifiable terms. One European manager [observed] that "U.S. managers want everything to be simple. But sometimes business situations are not simple. . . . They are messy, and one must try to understand all the facets."[29]

The third perspective is that American management has on its own volition taken the wrong road, while the right road leads to Japan. Like the first two perspectives, it criticizes the alleged myopic vision of American management, contrasting it with the long view of Japanese managers. It stresses the quality control techniques of W. Edwards Deming, an American statistician and consultant whose work received the highest honors in Japan, including that of widespread adoption of his methods, but whose ideas (and even the objective of defect-free production) were ignored or rejected in America.[30] Poor

quality, in the sense of the presence of defects, is seen as not only impairing customer acceptance of products but also lowering productivity, for the costs of correcting defects exceed the expense that would be incurred in preventing them. There is frequent reference to firms' "hidden factories" that engage only in correcting flaws. Defects in materials, parts, and capital goods such as motor vehicles sold to other firms lower productivity in the purchasing industries. Another Japanese practice, "management by consensus," is one way to minimize the bad effects, described by Hayes and Abernathy, of separating decisionmaking from hands-on knowledge and of deciding complex issues on the basis of executive summaries. Other features of Japanese management stressed by its admirers include "just in time" arrival of the raw materials and parts used in production and a variety of practices in personnel management and labor relations, including lifetime employment for a select group of workers, quality circles to promote productivity and the quality of working life, and techniques to promote company loyalty.

All three perspectives point to a conclusion that, in the words of Deming, "the basic cause of sickness in American industry . . . is failure of top management to manage."[31] Businessmen themselves are widely inclined to accept much of the responsibility for lagging productivity. Not that all who do so accept *blame* for managerial deficiencies: some stress the first perspective, which views managerial behavior as a response to external conditions.

The position that American management took the wrong turn is only informed opinion, and obviously it is contested.[32] I do not know whether this belief is correct, but I do find it sufficiently plausible, the importance of management great enough, and the timing of the change consistent enough, to include it among the more probable main causes of the slow-

26. Ibid.
27. Ibid., p. 72.
28. Ibid., p. 74.
29. Ibid., p. 75.
30. Deming's recommendations to top management for improvement of quality, productivity, and performance generally are contained in W. Edwards Deming, *Quality, Productivity, and Competitive Position* (Massachusetts Institute of Technology Center for Advanced Engineering Study, 1982). For the most part his ideas are consistent with those of Hayes and Abernathy. He includes a great many illustrations of what does and does not work.

31. Ibid., p. i.
32. For example, a survey of chief executives found a majority of the 230 queried critical of American management, notably of its emphasis on the short run, but also many vigorous dissenters. See John Perham, "What's Wrong with Management," *Dun's Business Month* (April 1982), pp. 48–52. Gordon Donaldson and Jay W. Lorsch firmly deny that American management pays undue attention to short-term financial results; they believe long-term self-sustaining growth is its guiding objective. See Gordon Donaldson and Jay W. Lorsch, *Decision Making at the Top: The Shaping of Strategic Direction* (Basic Books, 1983). Richard Tanner Pascale and Mary Ann Maguire found that, although five of ten Japanese-managed firms operating in the United States had higher "quantitative" productivity than American-managed counterparts, an equal number had lower productivity. However, Japanese-managed firms had an edge in other respects, including scarcity of defects. See New York Stock Exchange Office of Economic Research, *People and Productivity: A Challenge to Corporate America* (New York, 1982), p. 20.

down in the growth of residual productivity. As with most other explanations, however, the suddenness of the change in the growth rate is a difficulty. Nor is it obvious how management deterioration relates to the international character of the productivity slowdown, although multinational corporations might have contributed to dissemination of the criticized practices among Western free-market economies.

Work Effort

I reported in *Slower Growth* that most of the public and some economists, including Arthur F. Burns, believe that the main reason for the productivity slowdown was that "people don't want to work any more." To slow the growth of residual productivity, it should be understood, intensity of work while at work, not time at work, would have to drop—and more rapidly than in the past.[33] I noted in *Slower Growth* that the evidence of lessened effort was impressionistic and that the impressions carry little weight because similar judgments about deteriorating work effort have been expressed many times in many countries, often in situations characterized by rapid productivity advance.[34] More recent publications that I reviewed at a later date carried no evidence of reduced effort that was any more conclusive.[35] Still more recent publications provide no firmer answers. Neither Sar Levitan and Clifford Johnson nor Janice Hedges, for example, could find any strong evidence of reduced effort.[36] Surveys about job satisfaction yield mixed results; one new one, reported by Norval D. Glenn and Charles N. Weaver, reports less satisfaction in 1980 than in 1955.[37] However, many observers, including Levitan and Johnson, have noted the absence of evidence that there is a systematic relationship between job satisfaction and either productivity or work effort (or various proxies sometimes used to represent them). Ted Mills reviewed the movements to "restructure work" that swept Western Europe and, in

different forms, North America in the 1970s and early 1980s and found no demonstrable effects on productivity; he doubted that the effects were economic at all.[38]

Thomas E. Weisskopf, Samuel Bowles, and David M. Gordon incorporated into an econometric model proxies that were intended to indicate work intensity and concluded that changes in work intensity reduced the growth rate of output per production worker hour in nonfarm business by 0.6 percentage points from 1948–66 to 1966–73 (when the change that needs to be explained, according to my index for residual productivity, was a 0.1 percentage point increase) and by an additional 0.6 percentage points from 1966–73 to 1973–79 (when my residual indicates that a drop of 1.2 percentage points needs explanation). Discussants of this study did not rule out the possibility that work effort declined but found, as I do, that the combination of proxies whose applicability is unproven with regression analysis can hardly provide evidence that the decline actually happened.[39]

A variant of the "people don't want to work any more" explanation is "young people don't work like we did."

Martin Baily addressed the question of whether the productivity slowdown up to 1980 could be explained by deterioration in the labor provided by each successive age cohort of workers after those born in 1942—whether the deterioration resulted from increasing aversion to work or something else. His conclusion that the deterioration would have to have been implausibly sharp to explain more than a small fraction of the slowdown is convincing.[40]

Misallocation of Resources

The amount by which the actual allocation of resources departs from the income-maximizing allocation, except from overallocation of labor to farming and nonfarm self-employment, is the fourth of my miscellaneous determinants of output. Four reasons why misallocation may have increased and

33. This sentence disregards the effect of shorter hours upon the amount of work done in an hour, which would have to be removed if one were to try to measure the effect of changes in attitudes upon work intensity.

34. *Slower Growth*, pp. 34–35.

35. Denison, "Accounting for Slower Economic Growth: An Update," pp. 27–29.

36. Sar A. Levitan and Clifford M. Johnson, *Second Thoughts on Work* (Kalamazoo, Mich.: W. E. Upjohn Institute for Employment Research, 1982), especially chap. 4; and Janice Neipert Hedges, "Job Commitment in America: Is It Waxing or Waning?" *Monthly Labor Review*, vol. 106 (July 1983), pp. 17–24. Most indicators examined by these authors are pertinent only if there is a positive association between hours worked and work effort.

37. Norval D. Glenn and Charles N. Weaver, "Enjoyment of Work by Full-Time Workers in the U.S., 1955 and 1980," *Public Opinion Quarterly*, vol. 46 (Winter 1982), pp. 459–70.

38. Ted Mills, "U.S. and European Approaches to Improving Labor Productivity and the Quality of Working Life," in John W. Kendrick, ed., *International Comparisons of Productivity and Causes of the Slowdown* (American Enterprise Institute/Ballinger, 1984), pp. 361–91.

39. Thomas E. Weisskopf, Samuel Bowles, and David M. Gordon, "Hearts and Minds: A Social Model of U.S. Productivity Growth"; Martin Neil Baily and Albert Rees, "Comments and Discussion"; William C. Brainard and George L. Perry, "Editors' Summary"; all in *BPEA, 2:1983*, pp. ix–xxvi, 381–450. Discussants also had problems with the particular model used.

40. Martin Neil Baily, "Productivity and the Services of Capital and Labor," *BPEA, 1:1981*, pp. 11–14.

contributed to the slowdown in growth of residual productivity deserve discussion.

ROUND PEGS IN SQUARE HOLES. Frank L. Schmidt of George Washington University and John E. Hunter of Michigan State University, both industrial psychologists, believe that the federal government's restrictions against the use of tests in job placement led to a great decrease in the ability of employers to fill jobs with the best qualified workers and that this problem has been a major cause of the productivity slowdown. Their analysis stems from five propositions for which they offer substantial evidence.[41]

1. The output of individual workers in any group varies substantially. Typically the distribution approximates a normal curve, with output at the ninety-fifth percentile about double output at the fifth percentile.

2. Average earnings (and, presumptively, contributions to the value of output) are far higher in some occupations than others.

3. The ratio of each person's output to the output of each other person would change considerably if individuals were moved from one occupation to another (even after the provision of training and experience).

4. It has been firmly established that mental abilities and skills of various kinds are important determinants of performance on many jobs. General aptitude tests succeed in predicting which individuals in an applicant pool will do well in a particular job even when the tests have not been shown to measure directly the skills required for that job and have not been validated for a particular job in a particular

setting.[42] To be valid, job aptitude tests do not need to be situation-specific (validated anew for each setting, company, or agency) or occupation-specific or race-specific. Moreover, when an employer selects people who will do well in a job training program, he is also selecting people who will do well on the job. Schmidt and Hunter quantify the improvement in selection that testing introduces.

5. Many employers who formerly used tests for selection and assignment of workers stopped doing so after successive federal guidelines on employee selection procedures interpreting Title VII of the Civil Rights Act of 1964 (most recently, the 1978 Uniform Guidelines), and similar interpretations of Executive Order 11246 by the Office of Federal Contract Compliance Programs, which deals with federal contractors, forbade use of tests that were not separately validated for each situation and also shown to be fair in that situation to the different races. Agencies and courts often ruled that the selection procedure must be shown to be correlated not only with training success but also with performance on the job or that training success correlates with job performance.

From propositions 1 and 4 Schmidt and Hunter show that proper use of general tests improves selection enough to raise productivity in any group much above what it would be without testing. Combined with proposition 2 (that earnings vary by occupation), this means that use of testing to select people for the highest paying jobs, leaving the less capable for the lower paying, would raise output in the whole economy even if output ratios were the same in all jobs and/or a single test with the same weighting of its parts were used for all jobs. The average value of output in the higher paying jobs would be raised by a larger dollar amount, although by the same percentage, than the average value in the lower paying jobs would be reduced. The gains from testing are far more dramatic when proposition 3 (output ratios vary among occupations) is introduced along with tests of somewhat more specialized abilities (for example, special as well as general ability for skilled trades, or perceptual speed as well as general ability for clerical jobs). Schmidt and Hunter show that, when numbers they consider realistic are used, economywide gains from the better placement that results from testing become very large under these conditions, even when relative produc-

41. This section is based on research appearing in the following publications. Frank L. Schmidt and John E. Hunter, "New Research Findings in Personnel Selection: Myths Meet Realities in the '80's," *Public Personnel Administration—Policies and Practices for Personnel Service* (Prentice-Hall, 1980); Frank L. Schmidt and John E. Hunter, "Individual Differences in Productivity: An Empirical Test of Estimates Derived from Studies of Selection Procedure Utility," *Journal of Applied Psychology*, vol. 68, no. 3 (1983), pp. 407–14; John E. Hunter and Frank L. Schmidt, "Fitting People to Jobs: The Impact of Personnel Selection on National Productivity," in Marvin D. Dunnette and E. A. Fleishman, eds., *Human Performance and Productivity*, vol. 1 (Hillsdale, N.J.: Lawrence Erlbaum Associates, 1982), pp. 233–84; Frank L. Schmidt and John E. Hunter, "Poor Hiring Decisions Lower Productivity," *Civil Service Journal*, vol. 19 (January–March, 1979), p. 9; Frank L. Schmidt, John E. Hunter, Robert C. McKenzie, and Tressie W. Muldrow, "Impact of Valid Selection Procedures on Work-Force Productivity," *Journal of Applied Psychology*, vol. 64, no. 6 (1979), pp. 609–26; John E. Hunter and Frank L. Schmidt, "Quantifying the Effects of Psychological Interventions on Employee Job Performance and Work-Force Productivity," *American Psychologist*, vol. 38 (April 1983), pp. 473–78; and Frank L. Schmidt and John E. Hunter, "Employment Testing: Old Theories and New Research Findings," *American Psychologist*, vol. 36 (October 1981), pp. 1128–37.

42. "The applicant pool is made up of all who have survived screening or any prior selection hurdles that might be employed (e.g., minimum educational requirements or physical examinations)." (Hunter and Schmidt, "Fitting People to Jobs," p. 239.)

tivities of individuals in different occupations are highly correlated.

As federal regulation reduced testing, Schmidt and Hunter argue, the selection of new workers became much less accurate.[43] As workers left their jobs and were replaced by new ones, misallocation among all employed persons constantly worsened, and this held down the growth rate of productivity. "A major reason for the marked decline in U.S. productivity growth in the last few years is the decline in the accuracy with which employers have been sorting people into jobs. And this decline in accuracy is caused by substantial reductions in the use of valid job aptitude tests."[44]

Schmidt and Hunter add another point. Employers have been told "that as long as you hire qualified people it doesn't matter whom you hire." They have been pressured not to hire from the best qualified down but instead to set low minimum qualification levels and hire on the basis of other factors from among those who meet the minimum levels. "But there is no real dividing line between the 'qualified' and the 'unqualified'; employee productivity is on a continuum from very high to very low, and a decline from superior to average productivity is as costly as a decline from average to poor." Moreover, employers have also been pressured to lower their minimum standards. In correspondence with me Schmidt summarized and amplified the case for loss of testing as a cause of the slowdown in residual productivity:

I would like to add [another] suggested reason for the slowdown in the growth of your "residual": a decline in the accuracy with which the abilities of employees are matched to the requirements of jobs in the U.S. economy . . . as a result of efforts by EEOC [Equal Employment Opportunity Commission] and of OFCCP [Office of Federal Contract Compliance Programs] to promote minority employment. . . .

We believe the effects produced by this cause could appear simultaneously and suddenly in all major segments of the economy. These effects could be expected to appear roughly simultaneously because all segments of industry were subjected to the same pressures to abandon valid selection methods beginning at the same time and following the same trajectory of escalation. Accounting for the sudden onset of productivity decline in 1974 requires an hypothesis involving the concept of "critical mass." Up to a certain point, as new, less competent employees appear on a job or in an organization, the lowered performance and output standards are confined to this group. But when the less competent employees reach a

critical mass, their lower performance standards become the standards of the organization. That is, at this point the older (more tenured) employees whose abilities *are* well matched to the job requirements abandon their older and higher performance standards quite quickly and conform to the newer, lower standards. They no longer have the numbers necessary to maintain a separate high-performance "subculture" in the organization.[45]

Schmidt and Hunter make a logical case. One crucial point—that general tests are valid predictors of performance in specific situations—has been accepted by the Division of Industrial and Organizational Psychology of the American Psychological Association.[46] Another point—that the civil rights legislation in fact forced abandonment of a great deal of testing—is documented by a report of the National Research Council, but that same report stresses the inadequacy of quantitative information concerning the change in the proportion of workers whose employers used testing in selection. The scattered studies cited clearly indicate a reduction but seem to suggest that not more than (say) one-fifth of employment could have been in groups formerly but no longer selected by testing.[47] The figure may be much smaller. There can be little doubt that less testing is a factor in the productivity slowdown. I reserve judgment as to whether it is a major factor, of the order of magnitude that Schmidt and Hunter suggest, until it has received more examination by economists.[48]

45. Letter from Frank L. Schmidt to Edward F. Denison, November 25, 1980. The hypothesized spread of lower standards from new, less competent employees to the mass of workers brings us back to work intensity, and I have previously described the phenomenon under that heading. See *Accounting for Growth*, p. 79, and *Slower Growth*, p. 135. Elimination of testing would provide a "shock" such as that which Harvey Leibenstein says could lower "peer standards" in many firms, a lowering that would depress productivity widely—a point I discussed in "Accounting for Slower Economic Growth: An Update," p. 28.

46. Schmidt and Hunter report that the organization revised its standards on employment testing and selection to reflect the new findings, which stemmed from the organization's Committee on Psychological Tests and Assessment and were endorsed by the APA Board of Scientific Affairs. Schmidt and Hunter, "New Research Findings," p. 261. Based partly on the APA's recommendation, the General Accounting Office recommended revision of the EEOC Guidelines on Employee Selection Procedures to bring them into conformity with professionally accepted findings. See General Accounting Office, *Uniform Guidelines on Employee Selection Procedures Should Be Reviewed and Revised*, GAO/FPCD-82-26 (GAO, 1982).

47. Committee on Ability Testing, Assembly of Behavioral and Social Sciences, National Research Council, *Ability Testing: Uses, Consequences, and Controversies* (Washington, D.C.: National Academy Press, 1982).

48. I shall not review the quantitative estimates by Schmidt and Hunter. I believe these authors overestimate the effects even if their judgments about testing and its abandonment are correct, but I nevertheless believe that they have demonstrated that the costs of stopping testing *may* be large, even without allowance for a spread of lower standards to the work force as a whole.

43. Others have noted that the value of letters of recommendation deteriorated as teachers, former employers, and others became hesitant about providing candid appraisals because of privacy legislation denying confidentiality to their words and from fear that ex-employees might sue. The reduction in the value of reference letters prompted some employers to stop requiring them.

44. Schmidt and Hunter, "New Research Findings," p. 432.

MISALLOCATION OF CAPITAL: TAX DISTORTIONS. Capital (structures, equipment, and inventories) takes many forms and has many uses. Its efficient allocation requires that after-tax net earnings of capital derived from current production be proportional to before-tax net earnings, a condition that implies that all capital must bear the same effective tax rate. Otherwise, efforts by individuals and firms to maximize their after-tax earnings will not lead to equalization of expected before-tax rates of return, a requirement for maximization of output per unit of input. In the context of my analysis of the residual productivity series, these statements can be confined to nonresidential business capital.

The correspondence between before-tax returns and the income taxes imposed upon them has been severed by changes in the tax code that date back to the introduction of accelerated depreciation in 1954 and of the investment tax credit in 1962. Subsequently, use of objective estimates of actual service lives and realistic depreciation formulas for capital goods was progressively discarded, a trend that culminated, when the Accelerated Cost Recovery System was adopted in 1981, in the abandonment of all pretext of measuring economic depreciation. That same year saw an explosion of possibilities for tax-favored investments, known as tax shelters, on which part of the associated costs can be deducted from fully taxable income. (The 1982 Tax Equity and Fiscal Responsibility Act modified some of the worst features.) The system discriminates not only in favor of fixed capital over inventories, and equipment over structures, but also among components of the capital stock classified by use, type, and firm.

As tax expert Richard Goode says, "Economists point to inefficiencies in resource use attributable to provisions of both the individual income tax and the corporate tax. Most of those who have studied the subject think that these inefficiencies have recently increased greatly. . . . The presumption of economic inefficiency is especially strong for [tax-sheltered investments] because tax-sheltered investments that would produce not merely low returns but losses in the absence of taxation can be advantageous solely because of the tax saving."[49] Accelerated inflation also helped to weaken the connection between before-tax earnings and current production and taxes. Some of the changes in the provisions controlling capital consumption deductions in the tax code were rationalized, in part, as offsets to distortions resulting

from inflation, but there is no reason to think the changes helped restore tax neutrality among firms and types of investment. Under present tax law, effective tax rates on current earnings are so diverse, and, as a consequence, ratios of after-tax to before-tax earnings vary so much, that there can be no question that increased misallocation of capital contributed to the slowdown in the growth rate of the residual.[50] The question is how much.

To answer this question would require a more detailed study than has yet been made. An artificial example can help illustrate the possible order of magnitude, however. Suppose that sometime between 1973 and 1982 a single change had been made in the tax code and that one-third of all capital input in 1982 came from capital invested under the new code. Suppose, also, that the new code increased misallocation so much that, on average, capital invested under it contributed one-third less to output than the same amount of capital would have contributed if invested under the former code. The contribution of the *whole* capital stock to nonresidential business output in 1982 would then have been one-ninth lower than it would have been with the previous degree of misallocation (so the hypothetical contribution was one-eighth above the actual contribution). The weight of capital in total input in the sector was 13.1 percent in 1982 (table G-2). Hence in 1982 output would have been about 1.64 percent higher ($\frac{1}{8} \times 13.1$) without the tax change. Increased misallocation of capital would then have reduced the growth rate of residual productivity by 0.18 percentage points over the nine years from 1973 to 1982. I doubt that the actual figure could have been this big.[51]

49. Richard Goode, "Lessons from Seven Decades of Income Taxation," in Joseph A. Pechman, ed., *Options for Tax Reform* (Brookings, 1984), p. 15.

50. Studies showing the diversity of tax rates or the ratios of after-tax to before-tax earnings include Mervyn A. King and Don Fullerton, *The Taxation of Income from Capital: A Comparative Study of the United States, the United Kingdom, Sweden, and West Germany* (University of Chicago Press, 1984); Dale W. Jorgenson and Martin A. Sullivan, "Inflation and Corporate Capital Recovery," in Charles R. Hulten, ed., *Depreciation, Inflation, and the Taxation of Income from Capital* (Washington, D.C.: Urban Institute Press, 1981); and Alan J. Auerbach, "Corporate Taxation in the United States," *BPEA, 2:1983*, pp. 451–505.

51. A comment is necessary here on a series for 1953–82 that Auerbach ("Corporate Taxation," table 6, p. 471) developed. It measures what the welfare (misallocation) cost of differential corporate taxation would have been each year if the total corporate capital stock (not just investment made in that year) had been made under the conditions prevailing in that year. Auerbach calculates that under the conditions prevailing in 1953 the loss would have been equivalent to throwing away 0.72 percent of the corporate capital stock; under 1973 conditions, 3.90 percent; and under 1982 conditions, 1.54 percent. He notes that the 1982 percentage assumes, contrary to fact, that the moderating impact of the Tax Equity and Fiscal Responsibility Act of 1982 (TEFRA)

MISALLOCATION OF CAPITAL: ECONOMIC CHANGE. One reason for misallocation of resources is that patterns of demand and techniques of production are constantly changing. As a consequence, the output-maximizing distribution of resources is also changing. The actual distribution lags behind it, because resources are not instantly mobile, and tends to mirror the income-maximizing distribution of earlier years. If the actual distribution of resources is closer to the output-maximizing distribution in one year, given the demand patterns and production techniques of that year, than it had been in an earlier year, given the demand and production situation in that earlier year, then between the two years this improvement will be a source of output growth that is included in the residual productivity series. If, on the other hand, the gap widens, then this deterioration is a negative source of growth. In practice, it is difficult to identify or measure departures from the income-maximizing distribution. My general assumption has been that, apart from the overallocation of labor to farming and self-employment, the percentage by which misallocation stemming from this lag reduced nonresidential business output has not changed and consequently such misallocation did not affect the growth rate.

Martin Baily and, in somewhat different form, Ernst R. Berndt have argued that accelerated economic change, presumably unmatched by acceleration in the reallocation of capital, may have greatly widened the wedge between the actual and the income-maximizing distribution of capital.[52] Put differently, it has increased the rate of obsolescence and even caused early discarding.[53] Baily pointed to increases in government regulation and foreign competition, and to changes in relative prices, especially that of energy, as examples of accelerated change, while Berndt focused on energy.

Capital stock data allow for normal obsolescence at the rate it has occurred in the past. Whether economic change from all causes that affect capital (other than changes in taxation) accelerated from 1948–73 to 1973–82, receded, or stayed the same, I do not know. All things considered, I see no reason to assume acceleration. I have reviewed the composition of nonresidential business capital, including the distribution of fixed capital by industry and among types of structure or producers' durable goods, and found that most of the stock could not have been affected by oil prices. It is also germane that a large part of the 1982 stock included in the BEA capital stock series upon which I rely was acquired after the 1973 oil crisis. My conclusion is that changes in the misallocation of capital resulting from the reasons suggested could not have had a sizable effect on output per unit of input in nonresidential business. The illustrative calculation for the effect on the growth rate of misallocation of capital due to tax distortions is equally applicable to this case.

BARRIERS TO INTERNATIONAL TRADE. "The United States—and many of its trading partners—are drifting to protectionism," according to Murray L. Weidenbaum, who was President Reagan's first chairman of the Council of Economic Advisers.[54] Few would dissent from a judgment that barriers to U.S. imports and exports have risen since 1973. Nor is this judgment brought into question by the substantial increases that have occurred in ratios of imports

---

was in effect, but even his 1981 estimate, 3.19 percent, was below his estimate for 1973 conditions. Thus Auerbach's figures imply that the allocation effects of the corporate income tax became more adverse to productivity from 1953 to 1973 and less adverse from 1973 to 1981 (and much less so after passage of TEFRA). Even though the average tax rate was down, I would doubt this result. It may be noted that the biggest change in Auerbach's series prior to 1982 is a large jump in its level in 1972, when the Asset Depreciation Range was introduced. The series is disconcertingly jumpy from year to year.

Suppose misallocation of the capital stock in 1973 could be measured by the average of Auerbach's percentages for the tax laws of 1953–72, or 0.82 percent, and misallocation in 1982 by the average of his percentages for 1973–81, or 3.15 percent. Then, based on the procedure used for the example in the text, if misallocation had not worsened after 1973, capital would have contributed 2.41 percent more than it actually did to 1982 output, output per unit of input would have been 0.32 percent higher, and increased misallocation would have reduced the 1973–82 growth rate of the residual by 0.04 percentage points.

Auerbach's estimates are incomplete, however. They exclude differences between the tax burdens on fixed capital and inventories and on firms within an industry; many detailed points of discrimination in the corporate income tax; and (relevant to my calculations although not to his) the effects of the individual income tax, including tax loopholes, and discrimination between corporate and noncorporate firms within nonresidential business. See also the comments by Henry J. Aaron in *BPEA, 2:1983*, pp. 506–10.

52. Baily, "Productivity and the Services of Capital and Labor," pp. 1–50; Ernst Berndt, "Comment," in John W. Kendrick, ed., *International Comparisons of Productivity and Causes of the Slowdown*, pp. 331–33; and Ernst R. Berndt and David O. Wood, "Interindustry Differences in the Effects of Energy Price-Induced Capital Revaluation on Multifactor Productivity Measurement," (Massachusetts Institute of Technology Center for Energy Policy Research, 1984). I commented upon the paper by Baily in "Accounting for Slower Economic Growth: An Update," pp. 13–14.

53. The loss of output that would occur if capital became less appropriate is sometimes considered to result from an overstatement of the growth of capital input instead of from an increase in misallocation when the measure of capital input is given. The classification does not change the analysis.

54. Murray L. Weidenbaum with Michael C. Munger and Ronald J. Penoyer, *Toward A More Open Trade Policy* (Washington University, Center for the Study of American Business, 1984), p. 1.

and exports to GNP. These increases simply mean that the opportunities for gains from trade have expanded, a situation that implies that the costs of imposing the same level of trade barriers are greater than before.

Restrictions against international trade prevent full realization of its potential advantages of concentrating production of commodities in countries having the greatest comparative advantage in their production and of broadening markets and thus allowing more specialization. Changes between two dates in artificial barriers to trade can consequently add to or subtract from growth rates between those dates. Calculation of this contribution to the growth rate would require knowledge of the amount of trade that would have taken place at one date with the barriers of the other date and of the increased costs that were imposed because that trade did not take place.

I know of no recent comprehensive estimate of the change in the cost of protection. The difficulty of making such an estimate is enhanced because increased barriers are concentrated in quotas and other nontariff barriers, whose costs are even harder to appraise than those of tariffs. The recent emergence of exchange rates that permit imports to exceed exports greatly, altering the economy's industrial structure, is especially hard to handle, as is the effect of large fluctuations in exchange rates.[55] Although I do not doubt that heightened trade barriers helped retard the 1973–82 growth of the residual, I do doubt that the amount was appreciable. First, the rapid rise

domestic and foreign restrictions against trade may have reduced our national income in 1957 by 1.5 percent.[57] If the cost were still 1.5 percent in 1973, and were then increased by half to 2.25 percent in 1982, this growth would have curtailed the 1973–82 growth rate of the residual in nonresidential business by 0.11 percentage points.[58] I do not think the true figure could be higher.

Energy Prices and Use[59]

Increases in energy prices have had major adverse consequences for the American economy, but the question here is how much declines in the use of energy associated with them contributed to the decline in the growth rate of residual productivity. My view is that they made a contribution but that it was not major until after 1979, and that even then it was not the dominant cause of the productivity slowdown.

TIMING. Casual observers citing the energy situation as the chief cause of the slowdown derive their belief from timing: the sharp decline in the rate of productivity increase that began in 1974 followed the 1973 oil crisis, and the further decline in the rate of productivity increase that began in 1980 followed the 1979 oil shock. This pattern is what the annual data show. However, the quarterly data display a different pattern. The following informal table shows the seasonally adjusted annual rate of change (in percent) from the previous quarter in output per hour in the nonfarm business sector, as calculated by the BLS.[60]

Quarter	1972	1973	1974	1978	1979	1980
1	4.4	6.1	−4.4	−0.1	−2.3	0.3
2	4.7	−3.2	−3.1	1.6	−3.7	−3.5
3	5.2	−1.6	−2.9	−0.9	−2.3	2.7
4	4.7	−0.4	−0.4	0.3	−0.2	1.2

in trade suggests that the increase in barriers against trade as a whole was not enormous, even though it does not preclude some increase in obstacles.[56] Second, past estimates of the costs of trade barriers are not large, and estimates of changes in costs over periods as long as nine years are rather small. For example, I once "guesstimated" that the cost of all

The first steps by oil exporting countries to curtail shipments and raise prices were taken in October 1973.[61] However, the change in the course of produc-

55. Edward M. Bernstein discussed the latter subject, although without quantification, in *The Economics of Fluctuating Exchange Rates*, Report 76/7 (EMB Ltd., 1976).

56. Moreover, as Angus Maddison says, "One striking feature of the conjunctural situation that is different from the 1930s is that there have not been *massive* trade restrictions that would have adversely affected productivity. The liberal international economic order has held remarkably firm. . . ." (Italics added.) (Angus Maddison, "Comparative Analysis of the Productivity Situation in the Advanced Capitalist Countries" in John W. Kendrick, ed., *International Comparisons of Productivity and Causes of the Slowdown*, pp. 62–63.)

57. Denison, *Sources of Growth*, pp. 188–91.

58. This calculation takes into account the fact that the percentages refer to the whole economy but all the losses would appear in nonresidential business.

59. See also the section on p. 51, "Misallocation of Capital: Economic Change."

60. Exclusion of farms removes an irrelevant source of erratic change in the quarterly series that is, even so, subject to much greater possible error than the annual data. Output is measured by gross product, and the sector covered by these data includes tenant-occupied nonfarm housing.

61. Previously a two-price system had been introduced for oil as part of the Nixon price controls. Regional shortages of gasoline occasionally resulted, necessitating a direct allocation scheme, but could hardly have had a significant effect on national productivity before October.

tivity had occurred six months earlier. Productivity declined at an annual rate of 3.2 percent in the second quarter of 1973 and continued to decline through the fourth quarter of 1974. In the five preceding quarters it had increased at an average rate of 5.0 percent. In the second episode of oil price increases the productivity reversal began with a 2.3 percent drop in the first quarter of 1979 or perhaps even two quarters earlier, depending on how one interprets the series. Although not as unambiguous as the 1973 timing, this drop also seems too early to be a consequence of the oil situation. As late as December 1978 an OPEC announcement envisaged only a gradual increase in the average price of crude oil from about $13 per barrel to about $14.50 by the end of 1979. Only after the temporary interruption of Iranian oil supplies at year's end did prices start to rise, and although the refiner acquisition cost of imported crude oil almost doubled from January 1979 to January 1980, over seven-eighths of the increase occurred after April.[62]

Nor is the period since 1973 the only one in which the amount of energy used per unit of output showed a marked decline. Jack Alterman has developed important new data for energy use.[63] They show that from 1947 to 1954, when productivity was increasing at an especially fast rate, the energy-output ratio was dropping at a rate comparable to that from 1973 to 1981. Hence, even annual data show that worsened productivity does not always accompany a decline in energy intensity. More generally, Alterman has shown that when subperiods within the time span from 1929 (when his new data for nonresidential business start) to 1973 are compared, no systematic association between the growth rates of factor input per unit of output and energy input per unit of output is present. Alterman further found that, although energy per unit of factor input rose in all periods before 1973 and fell thereafter, there was no consistent relationship between the *size* of the changes in energy per unit of factor input and output per unit of factor input.

BUSINESS OPINION. If reduced energy use were the major cause of the productivity slowdown, management should be aware of it. Significant changes in energy use would have required explicit management decisions, and the effects would have been ascertainable. Hence opinions of management should be relatively reliable in this case.

The report on the results of a survey of the Fellows of the Academy of International Management to elicit their opinions of the causes of the productivity slowdown makes no mention of energy as such. Among eleven reasons for the decline in productivity growth in the United States ranked by U.S. fellows, a "shift from labor to raw materials saving," which might have included any energy effect, ranks above only "increased government request for information and data."[64]

A survey by the National Institute of Economic and Social Research of the manufacturing firms that are members of its Industrial Panel, conducted in the United Kingdom at the end of 1981, was also designed to obtain information about productivity changes. It provides more precise information, although for the United Kingdom only, because a question was included "to find out whether respondents attributed any of their reduced productivity growth" to the rise in fuel prices of 1973–74 and later. "The answers . . . suggest that considerable reorganization had taken place in some companies' production, although the most common reaction to the energy price rise was increased effort to save fuel generally (e.g. by remembering to switch lights off) and more attention to all-round efficiency. Only two [out of fifty-two], however, perceived any effect on labour productivity, and both these said that changes made to take account of high energy prices involved a significant *decrease* in their labour requirements. This implies that, in these cases, adjustments arising from higher fuel prices had had a beneficial effect on labour productivity."

The report also refers to an earlier study by the institute that found that, through 1979, reactions to the rise in energy prices were limited because of the low profitability of conservation measures. Major changes in production techniques, they reported, would be made only if the new price structure was thought to be permanent, and would take place only as old equipment needed to be replaced. This lag in reacting to the rise in the oil price suggests that major energy-related investment expenditures, made at the expense of increasing productivity directly, could not have been the cause of the slowdown in labor-productivity growth of the mid- and late-seventies.[65]

62. *Monthly Energy Review* (December 1980), p. 72.

63. Jack Alterman, principal investigator, *A Historical Perspective on Changes in U.S. Energy-Output Ratios,* report by Resources for the Future to the Electric Power Research Institute, Palo Alto, 1985.

64. Michel A. Amsalem, "The Decline in Productivity Growth—Causes, Consequences and Possible Remedies," *Columbia Journal of World Business,* vol. 16 (Winter 1981), pp. 48–56.

65. G. C. Wenban-Smith, "Factors Influencing Recent Productivity Growth—Report on a Survey of Companies," *National Institute Economic Review,* no. 101 (August 1982), pp. 57–66. The earlier study was G. Ray and J. Morel, "Energy Conservation in the UK," National Institute Discussion Paper no. 44 (National Institute of Economic and Social Research, 1981).

Responses from American businessmen would probably be similar to those of the British, and the two surveys together provide substantial evidence that energy was not the major cause of the slowdown. They need not mean, however, that energy contributed nothing to it.

ESTIMATED EFFECT OF CHANGED ENERGY CONDITIONS. The effect of the energy price increases, together with such related developments as government regulations to conserve energy, can be approximated if one knows the share of energy in the total unduplicated costs of the nonresidential business sector, can judge the effect of changed energy prices and controls upon the amount of energy the sector consumed, and accepts the proposition that keeping output per combined unit of factor input and energy unchanged when energy per unit of input is reduced requires substitution of additional factor input with a current value equal to that of the energy eliminated. To appraise the effect of the first price rise, I cited in *Slower Growth* calculations of this type by a number of writers and, when necessary, adjusted their results to conform to my framework.[66] The estimated effect on the growth rate of output per unit of input from 1973 to 1976 was not large—about 0.1 percentage

extraction stage, of mineral fuels acquired by the nonresidential business sector, measured in constant (1972) prices, to the net national product (net value added) of the nonresidential business sector, also measured in constant (1972) prices. This ratio declined by average annual amounts of 0.3 percent from 1948 to 1973, 1.6 percent from 1973 to 1979, 4.8 percent from 1979 to 1981, and 2.4 percent from 1973 to 1981.[67] One cannot be sure what would have happened to energy use if previous energy price trends and associated conditions had continued, and use of the past trend in the energy-output ratio as the basis for judgment is not very satisfactory because the trend was unstable. Moreover, the ratios may be affected by the business cycle; this possibility is especially troublesome in the short 1979–81 period. Suppose we nevertheless assume that, in the absence of a shift in price relationships and controls, the energy-output ratio would have continued to decline at 0.3 percent a year after 1973, so that the effect of the shift was to reduce the growth rate of the ratio by 1.3 percentage points in 1973–79, 4.5 points in 1979–81, and 2.1 points in 1973–81, as shown for variant A in the top panel of the following informal table.[68] The estimates by Alterman of the value of

	1973–79	1979–81	1973–81
Change from 1948–73 in growth rate of energy-output ratio (in percentage points) based on:			
A. Mineral fuels, constant dollars	−1.3	−4.5	−2.1
B. Mineral fuels, BTUs	−1.4	−3.4	−1.9
C. End use by nonresidential business, constant dollars	−1.2	−4.0	−1.7
D. End use by nonresidential business, BTUs	−0.3	−3.0	−1.0
Energy-output value ratio			
A, B. Mineral fuels	0.075	0.119	0.086
C, D. End use by nonresidential business	0.070	0.091	0.075
Change from 1948–73 in growth rate of residual productivity due to energy, based on:			
A. Mineral fuels, constant dollars	−0.10	−0.53	−0.18
B. Mineral fuels, BTUs	−0.11	−0.40	−0.16
C. End use by nonresidential business, constant dollars	−0.09	−0.36	−0.13
D. End use by nonresidential business, BTUs	−0.02	−0.27	−0.07
Average	−0.08	−0.39	−0.14

point—because energy was only a small part of costs and the change in energy use was not great. The new energy data by Alterman and his clarification of concepts of energy use permit improved calculations and their extension to 1981. Indeed, they permit alternative calculations for nonresidential business based on four variants of the energy-output ratio.

What happened to energy use? One variant of the energy-output ratio is the ratio of the value, at the

66. *Slower Growth*, pp. 138–40.

67. These energy data erroneously include mineral fuels used by the whole economy, but their inclusion is only a minor defect because sectors other than nonresidential business use very little mineral fuel. The energy they acquire consists almost entirely of electricity, gas, gasoline, oil, etc., that is provided by energy-processing industries (mainly electric and gas utilities and oil refineries) within nonresidential business.

68. The energy data used to compute the energy-output ratios in rows A–D, respectively, of the table are from Alterman, *Historical Perspective on Changes*, tables AT-5-3, column 1; AT-2-3, column 1; AT-5-21, column 6; and AT-5-21, column 3. The energy data used to compute the energy-output value ratios in line A, B are from his table AT-5-6, column 1, and in line C, D from his unpublished table underlying page 5-3 of his text. The

mineral fuels in current prices yield ratios of this value to net national product of nonresidential business in current market prices that averaged 0.075 in 1973–79, 0.119 in 1979–81, and 0.086 in 1973–81, as shown for variant A in the second panel of the informal table.[69] The products of the data in the first and second panels are estimates, shown in the bottom panel, of the change in the growth rates of output per unit of input and residual productivity that resulted from the change in the course of energy prices and related controls. According to variant A, they were responsible for drops of 0.10 and 0.18 percentage points from 1948–73 to 1973–79 and 1973–81, respectively. The changes from 1948–73 to 1979–81 (0.53 percentage points) and, by subtraction, from 1973–79 to 1979–81 (0.43 points) were larger.

Variant B follows the more traditional practice of measuring use of mineral fuels in British thermal units (BTUs) rather than in constant dollars. The decline in the constant-dollar series for mineral fuels from 1979 to 1981 was larger than that in the BTU series because use of coal and natural gas increased at the expense of crude oil, which was more expensive per BTU. The estimated effect on productivity is smaller in 1979–81 when the BTU series is used but about the same in 1973–79 and 1973–81.[70]

Although the decline in the energy-output ratio based on primary energy BTUs continued until at least 1983, the decline was at a reduced pace, so that the estimated energy effects based on BTUs are smaller for 1979–82 or 1979–83 than for 1979–81.[71] Moreover, extending the latest period beyond 1981 reduces the energy effect even more when it is based on variant A, because the shift from petroleum to coal and natural gas nearly stopped after 1981.

Variants C and D base the calculations not on mineral fuels or primary energy but on "finished" energy used for fuel and power by nonresidential business.[72] The informal table on the preceding page shows calculations for variant C, in which the numerator of the finished energy-output ratio is based on value in constant (1972) dollars, and for variant D, in which it is based on BTUs. All four variants yield rather similar energy effects except for the 1979–81 estimate based on variant A, but the last two sets are moderately smaller than the first two.

Two consideration suggest that, as a group, these results may be generous. First, if a computed pre-1973 trend line rather than the 1948–73 growth rate based on end years is used as the standard from which departures of the energy-output ratio in later years are judged, these departures are smaller. Second, the calculations assume that, per unit of output, additional factor input had to make good all of the energy reduction. Actually, some of the reduction was achieved by eliminating the waste that was present up to 1973, when energy was so cheap and so trifling a component of cost in most activities that little attention was paid to its conservation. Production was not affected by shutting doors, turning off lights, or eliminating the heating of materials to temperatures above the minimum necessary in processes such as making candy.

Despite the limitations of these calculations and differences among them, they give a useful indication of the importance of energy prices in the slowdown of residual productivity. Without knowing which energy-output ratio would have changed trend least after 1973 in the absence of altered price relationships, it is not possible to choose among the variants. The estimates are averaged at the bottom of the informal table. The effect in 1979–81 is then lessened by 0.05 percentage points, to −0.34, to represent 1979–82. If some allowance for the probable overstatement discussed in the preceding paragraph is

---

output data for the energy-output ratios are net national product in constant prices from NIPA, table 1.8, and those for energy-output value ratios are net national product in current prices from NIPA, table 1.7.

69. The first and last years of each period are given half the weight of other years because they enter the calculation of weights for only one rather than two annual changes. The 1973 ratio was only 0.037.

70. It is also possible to base the BTU calculation on data for primary energy, which includes primary energy equivalents of hydroelectric and nuclear electric power in addition to mineral fuels. This procedure, not shown in the table, yields slightly smaller effects of the changed energy situation on the growth rate of the residual. They are −0.08 percentage points for 1973–79, −0.38 points for 1979–81, and −0.10 points for 1973–81. Energy data are from Alterman, *Historical Perspective on Changes*, table AT-2-3, col. 6.

71. The ratio shows almost no drop in 1982, followed by a renewed drop in 1983. A calculation yields a reduction in the contribution from 1948–73 to 1979–82 of 0.32 percentage points as against 0.40 points to 1979–81, despite a higher weight for energy. This difference may be too small, because the irregularity of the annual drop in the energy-output ratio may be due to the business cycle, but even a calculation based on 1979–83 yields only 0.34 points.

72. Finished energy compares with primary energy as follows. The primary energy used for fuel and power by nonresidential business enterprises outside the energy sector is retained. Instead of fuels acquired by utilities, oil refineries, and other processors, one counts the electricity, gas, gasoline, oil, etc., that they produce, but only the portion that is used by nonresidential business for fuel and power. Finished energy sold for residential use and other uses by households, sales to governments and nonprofit organizations, sales to nonresidential business for use as a raw material, and BTUs lost in processing and delivery are eliminated. In the value series there is a partial offset to these deductions because the average price per BTU of energy delivered by utilities and refiners is much higher than that of the energy they buy.

made, the estimates suggest that energy prices were responsible for something over 0.1 percentage point of the decline of 1.4 percentage points in the growth rate of the residual from 1948–73 to 1973–82, less than 0.1 percentage point of the decline of 1.1 points from 1948–73 to 1973–79, perhaps 0.3 points of the total decline of 2.1 points from 1948–73 to 1979–82, and perhaps 0.2 points of the decline of 1.0 point from 1973–79 to 1979–82.[73] Thus, energy prices were a small factor in the slowdown after 1973 but more important to the further slowdown after 1979. The effect of the 1979 price rise seems to have been concentrated in a short period. By 1984 the decline in energy-output ratios had slowed greatly and may have stopped.

Background Conditions and Additional Causes of Slowdown

The rate of increase in output is often thought to have been cut by changes in such general conditions of the economy or society as the rate of inflation, level of unemployment, composition of families, social attitudes, government regulations, or the burden of taxation, government expenditures, or national defense. To have had this consequence, these changes would have to have affected adversely the direct determinants of output, such as employment, the age-sex composition of labor, its composition by amount of education, the amount of capital, the cost of misallocation, the intensity of utilization of employed resources, or the state of knowledge as to how to produce at low cost.[74]

The effects of changes in most direct determinants were separately estimated, and thus they are not included in the residual. Only advances in knowledge and the miscellaneous direct determinants affect residual productivity, and in this chapter I have included the main plausible hypotheses concerning the ways in which they may have changed and reduced the growth rate of the residual.

The discussion was not exhaustive, however, and there are other ways in which changes in background conditions may have affected residual productivity.

For example, besides ways previously discussed, intensified inflation may have raised the costs of information, prediction, and transactions. Further, inflation may have worsened decisionmaking despite acceptance of increased costs, a situation that leads to greater misallocation of labor and capital. In the case of government regulation the effect of a diversion of labor and capital to comply with regulations to protect the physical environment and worker safety and health were estimated, but similar costs (believed to be smaller) of compliance with other regulations affect residual productivity. Regulation may impose other types of costs not previously discussed. It may delay projects and the introduction of products and methods that raise productivity; raise paperwork costs; reduce the efficiency of production; and prevent resources from being allocated among uses in such a way as to maximize output. Some of these costs are imposed deliberately in order to protect regional, industrial, or other special interests.

Apart from the varied effects of changes in such broad background conditions, numerous specific developments doubtless had their effects. For example, government services to business apparently became less adequate as delays in the court system lengthened and the federal highway system, whose extension had been a positive element in growth, began to deteriorate from wear. I have discussed many such possibilities elsewhere.[75]

It is not likely that any one output determinant was responsible for the decline in the growth rate of residual productivity after 1973. My impression is that it is more likely to have resulted from small to moderate adverse changes in many of the unmeasured output determinants, just as nearly all measured determinants contributed to the lowering of the growth rate of output per person employed.

ACCURACY OF THE DATA. It is occasionally suggested that the productivity slowdown never happened and is merely the product of bad statistics. This cheerful illusion has no basis in reality. Although estimates of changes in output and input are subject to error even over periods of several years, the size of the slowdown since 1973 is too big for any appreciable part of it to have been caused by statistical error. Although long obvious, this fact is further confirmed by the latest information. National income

---

73. Alterman obtains estimates consistent with these. Alterman, *Historical Perspective on Changes,* p. 5-32. He estimates that 0.1–0.2 percentage points, or 6–12 percent, of the slowdown from 1948–73 to 1973–81 in the growth rate of nonresidential business gross product per unit of factor input resulted from the rise in energy prices.

74. Indeed, as I have stressed before, I believe it is impossible to appraise the effect of a change in such a background condition except by identifying the direct determinants it changes, estimating the amounts by which it changes each of them, and estimating the effects of these changes upon output. Usually, changes in one background condition will also lead to changes in another.

75. See, especially, Denison, *Slower Growth;* "Accounting for Slower Economic Growth: An Update"; and "Research Concerning the Effect of Regulation on Productivity." Barry P. Bosworth, in *Tax Incentives and Economic Growth,* surveys much of the pertinent literature.

and product statistics are revised periodically because increasingly reliable data for any year become available with the passage of time. The most definitive data appear only after a long time lag and refer to every fifth year, the dates for which industrial censuses are taken and input-output tables are prepared. Such benchmark data were recently completed for 1977 by the BEA but have not yet been incorporated into the official series. Based on the procedures used for the previous benchmark year, 1972, the 1977 national income estimate is raised by $2.7 billion (in current prices), or 0.2 percent, enough to raise the 1972–77 growth rate (which includes the first four years of the slowdown) by a trivial 0.03 percentage points.[76] The BEA's regular annual revisions for the years 1981 and 1982, reported in July 1984, are also small and, this time, downward. (These data are not incorporated into this study.)

Some journalists and economists, unfamiliar with the way economic time series are obtained, had supposed that statistical errors deriving from the presence of what they call the "underground economy" had caused the growth of productivity and other magnitudes to be enormously understated in the last decade or so. However, no logical support for this view has been provided, as I have explained elsewhere.[77] Subsequent careful studies by experts familiar with economic statistics document this conclusion more exhaustively. Richard D. Porter and Amanda S. Bayer of the Federal Reserve Board research staff show that financial series (including the number of large bills outstanding), which usually have been the foundation for the houses of straw erected by the underground economists, provide no support at all.[78] Robert P. Parker of the BEA, using all available evidence pertinent to the way the official national income and product series are measured, put the best (not conservative) estimates of the amounts by which the levels of national income and GNP are understated as a direct or indirect consequence of misreporting of tax return information at only 3 percent and 1 percent, respectively.[79] The BEA has not yet decided how to change these percentages over time, but they are too small for any reasonable change to alter growth rates appreciably. Richard J. McDonald found no indication of bias resulting from the underground economy in the price, employment, or other series prepared by the BLS.[80]

America's Response to the Slowdown

The growth of American production has been slow for over a decade, and the record becomes highly disappointing when the high rate of increase in the supply of labor is taken into account. That our performance was poor is suggested by two aspects of this record: the increase in the portion of our productive resources that went unused, culminating in 1982–83 in a huge gap between actual and potential output; and the drastic slowdown in productivity growth, especially the absence of any increase after 1973 in residual productivity in nonresidential business, a series that had grown a steady 1.4 percent a year since 1948.

How has America responded? It would unduly expand the scope of this study to examine further the problem of unused resources and the inflation-unemployment dilemma.[81] But America's response to the slowing of productivity growth deserves comment.

Preliminary Observations

Private enterprises produce 98 percent and government enterprises 2 percent of the output of nonresidential business. The sector's growth and productivity are determined by billions of decisions made by millions of private firms and over 100 million individuals who provide or deny their labor or prop-

76. Gerald F. Donahoe, "The National Income and Product Accounts: Preliminary Revised Estimates, 1977," *Survey of Current Business,* vol. 64 (May 1984), pp. 38–41. The $2.7 billion figure is obtained by subtracting the revision in compensation of employees and proprietors' income that was due to improved adjustments for misreporting on tax returns, shown in the table on p. 40 of Donahoe's article, from the total revision in national income shown in his table A.

77. Denison, "Accounting for Slower Economic Growth: An Update," pp. 32, 34–37, cites and comments upon a number of writings on this subject, and some evidence is provided in Edward F. Denison, "Is U.S. Growth Understated Because of the Underground Economy? Employment Ratios Suggest Not," *Review of Income and Wealth,* Series 28 (March 1982), pp. 1–16. A review of U.S. and foreign literature is provided by Carol S. Carson, "The Underground Economy: An Introduction," *Survey of Current Business,* vol. 64 (May 1984), pp. 21–37 and vol. 64 (July 1984), pp. 106–17.

78. Richard D. Porter and Amanda S. Bayer, "A Monetary Perspective on Underground Economic Activity in the United States," *Federal Reserve Bulletin,* vol. 70 (March 1984), pp. 177–89.

79. Robert P. Parker, "Improved Adjustments for the Misreporting of Tax Return Information Used to Estimate the National Income and Product Accounts, 1977," *Survey of Current Business,* vol. 64 (June 1984), pp. 17–25.

80. Richard J. McDonald, "The 'Underground Economy' and BLS Statistical Data," *Monthly Labor Review,* vol. 107 (January 1984), pp. 14–18.

81. This is primarily a responsibility of the federal government, including the Federal Reserve Board. For an excellent history of government policy see Herbert Stein, *Presidential Economics: The Making of Economic Policy from Roosevelt to Reagan and Beyond* (Simon and Schuster, 1984).

erty. Many decisions pertinent to present output were made years ago. Decisions relate to: organization and techniques of production; how much, how hard, and where to work; saving and investment; amount and type of education to be sought and the effort to be applied to it; research; and a host of other matters.

Governments—federal, state, and local—also influence business productivity. In the first place, they have positive responsibilities. Most students attend schools and colleges operated and supported by government. Government is responsible for the law enforcement and criminal justice systems, and for the civil law courts that are vital to business operations. It is responsible for streets and roads, harbors and rivers, airports, most local transit, some railroad transportation, and much of the water supply, trash disposal, and sewerage. In these broad areas, primary responsibility is largely with the states and localities, but federal participation and support are important. Direct federal responsibilities include maintenance of competition and a patent system; provision of accurate and timely economic information that is needed for informed private decisions as well as for formation of public policy; and provision and support of much research. The system of county agents to disseminate information to farmers and advise them is of long standing and widely approved but has been little imitated in other activities. All these responsibilities are in addition to the federal responsibility to use macroeconomic measures to achieve an economy in which wide fluctuations in output, large price changes, and excessive unemployment are avoided.

Second, in trying to meet its citizens' wishes for protection, other services, and the redistribution of income, government has responsibility to inflict as little damage as possible on business efficiency. Problems arise mainly from government regulation and taxation, although transfer programs may sometimes impair incentives.

The extent, if any, to which government has a third responsibility—to intervene to try to raise business productivity—remains a matter of dispute.

Government Response

The seriousness of the post-1973 setback to secular productivity growth was initially in doubt. The trend change was obscured by the 1974–75 recession, and the new situation was not clearly distinguished from the much milder and analytically different retardation that began about 1967. Moreover, energy needs, inflation, and unemployment posed more pressing problems than productivity. However, by 1978 or 1979 the presence of a new and serious productivity problem was generally recognized.

Given the great number of determinants of productivity, the many that contributed importantly to its advance before 1973, and the probable dispersion among many sources of the responsibility for the cessation of its advance, one might have expected that if there was to be any government program to restore productivity growth, it would be many-faceted. One might also have expected concentration on the government's own positive responsibilities, particularly in view of glaring declines in the educational achievement of students, greatly increased crime, long delays in civil suits, deterioration of the new interstate highway system for lack of maintenance, and congestion on the streets—not to mention macroeconomic failures.

In fact, the government's response has concentrated to an overwhelming extent on a single output determinant, and one that has been commonly regarded as peculiarly a province for private decision-making—namely, investment. I shall return to investment shortly.

Reduction of the burden of regulation has held a rather distant second place in government productivity policy. It has received attention at least since the Ford administration and increasingly in the Carter and Reagan years.[82] One way and another, regulation has contributed appreciably to worsened productivity performance, and emphasis upon finding ways to achieve important regulatory objectives at reduced cost is warranted. As yet, however, progress toward that objective has been painfully small, and probably the best that can be said is that the rise in the costs of regulation has been slowed.

Research, already favored by permission to deduct outlays currently rather than capitalize them, received a new tax credit in the 1981 Economic Recovery Tax Act. The credit is equal to 25 percent of eligible expenditures for research in excess of the annual average of similar expenditures in a base period (the three preceding years, after a transition period) but in no case more than half the current year's eligible expenditures. Eligible expenditures include a firm's own in-house research expenditures, expenditures for research use of computers and laboratory equipment, and 65 percent of the amounts

82. As Stein points out, the Nixon administration had earlier made a number of attempts to cut regulatory costs. (Stein, *Presidential Economics,* pp. 190–96.) However, its introduction of new regulations, especially price controls, was far more important.

paid for contract research or for grants for basic research to universities or certain scientific research organizations. Use of incremental outlays to compute the research credit contrasts with the use of total outlays in the calculation of the investment tax credit—which is, however, computed at a lower rate.[83]

Expenditures by the federal government for growth-promoting activities were not increased.[84] Most were cut back, although not because of any deliberate effort to reduce growth-promoting expenditures as such; they were victims of the general cut in nondefense expenditures.

The federal government's almost single-minded emphasis on investment to stimulate growth could hardly be described as assaulting the heart of the problem, because very little of the decline in the growth of labor productivity is ascribable to capital.[85] Nevertheless, whatever the source of the problem, one way to increase output is to increase business capital. I share with most economists the belief that more investment would be helpful if the cost of attaining it were not high, but before the government selected investment as its vehicle to increase growth, it should have asked how much additional growth would be obtained from a given amount of extra investment, how that extra investment could be obtained, and what the costs would be.

The following calculations yield an approximate answer, as of 1980, to the question of how much an increase in investment will raise national income and productivity. (The rate of resource utilization is assumed to be unaffected.) The apparent precision of the calculations is only to help the reader follow them; a very approximate result is all that is needed.[86]

Given 13.1 percent as the estimated share of nonresidential business national income that capital (fixed capital and inventories) would have earned, before taxes, under conditions of reasonably high employment, and 1.125 percent as the estimated increase in the output of the sector that would have resulted from a 1 percent increase in all inputs, a 1 percent increase in capital input alone would raise output by 0.147 percent, the product of these numbers.

In the long run a 1 percent increase in capital input requires a 1 percent increase in net stock. (Introducing refinements pertinent to the short run would raise the required increase in net stock.)[87] One percent of the net capital stock of the nonresidential business sector is equal to 1.28 percent of the annual net national product of the whole economy. Investment of an additional 1.28 percent of the nation's net national product, with all the incremental investment going to nonresidential business and none to housing or net foreign investment, would therefore raise the nonresidential business net capital stock by 1.0 percent and nonresidential business national income by 0.147 percent. Total national income would be raised by 0.115 percent. Labor input would be unchanged, so a 1.28 percentage point increase in the net national saving rate would also raise output per hour and per person employed by 0.147 percent in nonresidential business and 0.115 percent in the whole economy.

This calculation implies that to raise the long-run growth rate of national income per person employed, or per hour, in nonresidential business by even 0.2 percentage points would require raising the percentage of net national product that is saved and invested in nonresidential business by 1.75 percentage points ($1.28 \times 0.2/0.147$). Since total net private saving averaged only 7.8 percent of net national product even from 1948 to 1980, the required increase is equal to 22 percent of the average postwar net private saving rate.[88]

83. Robert Eisner, Steven H. Albert, and Martin A. Sullivan argue that the provision provides little incentive for R&D because additional spending, although rewarded with an immediate tax credit, increases the future base and reduces future credits. In practice, they say, the effects for individual firms are quite varied, with some of them "fairly bizarre." See Robert Eisner, Steven H. Albert, and Martin A. Sullivan, "The New Incremental Tax Credit for R&D: Incentive or Disincentive?" *National Tax Journal*, vol. 37 (June 1984), pp. 171–83.

84. Donald A. Nichols and Charles L. Schultze examined federal government expenditures and found no evidence of increases in growth-promoting expenditures. (Both, however, stress the difficulty of identifying such expenditures.) See Donald A. Nichols, "Federal Spending Priorities and Long-Term Economic Growth," and Charles L. Schultze, "Alternative Measures of Federal Investment Outlays," both in Charles R. Hulten and Isabel V. Sawhill, eds., *The Legacy of Reagonomics: Prospects for Long-Term Growth* (Washington, D.C.: Urban Institute Press, 1984), pp. 151–78.

85. This conclusion is, by now, shared by almost all serious students of productivity.

86. A fuller discussion of the role of capital in growth is provided in Edward F. Denison, "The Contribution of Capital to the Postwar Growth of Industrial Countries," in *U.S. Economic*

Growth from 1976 to 1986: Prospects, Problems and Patterns, vol. 3, *Capital* (GPO: Joint Economic Committee, November 15, 1976), pp. 45–83 (Brookings Reprint no. 324). See also Denison, "Accounting for Slower Economic Growth: An Update," pp. 10–17, for a discussion of various appraisals of capital in the slowdown. A valuable compendium is Board of Governors of the Federal Reserve System, *Public Policy and Capital Formation* (The Board, 1981).

87. For an explanation see Denison, *Sources of Growth*, chap. 12.

88. Similar arithmetic would tell us that the growth rate of output per hour could be raised by 1 percentage point (which is only two-fifths of the amount by which the rate has dropped) if the net saving rate were raised by 8.7 percentage points, but so large a change in saving would have a smaller proportional effect

This result does not make raising investment an appealing candidate to restore the growth rate of output per hour in nonresidential business, which fell by 2.5 percentage points from 1948–73 to 1973–82. But even if it did, the question would remain—how can investment be raised?

As explained in chapter 2, investment equals private saving plus the surplus or minus the deficit of governments. A program to increase the share of output invested implies a judgment as to whether its success would require greater incentives for investment, greater incentives for saving, or both, as well as means of bringing about the desired changes.

The stability of private saving ratios suggests that significant changes in the U.S. growth rate in the past cannot be ascribed to changes in the private propensity to save. Stability prevailed despite major changes in the rates of inflation, interest rates, the level and structure of taxes, real per capita income, government and private retirement programs, other forms of public and private insurance against contingencies, and many other aspects of the economic environment. It suggests that policymakers should be modest in appraising their ability to influence private saving behavior.

There is no similar difficulty in raising government saving, whether by increasing tax rates or reducing expenditures, if investment demand is known to be strong enough to assure that a more stringent fiscal policy will not instead simply reduce aggregate demand, production, and investment—and tax revenues as well. Much of the time this condition is not met. If monetary policy is taken as given, since 1973 the condition usually has not been met.

It seems clear to me that during the period of slow productivity growth, investment was limited only by investment demand and not by a saving propensity too weak to support larger investment. I also believe that any program to stimulate the growth of capital stock over an extended future period would do better to try to strengthen the incentives to invest than incentives to save. However, I do not suggest that acceptable measures are known that can be counted on with confidence to stimulate investment enough to raise the growth rate much.

The federal government's program to increase saving and investment consisted of tax inducements. Total federal corporate and personal taxes were reduced. The distribution of the tax burden was shifted by a host of special provisions that either distorted the measurement of property income so as to lower the taxes upon it or provided new or increased deductions and tax credits for selected types of investment and for switching assets from one form to another.

The effect of the tax reduction was to reduce national saving and investment because the tax reduction cut government saving without producing an offsetting increase in private saving. The special provisions in the tax code shifted the burden of taxation from property income to other income sources, mainly labor income. It is uncertain whether an additional dollar of net tax burden imposed upon labor reduces total factor input more or less than an additional dollar imposed upon property; both responses probably are small.[89] Private saving responded so little, if at all, to the tax cut that total input could hardly have been raised by the redistribution; it may or may not have been lowered. The more important effect of the special provisions, however, was to destroy the horizontal equity in the tax system, which requires that taxpayers with equal income pay equal taxes. These provisions impaired productivity by increasing the misallocation of capital and by increasing the amount of resources devoted by taxpayers to tax avoidance.

But this misallocation and waste were not the worst consequences of the failed government program of using tax breaks to promote growth by stimulating saving and investment.

As I wrote over two decades ago, "The cost of using the tax structure (as distinct from the level of taxes relative to expenditures) to stimulate growth, or for other purposes extraneous to raising necessary revenue in an equitable fashion, is a change in the income distribution that cannot be defended on the grounds of ability to pay. At least some supporters of any such proposal are inevitably those who gain by it, and the income distribution issue can never, as a practical matter, be removed from the discussion. This is especially so because the hoped-for benefits to growth are so hypothetical, unpredictable, and debatable, and all specific proposals that have favorable consequences also have adverse effects. In the long run discriminatory taxation must tend to weaken the tax system and respect for the impartiality of government."[90]

If there is one lesson that should have been learned by now, it is that proposals that the federal govern-

---

on the growth rate because the rise in the ratios of capital to other inputs would be greatly accelerated, a pattern that brings diminishing returns.

89. The evidence relating to this subject is reviewed in Bosworth, *Tax Incentives and Economic Growth.*

90. Denison, *Sources of Growth*, p. 281.

ment promote growth by special tax provisions or subsidies should be viewed with the greatest suspicion. The real purpose of such proposals almost invariably is to enlarge someone's income at someone else's expense. The claim that these tax changes are good for growth is incidental and usually wrong.

It is fortunate that recent administrations in Washington have had little enthusiasm for another possible area of government action: attempts to identify future "winners" and "losers" among industries and to use incentives and penalties to steer the industry distribution of production toward winners. Skepticism about the superiority of government foresight, and recognition that it is troubled industries that exert the strongest political pressures, backstop this attitude. Some recent proposals for industrial policy have, indeed, quite frankly espoused the protection of weak industries under the guise of an alleged need to prevent "deindustrialization."

Government probably influences private productivity for either good or ill less than public discussions would suggest. The extent to which it succeeds in the provision of education, largely a state and local responsibility, has the greatest impact in the long run. But government cannot have had very much to do with the recent slowdown in the growth rate of productivity computed on a potential basis. Whether the federal government provides an environment for business that is characterized by a high average level of employment, only moderate cyclical swings, and price stability is important to growth, but even the huge failures of the 1970s and early 1980s probably did not contribute much to the productivity slowdown. Neither did other government policies, unless (as is possible) it happens to be true that a big part of the slowdown was caused by faulty management stemming from the intricacies of government regulation, taxation, and financial market behavior (the viewpoint considered on pp. 44–45) or by misallocation resulting from the discontinuance of testing (the Schmidt-Hunter hypothesis described on pp. 48–49) and the government role in misallocation of capital.

Business Reaction

Whatever the causes of the productivity slowdown, any hope for restoration of an upward trend, except as a possible result of good luck, must depend mainly on actions by business. Only business management is in a strategic position to implement changes. Prospects are improved by the fact that many businessmen are inclined to accept much of the respon-

sibility for lagging productivity and to try to do something about it.

An astonishing number of businessmen have come to see the *problem* caused by poor productivity as Japanese competition, which they have viewed as an actual or imminent threat to the prosperity and even survival of every manufacturing enterprise. "Low" American productivity and poor quality of products, which they link, have been seen as the main reason for this threat. (In this context "quality" means absence of defects.) Low quality has been seen not only as hampering customer acceptance but also as lowering productivity by imposing costs to correct defects greater than would have been required to prevent them.

Economists can point out that output per man or per hour is much lower in Japan than in America in the economy as a whole and in most industries; that productivity growth has slowed in Japan as well as in America; that an undervalued yen has as much to do with the breadth of Japanese competition as productivity; and that the depth of the onslaught in the automobile market resulted in part from the high relative wage of American automobile workers. Businessmen may accept these points, and they welcome any government aid that they are able to extract to relieve the competitive pressure. But they nonetheless stress the urgency of improving productivity and product quality to meet Japanese competition and their own determination to do so. Whether and how this determination will be translated into action remains to be seen, but if our productivity is in fact reinvigorated, the credit may belong to Japanese competition.

Some managers expressing belief that survival now requires them to concentrate their firm's efforts on efficient production of reliable products and to pay attention to the long run apparently are beginning to act on this belief. The forgotten production engineer is promised new prestige and power, and incentive systems are to be restructured to reward long-term performance. Some changes in top management personnel are consistent with such a reemphasis. There is also great interest in Japanese management practices and labor relations (as in all things Japanese!) but no general view as to which are superior to American practices or transferable if they are.

The hope that management will raise the economy's productivity performance is only a hope. How serious and how successful management will be remains to be determined. The sad fact is that as yet the statistical record shows no improvement at all aside from effects of the business cycle.

APPENDIX

→>><<<←

Derivations of the Estimates

→>><<<←

The estimates in this book were prepared by procedures that were only slightly changed from those used in *Slower Growth*. Those, in turn, were slight modifications of the procedures used earlier in my *Accounting for Growth*. This appendix supplements the descriptions in *Slower Growth*; material that is unchanged is not repeated.

Since publication of *Slower Growth*, the BEA has revised the national income and product accounts. Some series were revised all the way back to 1929, although most remain unchanged prior to 1967. Series prepared by other statistical agencies have also been revised. The estimates presented here were recalculated to incorporate the new data, which are the origin of most of the changes in my series. It should be noted that, in the many series that are presented as indexes with 1972 equal to 100, a change in 1972 data changed the index values in all years.

The NIPA data used are from Bureau of Economic Analysis, *The National Income and Product Accounts of the United States, 1929–76 Statistical Tables* (1929–75 data) and *Survey of Current Business,* July 1982 (1976–78 data), July 1983 (1979–82 data), and March 1984 (1983 data), as corrected by errata (mainly in the July 1982 *Survey of Current Business,* pp. 130–33). Many table numbers in the NIPA have been changed since *Slower Growth* was published. The new numbers are used in the sources to my various tables.

National Income, by Sector, and Command

As in *Slower Growth,* national income in current and constant dollars is directly from the NIPA.

However, the NIPA series themselves have been changed by conceptual and procedural improvements introduced by the BEA, as well as by routine statistical revisions.

The most important conceptual change is the addition to national income of the amount by which the reinvested earnings of incorporated foreign affiliates of American direct investors exceed the reinvested earnings of incorporated American affiliates of foreign direct investors. Another change is the elimination of capital gains and losses from the net inflow of property income from abroad.[1] These improvements in the measurement of the net inflow of property income from abroad affect national income in both current and constant dollars. They bring national income into closer statistical conformity with its definition as the output attributable to the factors of production provided by U.S. residents (or the earnings accruing to resident suppliers of factors of production). Constant-dollar national income is also altered by a new method of deflating the net inflow of factor income from abroad: the use of the implicit deflator for the net national product as the deflator for this inflow.[2] Revisions in national income resulting from these changes are confined to the "international assets" sector (tables 2-5 and 2-6).

A procedural change that affects the constant-dollar values of total national income and its nonresidential business component concerns the statistical discrepancy between GNP measured as the sum of final products and GNP measured as the sum of gross product by industry. In the BEA series used in *Slower Growth* this discrepancy was included in constant-dollar national income; it is now excluded. The present procedure, which I had used in *Accounting for Growth* before the BEA introduced its series for real national income, is clearly superior. This change is mainly responsible for the irregular revisions, some of appreciable size, that appear in real national income before 1967.[3]

In the 1980 NIPA revision, correction of an error in the deflation procedure raised the BEA's series for housing national income in constant prices in the earlier years and lowered nonresidential business national income in constant prices by the same

---

1. The same changes were made in gross and net private saving and investment in table 4-3.
2. See Edward F. Denison, "International Transactions in Measures of the Nation's Production," *Survey of Current Business,* vol. 61 (May 1981), pp. 17–28, 34, for a fuller explanation of the changes described in this paragraph.
3. A complete description of the changes in BEA methodology is contained in Edward F. Denison and Robert P. Parker, "The National Income and Product Accounts of the United States: An Introduction to the Revised Estimates for 1929–80," *Survey of Current Business,* vol. 60 (December 1980), pp. 1–26.

amount; my series for these sectors are equally affected.

The value in 1972 prices of the nation's command over goods and services resulting from current production ("command" for short) had to be specially calculated for *Slower Growth*. The series is now published regularly by the BEA in the *Survey of Current Business* and is obtained from that source.[4]

Adjustment of Current Population Survey to 1980 Census of Population

This section describes a problem and decision that complicated the derivation of the labor input indexes but was of no importance to the analysis of growth.

Employment statistics are of two types: some are obtained mainly from establishment reports, others mainly from surveys of households. In 1982 the BLS raised its employment statistics of the second type—those based on data reported by households—in all years after 1969. The change resulted from a revision of the Census Bureau's series for total population, classified by demographic groups, to agree with the population count from the 1980 Decennial Census of Population, while also retaining agreement with the count from the 1970 census. The household-based employment estimates are, in effect, obtained by multiplying an estimated percentage of the population in each demographic group that is employed, obtained from the Current Population Survey (CPS) monthly sample of households, by the independently derived Census Bureau estimate of the total population in that demographic group. The 1981 household-based employment estimate was raised 2.1 percent by the revision of the population series. The BLS "wedged in" the difference between the two 1980 employment figures over the decade between the dates of the 1970 and 1980 censuses.

In preparing estimates for this book that make use of household survey data for employed persons and their characteristics, the unadjusted CPS series was used in preference to the revised series. (The revised series was used to extrapolate the unadjusted 1981 data to later dates.) This choice was made because (1) the consensus of expert opinion in and out of the Bureau of the Census is that more complete enumeration of the population in 1980 than in 1970 rather than an original understatement of the population

increase from 1970 to 1980 is probably the main reason that the 1980 census count exceeded the original estimate for 1980; and (2) my main concern is with consistency over time. However, use of the revised CPS series, instead, would scarcely alter the *movement* of my employment series because that movement rests almost entirely on establishment reports rather than on the CPS. CPS data are used only for unpaid family workers, for whom the employment revision is trivial.[5]

The *level* of my employment series (table 2-7) *is* affected by the decision concerning CPS data. The average level of the employment series is adjusted to that of the CPS series for the purpose of having it refer to the number of persons employed rather than the number of jobs. To make this conversion, the domestic civilian employment component of my employment series based mainly on establishment reports is multiplied by 0.96157, the average ratio of persons to jobs in 1947–75.[6] If the new CPS series and the revised establishment data were used, and the period of averaging extended to 1947–81, the ratio would become 0.9650 and would raise my domestic civilian employment by about 0.357 percent. Total employment in 1981 would then be 102,875,000 instead of 102,517,000. A third possibility, like the first requiring rejection of the new CPS series, is to assume (as I do) that the 1970–80 movement of the old Census Bureau population series was correct, but to base its level on the 1980 rather than the 1970 decennial census. Domestic civilian employment would be raised about 2 percent in all years, becoming about two million higher than I show in 1981.

CPS data are used in calculating all the indexes of labor input in table 3-1 except those for employment and average weekly hours and in calculating the average hours of the detailed employment groups shown in tables 3-7, 3-8, and 3-9; the latter enter into the indexes of gains from the reallocation of resources shown in table 5-1 as well as into the indexes

---

4. The series was introduced and fully described in Denison, "International Transactions in Measures of the Nation's Production."

5. CPS data also affect the movement of my employment series indirectly because the BEA uses CPS data to estimate the numbers of private household employees and active proprietors of unincorporated businesses, both of which are series that I use. However, the BEA estimates were last benchmarked before the CPS was revised and so are consistent with my treatment of the CPS revision.

6. This average is computed from data in *Slower Growth*, table B-1. The 1947–81 average based on table B-1 of the present book is slightly lower, 0.96059. Substitution of this ratio would lower domestic civilian employment by 0.10 percent in all years. Total employment in 1981 would be lowered from 102,646,000 to 102,542,000. To change the ratio every time another year passes or a revision occurs would require slight changes in my employment series all the way back to 1929, a process that is undesirable.

for offsets to changes in hours. In the calculations the unrevised CPS data were used through 1981, and the revised CPS data were used to extrapolate the 1981 data forward. Where absolute numbers are shown in tables, data are given on both bases for an overlap date, usually indicated by a footnote. The differences between indexes of age-sex composition on the old and new bases are slight, and for all other indexes the differences are trivial, so that a different procedure would scarcely change the results.

The statements about the handling of CPS revisions in deriving actual estimates of employment, labor input, and other series apply to the estimates on a potential basis as well as on an actual basis. Percentage differences between actual and potential values are not affected by my decisions concerning the CPS revision.

Total population is the sole exception to the preceding description of the handling of the 1980 census. The Census Bureau's official revised population series, which is benchmarked to both the 1970 and 1980 census counts, is used (tables 2-1 and 2-2). The 1970–80 increase in population is probably overstated, causing a probable understatement of the increase in national income per capita. There probably are no similar biases in the 1950–70 movements of these series because the decennial census enumerations are thought to be equally complete in 1950, 1960, and 1970.

Employment

There were no changes in the procedures used to obtain estimates of employment in the whole economy or by sector. The BEA provided full industrial detail for its estimates of full-time equivalent employment, and full-time and part-time employment, in nonprofit institutions. This addition permitted an improved table 6-2.

Total and Average Hours at Work

The same methods were used as in *Slower Growth*. The BEA provided statistics on hours worked in government after 1979 that are comparable to those for earlier years published in discontinued NIPA tables 6.12 and 6.13.

Ratios of hours at work to hours paid for are needed for employees in private nonagricultural establishments, separately for business and for nonprofit institutions. The ratios used in *Slower Growth*, which are unofficial BLS estimates, were retained through 1974. To obtain estimates representing the

average of 1976 and 1977, the 1974 ratios for all employees in private industries and in nonprofit institutions were extrapolated by "compensation" ratios for all private industries and for service industries, respectively. The compensation ratios are the ratio of "pay for working time" to the sum of such pay plus pay for vacations, holidays, civic and personal leave, and sick leave. Data are from the 1974, 1976, and 1977 surveys of expenditures for employee compensation from BLS, *Handbook of Labor Statistics 1980*, Bulletin 2070, table 132. (Survey data were not used to establish the change from 1976 to 1977 because the movement they showed appeared dubious and because the 1976 survey omitted small employers.) The average annual changes from 1974 to 1976–77 were used to estimate the annual figures for each year after 1974. Ratios for business were derived by subtracting total hours at work and total hours paid for in nonprofit institutions from similar data for all private nonagricultural establishments.

A new BLS survey provides information on hours at work and should provide a better basis for the at-work estimates when a series from it is available for a few years.

Age-Sex Composition

Only the weights used to combine total hours worked in nonresidential business by the ten age-sex groups shown in table 3-5 require comment. The weights used in *Slower Growth* for 1929–70 continue to be used for those years, while those formerly used for 1970–76 were used for 1970–75. New weights were used for 1975–82. The weights for the three periods are not very different. In fact, the weights for females 25–34 and 35–64 are the same (both 54) relative to males 35–64 (100) in all periods.

To arrive at the new weights, the annual estimates described in *Slower Growth*, pp. 157–58, were extended to 1979. The weights used for 1975–82 are based on 1975–79 averages.

Employment and Hours in Nonresidential Business by Sex and Work Status; Indexes of Efficiency as Affected by Changes in Hours

The detailed employment and hours data shown in tables 3-7, 3-8, and 3-9 were obtained, as in *Slower Growth*, by adjusting data derived from the CPS to conform to control totals based on establishment data. Revisions in 1966–76 stem from revisions in the control totals for employment and hours, which appear in tables 2-7 and C-1.

In *Slower Growth* one set of series was shown for 1929–66 and another for 1966–76, because definitions in the CPS were changed as of 1966. Only 1966–82 data are shown here. The former 1929–66 estimates may continue to be used, with the 1966 overlap, with the new 1966–82 data. (However, 1929–66 employment and hours totals derived from the tables in *Slower Growth* differ very slightly from the revised control totals shown in tables 2-7 and C-1 of the present book.)[7]

The indexes for the efficiency of an hour's work in table 3-1, columns 5 and 6, were calculated in the same way as in *Slower Growth*; the new data in the national income tables and tables 3-7, 3-8, and 3-9 were incorporated. Table E-1 was extended to cover the shortened hours prevailing in recent years.

Labor Input Index for Education

The education index from 1929 to 1972 is unchanged from *Slower Growth*. The procedures for 1973–82 were similar to those used for 1973–75 in *Slower Growth*. Slight changes in the 1973–75 indexes stem from recalculation of the lines of regression between the indexes for civilian employment and for the civilian labor force (table F-4). The previous regressions were based on data for March of the years 1972–76, the new regressions on data for March of 1972–82. The 1976 annual index was revised downward as a result of the incorporation of March 1977 data. Indexes based on the original and revised CPS series were linked at March 1980 by use of data provided by the BLS. Incomparability of the occupational classification used in March 1983 with that used in March 1982 (and earlier) necessitated use of a less detailed procedure to obtain the index for full-time equivalent business employment in 1983. The weights for education groups based on 1969 data were used through 1983. Data from the CPS for the years through 1979 (similar to those for earlier years discussed on pages 164–66 of *Slower Growth*) indicated no need for a change in weights. The pertinent earnings data for 1979 from the 1980 Census of Population were not available in time to use. They appear to indicate a moderate widening of earnings differentials up to the high school graduate level and a narrowing, by perhaps one-eighth, of the percentage differential between earnings of men completing

four years of high school and those completing four years of college.

Nonresidential Structures and Equipment and Inventories

The data for capital input in nonresidential business were derived from BEA data in the same way as in *Slower Growth*. A few words are required about prewar inventories. The value in 1972 prices of seasonally adjusted year-end inventories was reduced from $118.6 billion to $116.1 billion at the end of 1947, the earliest date shown in the NIPA, table 5.11. The dollar change in business inventories valued in 1972 prices in earlier years was not revised (NIPA, table 1.2). Because of the change in level, use of the dollar change to compute the level of the stock at earlier dates would have yielded slightly different and probably worse percentage changes and indexes than did the same procedure with the previous NIPA. I therefore retained the percentage changes from *Slower Growth* in the 1929 to 1947 period.

Weights to Combine Inputs in Nonresidential Business and Calculation of Total Input

The methodology employed to obtain the weights used to combine inputs (table G-2) and the procedures used to calculate total capital input and total factor input (table 4-6) were unchanged. Asset values in 1981 were used to allocate the nonlabor share among components in 1982.

The estimates for 1967 and later years were completely recalculated. (No new benchmark for the value of nonfarm land was available.) A shortcut was taken in revising the earlier years. Of the four types of income shown in table G-3, compensation of employees was kept the same as in *Slower Growth* in 1967 and before, other income originating in nonfarm corporations was raised beginning in 1948, and the noncorporate farm and nonfarm shares of income other than employee compensation were changed slightly. Comparison of the old and new dollar estimates that underlie table G-1 showed that of the total addition to the sector's national income in 1967, 5.3 percent was allocated to the labor share and 94.7 percent to the nonlabor share. The amounts added to sector national income in earlier years were allocated in the same proportions.

The period averages shown in table G-2 were calculated from annual labor shares that were ad-

---

7. Similar comments apply to the data on a potential basis, which are consistent with those on an actual basis.

justed to smooth out the effects of the business cycle. To derive them, the actual labor shares in 1930–47 and in the recession years 1949, 1954, 1958, 1961, 1970–71, and 1974–75 were first replaced by interpolated values. The 1979 share was used for subsequent years. Then a five-year moving average of the shares thus recalculated was substituted for the annual data, a small adjustment was made for Alaska and Hawaii (see *Accounting for Growth*, pages 260–61), and a uniform adjustment was introduced in all years to restore the average 1948–79 level of the series to that of the original unadjusted percentages. The new nonlabor weight in 1929–67 was initially distributed among its three component shares in proportion to the shares used in *Slower Growth*. The difference between the percentage thus computed for each share in 1967 and the corresponding new 1967 percentage was then added or subtracted to the initial percentage in earlier years.

The figures in table G-2 are averages of the adjusted percentages for the year shown and the preceding year.

Gains from Reallocation of Resources

Calculation of the indexes of gains from the reallocation of labor out of farming and out of nonfarm self-employment involved no changes in procedures.

Diversion of Resources to Pollution Abatement

These estimates, which I originally published in articles appearing in the *Survey of Current Business* for January 1978 and August 1979, were updated through 1981 by Frederick J. Dreiling, economist with the Environmental and Nonmarket Economics Division of the BEA, the main source of the underlying data. Dreiling also introduced improved series for pollution abatement capital (used in obtaining depreciation and net opportunity cost of invested capital) and a number of refinements in estimating procedures, and added R&D expenses to the pollution abatement costs. These changes affect all years. The new series (table 5-1, column 4) shows pollution abatement costs impairing productivity growth more from 1969 to 1972 and less from 1972 to 1975 than did the original series. The estimates, detailed in table 5-4, are closely related statistically to data appearing in tables 9 and 10 of Kit D. Farber, Frederick J. Dreiling, and Gary L. Rutledge, "Pollution Abatement and Control Expenditures, 1972–82," *Survey of Current Business*, February 1984, pp. 22–30.

Employee Safety and Health

Incremental costs for protection of employee safety and health of types that reduce national income per unit of input in nonresidential business are, as before, the sum of three components: safety equipment on motor vehicles, mining (except oil and gas), and other industries (table 5-5). Developments after 1975 and new evidence concerning regulatory costs necessitated some changes from the methods used to obtain my original results, which were published in the January 1978 *Survey of Current Business* and incorporated in *Slower Growth*.

Safety Equipment on Motor Vehicles

The method of estimating incremental costs incurred by business for required safety equipment on business motor vehicles (consisting of depreciation on, and cost of, invested capital) was similar to that followed previously, but revisions in the underlying series were incorporated. Refinements introduced by Dreiling in obtaining the corresponding components of pollution abatement costs (table 5-4, lines 6 and 9) were introduced here. In estimating the stock of safety equipment, no charge was made for air brakes on heavy trucks acquired after October 1978, when the air brake regulation was largely invalidated by the Supreme Court. The 1969–75 estimates are barely different from those in *Slower Growth*.

Mining (Except Oil and Gas)

As before, the percentage by which strengthening of safety and health controls in mining reduced output per unit of labor input each year was estimated, and the percentage reduction in output per unit of factor input was assumed to be the same.

Estimates of the additional employment that safety and health legislation made necessary in mining to produce the industry's actual output are shown in the informal table on the following page. The procedures were similar to those used before, but some changes, described below, were introduced, and revisions in both the NIPA and the BLS productivity series for mining were incorporated. The additional employment required in 1975 is now put at 0.17 percent of nonresidential business employment as against 0.24 percent in the original estimates. The percentage rises only a little after 1975.

COAL MINING. A number of studies of productivity in coal mining have been conducted since my original estimates for 1968–75 were prepared. My original estimates assumed that in the absence of the 1969 Coal Mine Health and Safety Act (CMHSA) and

	Employment required by strengthened controls (thousands)				Nonresidential business employment (thousands)	Col. 4 as percentage of col. 5
	Coal (1)	Nonmetal (2)	Metal (3)	Total mining (4)	(5)	(6)
1968	...	...	...	...	60,916	...
1969	4	...	...	4	62,809	0.01
1970	9	...	...	9	62,501	0.01
1971	18	...	...	18	62,278	0.03
1972	35	...	...	35	64,073	0.05
1973	41	...	4	45	67,077	0.07
1974	57	9	15	81	68,168	0.12
1975	82	15	17	114	66,077	0.17
1976	102	15	8	125	68,024	0.18
1977	108	13	13	134	70,815	0.19
1978	106	11	5	122	74,590	0.16
1979	118	17	7	142	77,424	0.18
1980	116	30	18	164	77,459	0.21
1981	109	32	13	154	78,218	0.20
1982	111	38	6	155	76,843	0.20

other safety and health restrictions, output per person employed would have increased 6.5 percent a year (the 1957–68 rate) from 1968 to 1975, instead of falling, and that the shortfall from that rate was due to safety and health restrictions. The consensus, if one can be said to exist, is that safety and health restrictions were indeed the main cause of poor productivity performance but that I overestimated their impact.

A survey of coal operators by John W. Stratton, for example, showed that they believed the CMHSA to be the major reason for productivity decline.[8] The general feeling at a 1978 conference of researchers from trade organizations, unions, government, the academic sector, coal companies, and research institutions called by the President's Commission on Coal was that the major causes of productivity decline had been the CMHSA (in deep mines) and reclamation laws (in surface mines).[9] Richard L. Gordon, citing work under his direction at Pennsylvania State University, expressed agreement with me that the CMHSA was the largest source of productivity decline but thought that my estimate of its impact appeared too large; observers consulted by Gordon believe my assumption as to the increase

in output per day that would have prevailed without the act is too high.[10] Joe G. Baker believes that in the period before the 1969 act the rate of productivity advance was exceptionally high (and therefore unsustainable) because depressed coal prices and markets were driving the industry toward a position of extreme efficiency, which was essential if the industry was to survive at all; labor peace and union-management cooperation prevailed, only the most efficient mines remained in operation, and safety and health considerations received short shrift.[11] Richard Gordon and associates estimated that the act increased section crews from twenty workers to thirty and reduced output per person by 12–23 percent, depending upon mining conditions.[12] Charles Fettig, like Gordon at Pennsylvania State University, concluded from such evidence that productivity was 45 percent lower than it would have been in the absence of the act, apparently referring to 1977.[13] Baker, whose analysis of coal mining productivity is espe-

8. Articles in *Mining Congress Journal*, vols. 58 (7), 61 (10), and 63 (7), summarized in a literature review in Joe G. Baker and Wayne L. Stevenson, "Determinants of Coal Mine Labor Productivity Change," prepared by Oak Ridge Associated Universities for U.S. Department of Energy and U.S. Department of Labor, November 1979.

9. This summary of the conference, which I attended, is paraphrased from Baker and Stevenson, "Coal Mine Labor Productivity Change," p. 12.

10. Richard L. Gordon, "Hobbling Coal—or How to Serve Two Masters Poorly," *Regulation* (July–August 1978), pp. 36–45.

11. Baker and Stevenson, "Coal Mine Labor Productivity Change." Also summarized in Joe G. Baker, "Sources of Deep Coal Mine Productivity Change, 1962–75," *Energy Journal*, vol. 2 (April 1981), pp. 95–106.

12. Gordon and others, "Simulating the Effects of the Coal Mine Health Safety Act" (Pennsylvania State University, n.d), cited by Baker and Stevenson in "Coal Mine Labor Productivity Change."

13. Charles Fettig, "Impacts on Output per Man-Day, Costs, and Price of the Coal Mine Health and Safety Act of 1969" (Pennsylvania State University, 1978), quoted by Baker and Stevenson, "Coal Mine Labor Productivity Change."

cially comprehensive, reported that strikes temporarily reduced productivity in 1971, 1974, and 1975.[14]

Against this background I have used the procedure detailed in the following informal table. Column 1 shows the BLS index of output per employee in coal mining. Column 2 shows that the costs imposed

	Output per employee, actual, BLS, 1977 = 100 (1)	Without CMSHA		Ratio of col. 1 to col. 3 (4)	Col. 4 adjusted (5)	Employment in coal mining		
		If it lowered 1977 productivity by 45 percent (2)	At 3.14 growth rate (3)			BEA (thousands) (6)	Without strengthened controls (col. 5 × col. 6) (7)	Required by strengthened controls (col. 6 − col. 7) (8)
1968	137.6	137.6	137.6	1.000	1.000	133	133	0
1969	137.4	. . .	141.9	0.968	0.968	136	132	4
1970	137.1	. . .	146.4	0.936	0.936	146	137	9
1971	125.1	. . .	151.0	0.828	0.858	148	130	18
1972	121.4	. . .	155.7	0.780	0.780	161	126	35
1973	119.8	. . .	160.6	0.746	0.746	161	120	41
1974	109.9	. . .	165.6	0.664	0.683	180	123	57
1975	99.6	. . .	170.8	0.583	0.619	214	132	82
1976	98.4	. . .	176.2	0.556	0.556	229	127	102
1977	100.0	181.8	181.8	0.550	0.550	240	132	108
1978	103.3	. . .	187.5	0.551	0.551	235	129	106
1979	97.5	. . .	193.3	0.504	0.539	255	137	118
1980	108.9	. . .	199.4	0.546	0.539	251	135	116
1981	118.9	. . .	205.7	0.578	0.539	237	128	109
1982	112.1	. . .	212.1	0.529	0.539	241	130	111

by regulation after 1968 had no effect on productivity in 1968, by definition, while in 1977, based on the Gordon-Fettig estimates, actual productivity was 55 percent of what it would have been in the absence of additional regulation. This conclusion implies that from 1968 to 1977 output per man would have risen an average of 3.14 percent a year without additional regulation. Column 3 shows what the index would have been if it had grown 3.14 percent a year until 1982, while column 4 shows the ratio of actual productivity to this hypothetical productivity. In column 5 the ratios are adjusted to provide a better measure of regulatory effects by replacing ratios for the strike years 1971, 1974, and 1975 with interpolated values, and replacing the 1979–82 ratios, which move irregularly, with the average value for those years. The impact of regulation on productivity *growth* was almost over by 1976, according to this result, implying that the 1977 Mine Safety and Health Act, dealing with training and certification, had only a small effect on productivity.

Column 6 shows actual employment, column 7 employment that would have been required to obtain the same output in the absence of safety and health

14. Ibid.

controls, and column 8 the additional employment that controls necessitated.

METAL AND NONMETAL MINING. The procedures to estimate the effects of the Metal Nonmetal Act paralleled those followed for the metal and nonmetal mining industries in the January 1978 *Survey of Current Business* article, with the following minor changes. For nonmetallic minerals and fuels it was assumed that output per employee in the absence of safety and health legislation would have been the same as actual output per employee in 1973 and would have grown thereafter at the same rate that the index had actually grown from 1955 to 1973. For copper and iron mining it was assumed that in the absence of safety and health legislation, output per employee on January 1, 1972, would have been the same as the 1970–73 average for actual output per employee and that it would have grown thereafter at the same rate that the actual index grew from its 1954–57 average to its 1970–73 average.

Other Industries

Incremental capital and labor costs were estimated by the same approach as before, but the McGraw-Hill Publications Co. has revised upward the level of its series for plant and equipment investment for employee safety and health (excluding mining), which series is the main input into my estimates. The McGraw-Hill investment series starts with 1972. As before, it was assumed that the ratio of such investment to nonfarm nonresidential business net national product was three-fourths as large in 1970 as in 1972 and that the 1970 ratio would not have changed in the absence of the Occupational Safety and Health Act (OSHA) effective April 28, 1971. The latter assumption was modified in 1976 and 1979–82, when the actual ratio fell below the assumed 1970 ratio; it was assumed that outlays in the absence of OSHA would have been the same as actual outlays in those years, so that the incremental outlays due to regulation were zero, not negative. The gross stock and net stock of safety and health capital resulting from regulation, from which were computed the annual depreciation on, and net opportunity cost of, invested capital, respectively, were derived from annual incremental investment by the perpetual inventory method. The annualized capital costs peaked as a percentage of nonresidential business net national product in 1979.

Until 1979 current costs were estimated (as before) by applying to annualized capital costs the ratio of current costs to capital costs obtained for air and water pollution abatement. However, the average pollution abatement percentage—75 percent of annualized capital costs—was now used to estimate current costs every year; previously the actual ratio for each year was used. For 1980–82 the procedure was changed because it seemed unlikely that current costs dropped after 1979 as capital costs did. Instead, nonfarm nonresidential business net national product was multipled by the 1979 ratio of current costs to nonfarm nonresidential business net national product.

The main implication of the estimates, as of the earlier ones, is that the costs imposed by OSHA are not large. This conclusion is supported by other evaluations. My earlier article noted that through 1975 OSHA regulations were in the field of safety and consisted mainly of the codification of standards previously adopted by trade and professional associations, and that health regulations were likely to be more costly because they would require greater changes in existing practices. However, few health regulations have as yet been implemented. John F. Morall III put the annual cost of the twelve health regulations issued through 1981 at only $1,384 million.[15] Morall deduces from the well-known Arthur Anderson study of regulatory costs that 62 percent of the OSHA-imposed costs were for occupational health regulations in 1977 and that, since there were only four health regulations in 1977, the percentage in later years was higher. If it was 75 percent in 1981, the total cost in 1981 was only $1,845 million.[16] The difference from my figure of $2,726 million is too small to have any noticeable effect on the estimated contribution to the post-1973 growth rate. W. Kip Viscusi found earlier that "the weak financial incentives associated with the present enforcement effort combines with the ill-conceived nature of the enforcement strategy to provide at best only very weak incentives for enterprises to alter their actions. No significant effect of OSHA was found in an examination of pooled time series and cross section data pertaining to health and safety investment, planned health and safety investments, and worker injuries from 1972 to 1975."[17]

Two investigations supported by the Department of Labor confirm that the costs are small. A thorough study of the asbestos regulation, the first of the health regulations and usually considered one of the more costly, was made by W. Curtis Priest and Sohail Bengali.[18] They put the annual cost to the asbestos industry at $22 million as of 1980, even less than the $75 million that Morall used for this regulation. Sixty-nine regulations with this average impact would have been required to reduce the 1971–80 growth rate of national income per unit of input in nonresidential business by 0.01 percentage point. A study by Joseph R. Morris of five establishments in the foundry industry, also thought to be among the industries most affected by OSHA regulations, found that such regulations had depressed the average growth rate of output per unit of input in these establishments by 0.15 percentage points.[19] The foundry industry is small, with negligible weight in nonresidential business as a whole, so this retardation had no effect on nonresidential business as a whole.

15. John F. Morall III, "OSHA after Ten Years," American Enterprise Institute Working Paper in Government Regulation, November 18, 1981. The figure cited omits the cost of the January 29, 1974, regulation concerning fourteen carcinogens, which Morall describes as "minimal," and of the "cancer policy regulation of January 22, 1981," for which he had no reliable estimate.

16. However, it is not clear that this amount is all valued in 1981 prices; part may be valued in earlier lower prices.
17. W. Kip Viscusi, "The Impact of Occupational Safety and Health Regulation," *Bell Journal of Economics,* vol. 10 (Spring 1979), pp. 117–40. The quotation is found at p. 136. Viscusi repeats the judgment that actual OSHA costs have been limited because enforcement is so weak that regulations have had little effect. See W. Kip Viscusi, *Risk by Choice: Regulating Health and Safety in the Workplace* (Harvard University Press, 1983), chap. 2.
18. W. Curtis Priest and Sohail Bengali, *A Microeconomic Study of Productivity: Impact of OSHA Regulation on the Asbestos Industry* (Massachusetts Institute of Technology, Center for Policy Alternatives, November 1981).
19. This figure is the average for the five foundries weighted by employment of production workers. Joseph R. Morris, "Productivity and OSHA Compliance: Case Studies in the Foundry Industry" (Washington, D.C.: Jack Faucett Associates, October 1981).

Dishonesty and Crime

As before, this series was constructed in two parts, covering the business costs of protection against crime and costs of losses, respectively. Table 5-6 shows the separate series, which are slightly revised for 1973–75. The procedures were similar to those originally described in my article in the January 1978 *Survey of Current Business* and used in *Slower Growth*.

1. *Costs of protection.* Receipts of detective agencies and protective services, armored car services, and burglar and fire alarm systems from the 1977 *Census of Business* were incorporated into the estimates, as were annual data through 1980 for payrolls of detective and protective services, all from *County Business Patterns*.

2. *Thefts of merchandise and damage to property.* Bureau of Domestic Commerce estimates of the cost of crime against business in 1971, 1973, 1974, and 1975, reduced to eliminate the estimated value of losses of cash and financial assets, are the benchmarks for both the previous and present estimates. Before the bureau (which was renamed the Industry and Trade Administration and later abolished) ended its program of research on business crime, it apparently prepared comparable estimates for 1976, which were published by Carl P. Simon and Ann D. Witte.[20] The total for thefts they show, $25.0 billion, becomes $25.4 billion if the Bureau of Domestic Commerce 1975 estimate of $0.4 billion for arson is added. This level is not inconsistent with the statement in a May 11, 1978, press release (ITA 78–85) of the Industry and Trade Administration that the total cost of crimes against business exceeded $30 billion in 1976, of which $5.8 billion was the cost of private security services. Use of the $25.4 billion figure for 1976 in my estimates is important because the increase from $19.1 billion in 1975 is unusually large. Estimates for the years from 1977 through 1981, for which no data from the Industry and Trade Administration were available, were based, as were the pre-1971 estimates, on the number of property crimes in the Federal Bureau of Investigation index.

Effect of Weather and Work Stoppages on Output per Unit of Input

The method of deriving fluctuations in output per unit of input stemming from the effects of weather on farm output and of work stoppages was unchanged from *Slower Growth*.

20. Carl P. Simon and Ann D. Witte, *Beating the System: The Underground Economy* (Boston, Mass.: Auburn House, 1982), p. 100.

Effect of Varying Intensity of Demand on Output per Unit of Input

The reasons that the intensity of use of resources employed in nonresidential business fluctuates with the intensity of demand pressures, the time pattern that these fluctuations impose upon output per unit of input, the method I devised to measure their effect, and the logic of this method were all described in *Accounting for Growth* and *Slower Growth*. Here I merely describe the mechanics of the method as it was adjusted to incorporate the revised and extended data used in the present study. As in *Slower Growth*, the estimates are described separately for three time periods. The index for the full 1929–82 period is shown in table 5-1, column 9.

The 1948–73 Period

Although the method for 1948–73 is the same as that used in *Slower Growth*, I repeat much of the description in light of revisions in the underlying series used, which are shown in table I-1. (The table shows data for years outside the 1948–73 period even though many of them were not used.) The first four columns all refer to nonfinancial corporations. Column 1 shows the nonlabor share of national income, column 2 the implicit deflator for national income, column 3 the index of compensation of employees per hour worked, and column 4 the ratio of column 3 to column 2. The last two columns refer to all nonresidential business. Column 6 shows the refined index of productivity that was obtained when the influence on output of all inputs and of all the determinants of output per unit of input previously considered was eliminated. Column 5 is the same except that the influence of labor disputes—which affect the intensity of utilization of employed resources and income shares in the same way as intensity of demand—was not eliminated.

The 1948–73 period appears to be homogeneous in the sense that there was no ascertainable change in the underlying trends of the three variables that are used—the nonlabor share, the ratio of hourly compensation to price, and adjusted output per unit of input—or in the relationships among deviations of the three variables from their trends.

TREND LINES. The first step in the estimation process was to compute least squares trend lines for columns 1, 4, and 5 of table I-1. As in *Slower Growth*, the trends were based on the 1947–69 period even though they were to be used for 1947–73, because the end of the latter period was dominated by years of weak demand whose inclusion would have erroneously tilted the trend lines downward over time. However, as in *Slower Growth,* I show below how the trends, and in tables I-2 and I-3 how the results for each year, would have changed if the entire 1947–73 period were included in the calculation of trends. (The years after 1973 clearly must be excluded because the period was one of very low utilization, whose inclusion would have distorted the trend lines even more strongly than 1970–73, and because the trends of two of the three series changed sharply after 1973.)

The trends for the nonlabor share are arithmetic so that the trend value changes (falls) by the same absolute amount each year, while the trends for the ratio of employee compensation to price and for adjusted productivity are logarithmic, so that the trend value changes (rises) by the same percentage each year. Use of logarithmic trends for the last two variables is indicated both on a priori grounds and by the data. Use of an arithmetic trend seemed preferable for the nonlabor share, but the choice was neither clear nor important to the result.

I now designate the deviation of the nonlabor share (measured in percentage points) from its trend by N, the deviation of the ratio of compensation per hour worked to prices (measured in percent) from its trend by W, and the deviation of adjusted output per unit of input (measured in percent) from its trend by P. I use the subscript 1 when the trends are based on 1947–69 or 1948–69 (used for the wage-price ratio because 1947 is not available) and 2 when they are based on 1947–73 or 1948–73. The formulas for the trend values that were used in computing N, W, and P are as follows, where log refers to natural logarithms and t to time (in years):

for N_1 the trend value is
$$21.67648 - 0.07616t \qquad t_1 = 1947;$$
for N_2 the trend value is
$$22.45436 - 0.16618t \qquad t_1 = 1947;$$
for W_1 the log of the trend value is
$$-0.75226 + 0.02987t \qquad t_1 = 1948;$$
for W_2 the log of the trend value is
$$-0.75420 + 0.03091t \qquad t_1 = 1948;$$
for P_1 the log of the trend value is
$$4.17345 + 0.01702t \qquad t_1 = 1947;$$
for P_2 the log of the trend value is
$$4.17806 + 0.01647t \qquad t_1 = 1947.$$

The differences from the formulas in *Slower Growth,* which stem from revisions in the underlying data, are slight. The 1947–69 trend value for the nonlabor share declines 0.02 percentage points a year less than it did before these revisions.

THE EFFECT OF FLUCTUATIONS IN UTILIZATION ON OUTPUT PER UNIT OF INPUT. On the basis of these data I next estimate the ratio of actual adjusted productivity each year to what adjusted productivity would have been if the intensity of utilization had been at its average level during the period on which the estimate is based. I designate this ratio U.

The simplest procedure, and one that is rather satisfactory when judged against the difficulty of the problem, is to correlate P, the deviation of adjusted output per unit of input from its trend, with N, the deviation of the nonlabor share from its trend. The justification, in a phrase, is that the fluctuation in intensity of utilization is the main reason that both series diverge from their trends. The regressions are based on the same time spans as those from which the trends were computed, except that 1947 was omitted because 1947 wage-price data are not available for subsequent steps.

If the correlation is based on 1948–69 data (and 1947–69 trends), the following relationship and value for $\bar{r}^2$ (r^2 corrected for degrees of freedom) are obtained:

(1) $$\log U = -0.00016 + 0.00950N_1$$
$$\bar{r}^2 = 0.867.$$

(The values of U obtained from this and the three following formulas are shown in table I-2, columns 7–10.)[21]

If, instead, the correlation is based on 1948–73 data (and 1947–73 trends), the following relationship is obtained:

(2) $$\log U = -0.00020 + 0.00905N_2$$
$$\bar{r}^2 = 0.828.$$

The estimates can be improved, on average, by introducing the wage-price ratio as a second independent variable in the equations. The rationale follows.

It is first necessary to stress that, as I showed in *Accounting for Growth* and *Slower Growth,* none of the correlation between the nonlabor share and adjusted productivity, which I ascribe to the influence of the intensity of utilization on both, is due to short-term wage-price movements being related to both. Annual changes in adjusted output per unit of input were highly correlated with annual changes in the nonlabor share but not correlated at all with annual changes in the wage-price ratio. Neither was the deviation of the wage-price ratio from its trend correlated with the deviation of the nonlabor share from its trend.

21. Table I-2 and I-3 are explained in *Slower Growth,* pp. 178–83.

The reason for devoting attention to the wage-price ratio is the possibility that erratic fluctuations in it, including any due to wage and price controls, might introduce random fluctuations in the nonlabor share that do not result from changes in the intensity of utilization. Such random fluctuations would introduce an error in the estimated value of U, which measures the effect of the intensity of utilization on productivity, if it is estimated from the nonlabor share alone.

One can reduce any such error by introducing as a second independent variable W, the deviation from its trend of the ratio of compensation per hour worked to price. Based on 1948–69 data the relationship is

$$\text{(3)} \quad \log U = -0.00019 + \\ 0.00976N_1 + 0.0031354W_1 \\ \bar{r}^2 = 0.898.$$

Evidently the suspected tendency is present because introduction of the wage-price ratio raises $\bar{r}^2$ from 0.867 to 0.898. The unexplained percentage of the deviations of adjusted productivity from its trend is thus reduced by nearly one-fourth, from 13.3 percent to 10.2 percent. The positive sign for the wage-price ratio, W_1, in the equation is expected. When W_1 is erratically high, the nonlabor share, N_1, will be erratically low. Intensity of utilization, U, will then be underestimated if it is calculated from the nonlabor share alone. This formula is the one I actually use.

A similar equation was computed from the 1948–73 data:

$$\text{(4)} \quad \log U = -0.00024 + \\ 0.00944N_2 + 0.0037231W_2 \\ \bar{r}^2 = 0.864.$$

Another possibility would be to use deviations from the 1947–69 trends, as I have done, but to base the regression line on 1948–73 instead of 1948–69. When both N and W are used, this regression line is:

$$\text{(5)} \quad \log U = 0.00074 + \\ 0.00909N_1 + 0.0038668W_1 \\ \bar{r}^2 = 0.863.$$

The ratio to the average for the 1948–73 period would not change by more than one-fourth of 1 percentage point in any year if this formula were used instead of formula 3.

The inclusion of W as an additional variable raises the values of $\bar{r}^2$ less now than was the case with the data used in *Slower Growth*. The reason is that adjusted productivity deviates less from its trend

value than it did before, apparently the result of the change in the BEA's treatment of the discrepancy between real national income derived from the income side of the accounts and real national income derived as the sum of industry estimates. The previous procedure introduced an inconsistency between input and output estimates that carried over to the adjusted productivity series and also introduced a corresponding error in the implicit deflator and hence the wage-price ratio. Use of the wage-price ratio in the utilization adjustment tended then to absorb the statistical error in adjusted productivity into the utilization adjustment.

Years before 1948

The estimates for 1929–47 were calculated in the same way as in *Slower Growth:* an intensity of utilization series calculated from formula 1, which uses only the nonlabor share, was used to extrapolate the 1948 index backward. The 1947 trend value of the nonlabor share was used in earlier years in implementing the formula. As before, the 1929 index was based on the difference from 1940 in the nonlabor share of all corporations rather than of nonfinancial corporations, the series shown in table I-1. Revisions in the movement of the index from 1929 to 1948 are trivial and stem from revisions in the data.

Years after 1973

It is obvious that the annual increases in the trend values of adjusted productivity and the ratio of employee compensation to prices were much smaller after 1973 than before, so their previous trends cannot be extended beyond 1973. However, the large and frequent fluctuations in the economy after 1973 prevent calculation by the least squares method of new trends that are at all satisfactory.

The first formula for estimating the effect of fluctuations in the intensity of utilization upon adjusted output per unit of input can still be applied after 1973 if two conditions, considered in the next paragraph, are met: first, that the 1948–69 trend of the nonlabor share can validly be extended to this period; and, second, that there is no change in the relationship between the effects of fluctuations in the intensity of utilization upon the nonlabor share and upon output per unit of input. Before the nonlabor share can be used in the formula, however, it must be adjusted to eliminate the special effect upon it of the sharp rise in petroleum prices, which elevated the nonlabor share in nonresidential business as a whole both by raising the nonlabor share in the oil and gas industries and by increasing the importance in current-dollar national income of those industries, in which the nonlabor share was already above average. The 1973 figure inclusive of oil and gas (16.73 percent) was simply moved to later years by the absolute change in the nonlabor share excluding oil and gas (which was 16.17 percent in 1973). Column 1 of table I-1 provides the data so adjusted; a footnote gives the unadjusted data. If this adjustment had not been made, the index of intensity of utilization that is obtained after 1973 would have been higher than I estimate, and the decline in the growth rate of the semiresidual would have been even greater than I estimate.

Extension to 1982 of the 1948–69 trend in the nonlabor share, which drops the estimated value of the share under conditions of constant intensity of utilization by 0.08 percentage points a year, is, of course, open to question. If, as is possible, the annual decline in the trend value had become larger, then the intensity of utilization in recent years would have been higher and the decline in the growth rate of the semiresidual even greater than I show.

I had no reason to believe that there was a change in the relationship between the effects of changes in intensity of utilization upon the nonlabor share and upon output per unit of input.

The possibility that irregular changes in the ratio of wages to prices might introduce errors in an estimate of intensity of utilization that was based only on the nonlabor share, a possibility that was minimized in 1948–73 by introduction of the wage-price ratio in the third formula, was also present thereafter. Hence, the first equation alone might not have produced a fully satisfactory annual series. But use of the third equation required estimates of the trend values of the wage-price ratio.

To deal with this dilemma, I adopted an expedient for 1973–82 that is rather similar to the one I adopted for 1973–76 in *Slower Growth*. I calculated the index of intensity of utilization in 1981, almost the end of the period, by use of the first formula, which requires only the nonlabor share; this estimate is my final one for 1981. I next derived the 1981 trend value of the wage-price ratio that would produce the same 1981 index of intensity of utilization if the third formula were used. I then computed the 1973–81 growth rate for the trend value of the wage-price ratio and applied this growth rate to the 1973 trend value to obtain the trend values for 1974–80 and 1982. The annual increase in the trend value of the wage-price ratio obtained in this way is 0.82 percent, as compared with a 3.03 percent annual increase in 1948–73. With trend values thus established, the intensity of utili-

zation index for each year was then derived by formula 3; this procedure provided my final series. The series was benchmarked on the formula 1 estimate for 1981, rather than for the end year of the series, 1982, because 1982 was a severe recession year; using it would have made a comparison with 1973 subject to greater uncertainty. However, in fact, use of 1982 would have changed the estimates very little.

Table I-8 compares the indexes of the effect of changes in intensity of utilization of employed resources resulting from fluctuations in the intensity of demand, that are obtained by formula 3 as adapted, and the series for the semiresiduals that are obtained when they are used, with the indexes that would be obtained if formula 1 were used. (The values for 1972 and 1981 are necessarily the same under both procedures.) The estimates differ as much as 1 percent only in 1975, and in most years are quite similar.

An inconsistency between the series for the nonlabor share and the wage-price ratio is present as a result of the failure, for lack of suitable data, to eliminate the oil and gas industries when the wage-price ratio was computed. This inconsistency does not affect the 1973–81 movement of the index for intensity of utilization but may impair its year-to-year movement and could help to explain why the index for intensity of demand based only on the nonlabor share, which is not subject to this particular defect, falls less from 1973 to 1975 than does the series adopted (see table I-8).

To change the 1973–81 growth rates of the indexes of the effect of demand intensity and of the residual by as much as 0.25 percentage points would require an error in the 1981 indexes, relative to 1973, of 2 percent. Even an error in either direction of this improbably large size would not greatly alter the picture presented by the semiresidual; its growth rate fell from 1.80 percent in 1948–73 to 0.37 percent in 1973–81 and 0.20 percent in 1973–82.

Revisions in the Index

Revisions in the underlying data are responsible for revisions in the demand intensity index since the preparation of *Slower Growth*. Revisions in 1972 data, it will be noted, affected the index in all other years.

Table I-5 shows the indexes for the effect of intensity of demand upon output per unit of input, with the years arranged from highest to lowest. It also shows the numerical rank of each year among years also covered in *Slower Growth* according to the new and former estimates. Only one year, 1969, shifts position by as much as three places. In *Slower Growth* the ranking of all the years up to 1976 was carefully examined for reasonableness. Since the ranking is scarcely changed, the exercise need not be repeated. The behavior of the index after 1976 seems to me sensible enough, given everything known about the period, but since no other series succeeds nearly as well as the nonlabor share in tracking the movements of adjusted productivity before 1973, there is no equally or more reliable way to derive a series with which mine can be compared in the recent troubled years.

Economies of Scale

The index of gains from economies of scale (table 5-1, column 11) was derived in the same way as in *Slower Growth*. Table J-1 shows the data used in its derivation.[22] To derive column 2 of table J-1 from column 1 in 1948–82, index values through recession years—1949, 1954, 1958, 1961, 1970, 1975, 1980, and 1982—were first replaced by interpolated values. For each year-to-year percentage change in column 1 so adjusted, the average of that percentage and the similar percentage for the previous year was substituted. These percentages were then linked to obtain a continuous index.

Components of Labor Input in General Government, Households, and Institutions

Table 6-1 was calculated by the same method as in *Slower Growth*,[23] except for column 4, "implied efficiency offset," in 1947–82. That series is now based only on nonprofit institutions, rather than on households and institutions as in *Slower Growth*,[24] because the movement of the real output of household employees is not based on full-time equivalent employment. Moreover, full-time equivalent employment in institutions was provided by the BEA for the whole 1948–82 period; previously, it had to be approximated for some years.

Analysis of the Services of Dwellings Sector

The procedure used to derive the index for the effect of changes in the dwellings occupancy ratio

(table 6-4, column 3) was the same as that described in *Slower Growth*[25] from 1929 through 1970, and substantially the same through 1975. In its latest benchmark revision the BEA did not continue its series for the numbers of vacant units. The numbers of vacant homeowner units and rental units (excluding reserved units) were extrapolated from 1975 to 1982 by use of vacancy ratios from the Census Bureau.[26] The series for 1975–79 and 1979–82 were linked to eliminate a discontinuity in the Census Bureau's series.

Potential National Income and Its Determinants

Potential national income and the indexes for the determinants of potential national income were derived from actual national income by the same procedures as in *Slower Growth*. A few details need to be specified, however.

Adjustment of Output per Unit of Input for Intensity of Utilization Resulting from Fluctuations in Demand Intensity

To set the level of potential output in nonresidential business, the value of the index for the effects of changes in intensity of employed resources resulting from fluctuations in intensity of demand (table 5-1, column 9) must be established. Its "potential" level was put at 102.91 when 1972 equals 100. This is the value of the index when the civilian unemployment rate is at 4 percent that is predicted by a regression line relating the index to the unemployment rate, based on 1948–69 data.[27] The approximate level is confirmed by another procedure. In the seventeen years from 1948 through 1982 in which unemployment was lowest, the unemployment rate was 4.0 percent in one year, lower in eight years, and higher in eight years, with an average of 4.05 percent, while the average value of the index was 102.72.[28] The latter figure becomes 102.75 if the regression is used to adjust for the 0.05 percentage point difference

22. In appendix J of *Slower Growth*, the description of the derivation of column 1 of table J-1 is in error. The description in the sources to table J-1 in the present book is correct.
23. *Slower Growth*, pp. 84–87, 191.
24. Ibid., p. 191.
25. Ibid., pp. 191–92.
26. U.S. Bureau of the Census, *Vacancy Ratios and Characteristics of Housing in the United States: Annual Statistics 1982*, Series H-111-82-5 (Government Printing Office, 1983), table 1, p. 13.
27. The correlation is poor because unemployment is not a good indicator of intensity of utilization. Values of 102.64 and 102.51 are obtained if, instead, the relation is based on 1948–73 and 1948–82, respectively. Results in these periods are unduly influenced by years of high unemployment. Nevertheless, the results are not greatly different.
28. The most recent year in this group is 1973. In these seventeen years the unemployment rate ranged from 2.7 percent to 4.9 percent and the index from 98.43 to 105.46.

between the average unemployment rate and 4 percent. This figure differs by only 0.16 percent from the index value—102.91— derived from the regression.

The index value under potential conditions, 102.91, is a little below that used in *Slower Growth,* 103.31, because the "actual" index in the base year, 1972, was lowered relative to the 1948–69 average.

Adjustment of Labor Input, Including Allocation of Labor

The elasticities, by sex and age, for the response of the labor force to differences in the civilian unemployment rate that are shown in *Slower Growth,* page 196, and that were originally estimated by George Perry, were retained. They continue to yield reasonable results. Also retained were the formulas used to estimate the potential average hours of nonfarm business wage and salary workers, by sex and full-time or part-time status.

The ratios of potential to actual values of determinants of nonresidential business national income (table L-5) were recalculated back to 1966. The revisions in dollar values of potential national income before 1966 stem from revisions in actual national income and in the adjustment for intensity of demand. Small changes in table 8-7 result, in addition, from the fact that components are "forced" to agree with the total computed from unrounded data, whereas they were not in *Slower Growth.*

Tables

-⟫⟪-

A list of the formal tables in this book appears in the table of contents, pages xii–xiv.

Table numbers are the same as those of the corresponding tables in *Slower Growth,* except that table 2-3 in that volume is replaced by table 1-1, which appears on page 4. All other tables are grouped in the present section. Table L-6, which provides

average potential hours at work, by sector, is new. Certain other tables have been expanded to provide additional information, such as national income per hour at work, by sector, which is shown in columns 11–13 of table 2-7. The following tables that appeared in *Slower Growth* have been replaced by informal tables appearing in the text or completely omitted, usually because no new data were available or because the tables were not needed for the present study: 2-3, 3-3, 3-11, 3-12, 3-13, 4-5, 7-5, 8-5, 8-6, 8-8, 8-9, 9-1, 9-2, F-1, I-4, I-6, I-7, and I-9.

Nearly three-fourths of the tables, including the more important ones, provide data for all the years or periods covered by the study. Others omit all or most of the earlier years; data for the omitted years can be otained from the table with the same number in *Slower Growth.*

The preface provides information about the numbering system, concepts, sectors, and definitions. Methods of estimate are described in *Slower Growth,* supplemented by the appendix to the present book, ''Derivations of the Estimates'' (cited as ''Derivations'' in the sources to the tables).

Table 2-1. Actual and Potential Total National Income in Current and Constant Prices, Unemployment, Population, Employment, and Hours Worked, 1929, 1940–41, and 1947–83

| Year | National income in current prices (billions of dollars) (1) | Output in constant (1972) prices (billions of dollars) | | | Percent of civilian labor force 16 and over unemployed (5) | Population, annual average (thousands) (6) | Employment, annual average (thousands) | | Total hours at work, weekly (millions) | |
		Actual national income (2)	Command over goods and services (3)	Potential national income (4)			Actual (7)	Potential (8)	Actual (9)	Potential (10)
				Excluding Alaska and Hawaii						
1929	84.8	255.1	254.0	250.6	3.0	121,878	47,729	46,990	2,310	2,268
1940[a]	79.7	278.2	279.0	302.9	9.3[b]	132,122	51,275	55,927	2,170	2,413
1940[c]	78.1	271.2	. . .	302.9	14.4[d]	. . .	48,445	55,927	2,100	2,413
1941[a]	102.7	332.2	333.0	331.6	5.7[b]	133,402	55,794	57,306	2,381	2,461
1941[c]	101.5	326.8	. . .	331.6	9.6[d]	. . .	53,585	57,306	2,328	2,461
1947	194.9	389.7	389.9	394.0	3.7	144,126	59,601	59,351	2,479	2,473
1948	219.9	410.9	410.4	406.0	3.6	146,631	60,578	60,211	2,503	2,483
1949	213.6	406.8	406.2	417.6	5.9	149,188	59,258	61,099	2,418	2,496
1950	237.6	442.2	439.7	438.9	5.2	151,684	60,945	62,143	2,487	2,527
1951	274.1	479.5	475.2	466.4	3.1	154,287	64,769	63,872	2,638	2,591
1952	287.9	499.1	495.6	493.8	2.8	156,954	66,000	64,766	2,677	2,625
1953	302.1	516.7	513.9	513.0	2.7	159,565	66,830	65,430	2,698	2,642
1954	301.1	506.6	503.4	522.4	5.4	162,391	65,075	66,433	2,600	2,665
1955	330.5	543.3	540.2	539.1	4.2	165,275	66,534	66,749	2,662	2,666
1956	349.4	558.0	554.9	564.7	4.0	168,221	67,986	67,953	2,697	2,707

Table 2-1. (*continued*)

Year	National income in current prices (billions of dollars) (1)	Output in constant (1972) prices (billions of dollars)			Percent of civilian labor force 16 and over unemployed (5)	Population, annual average (thousands) (6)	Employment, annual average (thousands)		Total hours at work, weekly (millions)	
		Actual national income (2)	Command over goods and services (3)	Potential national income (4)			Actual (7)	Potential (8)	Actual (9)	Potential (10)
1957	365.2	565.2	562.8	578.1	4.1	171,274	68,126	68,243	2,666	2,690
1958	366.9	558.3	557.1	598.9	6.7	174,141	66,381	69,240	2,571	2,717
1959	400.8	596.2	595.5	613.8	5.4	177,073	67,868	69,322	2,639	2,711
1960ᵉ	414.2	607.4	606.9	634.1	5.4	179,893	68,463	70,013	2,650	2,734
Including Alaska and Hawaii										
1960ᵉ	415.7	609.7	609.2	636.5	5.4	180,760	68,750	70,306	2,660	2,745
1961	428.8	622.5	622.8	656.9	6.6	183,742	68,781	71,644	2,642	2,776
1962	462.0	657.4	658.4	673.6	5.5	186,590	70,226	71,836	2,698	2,769
1963	488.5	684.9	685.5	695.1	5.6	189,300	70,830	72,610	2,715	2,784
1964	524.9	724.2	724.4	725.8	5.1	191,927	72,242	73,506	2,766	2,809
1965	572.4	770.9	772.0	759.4	4.4	194,347	74,485	74,976	2,854	2,860
1966	628.1	816.0	817.6	799.5	3.6	196,599	77,749	77,309	2,949	2,919
1967	662.2	836.4	838.7	832.6	3.8	198,752	79,502	79,275	2,980	2,969
1968	722.5	876.1	880.4	869.9	3.5	200,745	81,532	80,956	3,036	3,010
1969	779.3	899.5	903.2	908.7	3.5	202,736	83,774	83,083	3,105	3,087
1970	810.7	888.4	892.0	932.0	4.9	205,089	83,482	84,754	3,047	3.112
1971	871.5	911.8	914.2	957.0	5.9	207,692	83,322	86,027	3,024	3,133
1972	963.6	963.7	963.7	1,004.9	5.6	209,924	85,306	87,615	3,092	3,184
1973	1,086.2	1,023.5	1,020.5	1,057.8	4.8	211,939	88,561	89,792	3,201	3,256
1974	1,160.7	1,008.2	990.6	1,087.8	5.6	213,898	89,928	92,277	3,207	3,326
1975	1,239.4	986.7	971.4	1,081.5	8.5	215,981	88,380	95,149	3,115	3,373
1976	1,379.2	1,043.0	1,027.0	1,123.8	7.7	218,086	90,548	96,289	3,189	3,408
1977	1,550.5	1,105.4	1,084.0	1,170.2	7.1	220,289	93,727	98,564	3,290	3,471
1978	1,760.3	1,165.1	1,143.1	1,218.1	6.0	222,629	98,089	101,364	3,431	3,557
1979	1,966.7	1,194.8	1,166.4	1,263.7	5.8	225,106	101,219	104,153	3,524	3,645
1980	2,116.6	1,181.6	1,144.2	1,296.0	7.0	227,694	101,747	106,920	3,507	3,723
1981	2,373.0	1,212.6	1,182.2	1,319.1	7.5	229,916	102,517	108,571	3,520	3,761
1982	2,450.4	1,175.4	1,155.3	1,333.9	9.6	232,118	101,182	110,875	3,437	3,825
1983ᶠ	2,650.1	1,213.4	1,200.1	1,353.0	9.5	234,297	n.a.	n.a.	n.a.	n.a.

Sources: Column 1, NIPA, table 1.11; column 2, NIPA, table 1.10; column 3, Edward F. Denison, "International Transactions in Measures of the Nation's Production," *Survey of Current Business* (May 1981), p. 20, and later issues of the *Survey of Current Business;* column 4, table 2-4; column 5, Department of Labor, Bureau of Labor Statistics, with small adjustments by George L. Perry and Edward F. Denison; column 6, NIPA, table 8.2, except 1960 excluding Alaska and Hawaii, which is from "Estimates of the Population of the United States and Components of Change: 1940 to 1972," *Current Population Reports*, series P-25, no. 481 (GPO, 1972), table 2, p. 11; column 7, table B-1; column 8, column 7 plus table L-4, column 10; column 9, see "Derivations" and *Slower Growth*; column 10, column 9 plus table L-3, column 12.

n.a. Not available.

a. Including work relief.

b. Persons on work relief are counted as employed.

c. Excluding work relief. Work relief data are from NIPA or were provided directly by the Bureau of Economic Analysis.

d. Persons on work relief are counted as unemployed.

e. The difference between the two 1960 rows understates the true values for Alaska and Hawaii because the armed forces stationed in Alaska and Hawaii were included in the series throughout, as were some other components. Data for 1960 excluding Alaska and Hawaii were computed from data provided by the Bureau of Economic Analysis. See *Accounting for Growth* for details.

f. Preliminary.

Table 2-2. Indexes of Actual and Potential National Income in Constant Prices, Population, Employment, and Hours at Work, 1929, 1940–41, and 1947–83

Actual, 1972 = 100

	Actual national income				Potential national income					Employment		Hours at work	
Year	Total (1)	Per capita (2)	Per person employed (3)	Per hour at work (4)	Total (5)	Per capita (6)	Per person potentially employed (7)	Per potential hour at work (8)	Population (9)	Actual (10)	Potential (11)	Actual (12)	Potential (13)
1929	26.57	45.54	47.29	35.43	26.10	44.74	47.20	35.44	58.34	56.18	55.31	74.99	73.65
1940a	28.98	45.83	48.01	41.13	31.55	49.89	47.93	40.27	63.24	60.36	65.84	70.46	78.34
1940b	28.25	44.67	49.54	41.43	31.55	49.89	47.93	40.27	63.24	57.03	65.84	68.19	78.34
1941a	34.60	54.19	52.69	44.75	34.54	54.10	51.21	43.21	63.85	65.68	67.46	77.32	79.93
1941b	34.04	53.31	53.97	45.03	34.54	54.10	51.21	43.21	63.85	63.08	67.46	75.59	79.93
1947	40.59	58.83	57.87	50.43	41.04	59.49	58.75	51.11	68.99	70.16	69.87	80.49	80.29
1948	42.80	60.98	60.03	52.66	42.29	60.25	59.67	52.46	70.19	71.31	70.88	81.28	80.62
1949	42.37	59.33	60.74	53.96	43.50	60.92	60.49	53.67	71.41	69.76	71.92	78.52	81.04
1950	46.06	63.44	64.20	57.04	45.72	62.98	62.50	55.71	72.60	71.74	73.15	80.75	82.06
1951	49.94	67.62	65.52	58.31	48.58	65.78	64.62	57.75	73.85	76.24	75.19	85.65	84.12
1952	51.99	69.20	66.93	59.81	51.43	68.45	67.47	60.35	75.13	77.69	76.24	86.92	85.23
1953	53.82	70.46	68.43	61.43	53.43	69.95	69.39	62.29	76.38	78.67	77.02	87.61	85.78
1954	52.77	68.24	68.89	62.49	54.41	70.36	69.59	62.89	77.33	76.60	78.20	84.44	86.52
1955	56.59	71.50	72.26	65.47	56.15	70.98	71.47	64.86	79.11	78.32	78.57	86.44	86.58
1956	58.12	72.18	72.63	66.37	58.82	73.05	73.54	66.92	80.52	80.03	79.99	87.57	87.90
1957	58.87	71.81	73.42	67.99	60.21	73.44	74.97	68.94	81.98	80.20	80.33	86.58	87.35
1958	58.15	69.77	74.43	69.65	62.38	74.84	76.55	70.70	83.35	78.14	81.51	83.49	88.23
1959	62.10	73.27	77.74	72.47	63.93	75.42	78.36	72.63	84.76	79.89	81.60	85.69	88.03
1960	63.27	73.48	78.51	73.54	66.05	76.70	80.15	74.40	86.11	80.59	82.42	86.03	88.77
1961	64.59	73.79	80.12	75.60	68.16	77.87	81.17	75.93	87.53	80.63	83.98	85.44	89.78
1962	68.22	76.76	82.87	78.19	69.90	78.65	83.01	78.03	88.88	82.32	84.21	87.25	89.57
1963	71.07	78.81	85.60	80.95	72.13	79.98	84.75	80.10	90.18	83.03	85.12	87.80	90.05
1964	75.15	82.19	88.75	83.99	75.31	82.37	87.41	82.89	91.43	84.69	86.17	89.47	90.87
1965	79.99	86.40	91.62	86.66	78.80	85.12	89.67	85.18	92.58	87.32	87.89	92.30	92.51
1966	84.67	90.41	92.92	88.76	82.96	88.59	91.55	87.88	93.65	91.14	90.63	95.39	94.40
1967	86.79	91.67	93.14	90.05	86.40	91.25	92.98	89.98	94.68	93.20	92.93	96.38	96.02
1968	90.91	95.06	95.12	92.58	90.27	94.40	95.13	92.73	95.63	95.58	94.90	98.20	97.34
1969	93.34	96.65	95.05	92.95	94.29	97.63	96.82	94.43	96.58	98.20	97.39	100.42	99.85
1970	92.19	94.36	94.21	93.56	96.71	98.99	97.35	96.09	97.70	97.86	99.35	98.54	100.65
1971	94.61	95.62	96.88	96.73	99.30	100.36	98.48	98.01	98.94	97.67	100.85	97.81	101.32
1972	100.00	100.00	100.00	100.00	104.28	104.28	101.54	101.24	100.00	100.00	102.71	100.00	103.00
1973	106.21	105.20	102.31	102.58	109.76	108.72	104.29	104.23	100.96	103.82	105.26	103.53	105.31
1974	104.62	102.68	99.25	100.87	112.88	110.79	104.36	104.93	101.89	105.42	108.17	103.72	107.58
1975	102.39	99.51	98.83	101.75	112.22	109.07	100.62	102.87	102.89	103.60	111.54	100.76	109.09
1976	108.23	103.71	101.97	104.94	116.61	111.74	103.32	105.79	104.36	106.14	112.87	103.14	110.24
1977	114.70	109.30	104.41	107.81	121.43	115.71	105.10	108.16	104.94	109.87	115.54	106.39	112.26
1978	120.90	114.00	105.15	108.96	126.40	119.19	106.38	109.86	106.05	114.98	118.82	110.96	115.06
1979	123.98	115.62	104.50	108.77	131.13	122.29	107.41	111.23	107.23	118.65	122.09	113.98	117.89
1980	122.61	113.05	102.81	108.10	134.48	123.99	107.31	111.68	108.46	119.27	125.34	113.42	120.42
1981	125.83	114.89	104.71	110.53	136.88	124.98	107.56	112.54	109.52	120.18	127.27	113.84	121.63
1982	121.97	110.31	102.84	109.70	138.41	125.18	106.50	111.87	110.57	118.61	129.97	111.18	123.72
1983c	125.91	112.81	n.a.	n.a.	n.a.	n.a.	n.a.	n.a.	111.61	n.a.	n.a.	n.a.	n.a.

Source: Calculated from table 2-1 and underlying data.
n.a. Not available.
a. Including work relief.
b. Excluding work relief.
c. Preliminary.

Table 2-4. Derivation of Potential National Income at 4 Percent Unemployment, 1929, 1940–41, and 1947–82
Billions of 1972 dollars

Year	Actual national income (1)	Plus: Adjustment for intensity of utilization of employed inputs (2)	Plus: Adjustment for labor input[a] (3)	Equals: Potential national income (4)	Excess of actual over potential	
					Amount (5)	Percent (6)
Excluding Alaska and Hawaii						
1929	255.1	−1.3	−3.2	250.6	4.5	1.8
1940	271.2[b]	0.8	30.9[c]	302.9	−24.7[d]	−8.2[d]
1941	326.8[b]	−8.7	13.5[c]	331.6	0.6[d]	0.2[d]
1947	389.7	5.1	−0.8	394.0	−4.3	−1.1
1948	410.9	−2.8	−2.1	406.0	4.9	1.2
1949	406.8	2.0	8.8	417.6	−10.8	−2.6
1950	442.2	−8.3	5.0	438.9	3.3	0.8
1951	479.5	−7.5	−5.6	466.4	13.1	2.8
1952	499.1	1.4	−6.7	493.8	5.3	1.1
1953	516.7	3.9	−7.6	513.0	3.7	0.7
1954	506.6	7.0	8.8	522.4	−15.8	−3.0
1955	543.3	−5.1	0.9	539.1	4.2	0.8
1956	558.0	5.1	1.6	564.7	−6.7	−1.2
1957	565.2	9.3	3.6	578.1	−12.9	−2.2
1958	558.3	17.4	23.2	598.9	−40.6	−6.8
1959	596.2	6.1	11.5	613.8	−17.6	−2.9
1960[e]	607.4	12.9	13.8	634.1	−26.7	−4.2
Including Alaska and Hawaii						
1960[e]	609.7	12.9	13.9	636.5	−26.8	−4.2
1961	622.5	11.9	22.5	656.9	−34.4	−5.2
1962	657.4	3.9	12.3	673.6	−16.2	−2.4
1963	684.9	−1.9	12.1	695.1	−10.2	−1.5
1964	724.2	−6.0	7.6	725.8	−1.6	−0.2
1965	770.9	−12.7	1.2	759.4	11.5	1.5
1966	816.0	−11.1	−5.4	799.5	16.5	2.1
1967	836.4	−1.8	−2.0	832.6	3.8	0.5
1968	876.1	−1.3	−4.9	869.9	6.2	0.7
1969	899.5	12.5	−3.3	908.7	−9.2	−1.0
1970	888.4	30.3	13.3	932.0	−43.6	−4.7
1971	911.8	22.5	22.7	957.0	−45.2	−4.7
1972	963.7	21.3	19.9	1,004.9	−41.2	−4.1
1973	1,023.5	22.7	11.6	1,057.8	−34.3	−3.2
1974	1,008.2	52.1	27.5	1,087.8	−79.6	−7.3
1975	986.7	36.7	58.1	1,081.5	−94.8	−8.8
1976	1,043.0	30.0	50.8	1,123.8	−80.8	−7.2
1977	1,105.4	22.0	42.8	1,170.2	−64.8	−5.5
1978	1,165.1	22.8	30.2	1,218.1	−53.0	−4.4
1979	1,194.8	39.4	29.5	1,263.7	−68.9	−5.5
1980	1,181.6	59.1	55.3	1,296.0	−114.4	−8.8
1981	1,212.6	44.5	62.0	1,319.1	−106.5	−8.1
1982	1,175.4	56.2	102.3	1,333.9	−158.5	−11.9

Sources: Column 1, table 2-1, column 2; columns 2 and 3, table L-5; column 4, sum of columns 1, 2, and 3; column 5, column 1 minus column 4; column 6, column 5 divided by column 4.

a. Includes the effect on resource allocation of differences between actual and potential labor input.

b. Excluding work relief.

c. The actual output of employees on work relief ($7.0 billion in 1940 and $5.4 billion in 1941) is not offset here against their potential output because it is omitted from column 1.

d. Comparison is with actual national income including work relief; see table 2-1 for data.

e. See table 2-1, note e.

Table 2-5. National Income in Current Prices, by Sector of Origin and Industrial Branch, 1929, 1940–41, and 1947–82
Billions of dollars

Year	Whole economy (1)	General government, households, and institutions[a] (2)	Services of dwellings[b] (3)	International assets (4)	Nonresidential business Total[b] (5)	Nonresidential business Farm[c] (6)	Nonresidential business Nonfarm[b] (7)
			Excluding Alaska and Hawaii				
1929	84.8	7.2	5.4	0.8	71.4	8.6	62.8
1940[d]	79.7	10.2	3.3	0.4	65.8	6.2	59.6
1940[e]	78.1	8.6	3.3	0.4	65.8	6.2	59.6
1941[d]	102.7	11.9	3.6	0.5	86.7	8.7	78.0
1941[e]	101.5	10.7	3.6	0.5	86.7	8.7	78.0
1947	194.9	21.9	4.5	1.2	167.3	19.5	147.8
1948	219.9	23.1	5.1	1.5	190.2	22.1	168.1
1949	213.6	25.4	6.0	1.4	180.8	16.9	163.9
1950	237.6	27.4	7.0	1.5	201.7	17.9	183.8
1951	274.1	34.3	7.8	2.1	229.9	20.7	209.2
1952	287.9	38.4	9.2	2.3	238.0	19.7	218.3
1953	302.1	39.7	10.9	2.2	249.3	17.3	232.0
1954	301.1	40.5	12.5	2.4	245.7	16.6	229.1
1955	330.5	43.2	13.4	2.8	271.1	15.5	255.6
1956	349.4	46.3	14.1	3.3	285.7	15.3	270.4
1957	365.2	49.6	15.5	3.6	296.5	15.3	281.2
1958	366.9	53.5	17.0	3.1	293.3	17.7	275.6
1959	400.8	56.3	18.7	3.4	322.4	15.5	306.9
1960[f]	414.2	60.3	20.6	3.7	329.6	16.5	313.1
			Including Alaska and Hawaii				
1960[f]	415.7	60.6	20.6	3.7	330.8	16.5	314.3
1961	428.8	64.8	22.2	4.0	337.8	17.4	320.4
1962	462.0	69.8	24.3	4.6	363.3	18.0	345.3
1963	488.5	74.5	25.9	5.0	383.1	18.0	365.1
1964	524.9	80.6	27.4	5.5	411.4	17.2	394.2
1965	572.4	86.8	29.4	5.8	450.4	20.0	430.4
1966	628.1	97.8	31.4	5.6	493.3	21.4	471.9
1967	662.2	108.6	33.3	5.9	514.4	20.0	494.4
1968	722.5	121.3	34.6	6.7	559.9	20.4	539.5
1969	779.3	133.9	36.7	6.8	601.9	22.6	579.3
1970	810.7	148.1	38.5	7.3	616.8	22.9	593.9
1971	871.5	161.4	41.6	9.1	659.4	24.0	635.4
1972	963.6	176.4	45.7	10.9	730.6	29.5	701.1
1973	1,086.2	191.8	50.2	16.0	828.2	47.7	780.5
1974	1,160.7	208.0	56.1	19.8	876.8	41.5	835.3
1975	1,239.4	230.3	59.7	17.3	932.1	40.3	891.8
1976	1,379.2	250.2	66.4	20.5	1,042.1	35.4	1,006.7
1977	1,550.5	270.8	74.7	23.5	1,181.5	38.0	1,143.5
1978	1,760.3	297.0	85.9	29.7	1,347.7	47.9	1,299.8
1979	1,966.7	323.0	99.1	42.6	1,502.0	56.8	1,445.2
1980	2,116.6	358.1	116.0	45.4	1,597.1	49.4	1,547.7
1981	2,373.0	395.5	138.8	49.6	1,789.1	61.1	1,728.0
1982	2,450.4	431.1	159.7	47.4	1,812.2	52.9	1,759.3

Sources: Column 1, NIPA, table 1.12, line 1; column 2, NIPA, table 1.14, sum of rows 41, 45, and 49; column 3, NIPA, table 1.20, row 17 minus row 18; column 4, NIPA, table 1.12, sum of rows 50 and 51; column 5, column 1 minus columns 2 through 4; column 6, NIPA table 1.18, sum of rows 13 and 18, plus NIPA, table 1.9, sum of rows 17 and 23, plus total government payments from U.S. Department of Agriculture, Economic Research Service, *Economic Indicators of the Farm Sector,* various issues, minus NIPA, table 1.18, line 17, minus NIPA, table 1.9, row 14; column 7, column 5 minus column 6.
  a. Includes compensation of employees in the rest-of-the-world industry.
  b. The small amount of labor income in the dwellings industry is classified in nonfarm nonresidential business.
  c. Includes net rent and government payments to nonoperator landlords. Excludes farm housing.
  d. Including work relief.
  e. Excluding work relief. Work relief data are from NIPA, table 6.6A, rows 80 and 86.
  f. See table 2-1, note e.

Table 2-6. National Income in Constant Prices, by Sector of Origin and Industrial Branch, 1929, 1940–41, and 1947–82
Billions of 1972 dollars

Year	Whole economy (1)	General government, households, and institutions[a] (2)	Services of dwellings[b] (3)	International assets (4)	Nonresidential business		
					Total[b] (5)	Farm[c] (6)	Nonfarm[b] (7)
			Excluding Alaska and Hawaii				
1929	255.1	41.8	6.5	2.4	204.4	20.2	184.2
1940[d]	278.2	60.1	6.4	1.3	210.3	21.9	188.4
1940[e]	271.2	53.1	6.4	1.3	210.3	21.9	188.4
1941[d]	332.2	71.1	6.9	1.7	252.5	23.8	228.7
1941[e]	326.8	65.7	6.9	1.7	252.5	23.8	228.7
1947	389.7	74.1	9.4	2.4	303.8	20.9	282.9
1948	410.9	75.0	10.0	2.8	323.0	22.3	300.7
1949	406.8	79.7	11.3	2.6	313.2	21.5	291.7
1950	442.2	83.2	12.3	2.9	343.8	22.4	321.4
1951	479.5	97.7	13.3	3.7	364.8	20.9	343.9
1952	499.1	104.1	14.7	3.9	376.4	21.4	355.0
1953	516.7	104.2	15.8	3.8	392.9	22.3	370.6
1954	506.6	103.5	17.1	4.1	382.0	22.6	359.4
1955	543.3	105.8	18.1	4.7	414.6	23.3	391.3
1956	558.0	109.0	19.1	5.2	424.6	23.1	401.5
1957	565.2	112.1	20.5	5.6	427.0	22.5	404.5
1958	558.3	114.4	22.2	4.7	416.9	23.7	393.2
1959	596.2	116.8	23.6	5.0	450.8	22.5	428.3
1960[f]	607.4	120.4	25.2	5.4	456.3	24.0	432.3
			Including Alaska and Hawaii				
1960[f]	609.7	121.1	25.2	5.4	457.9	24.0	433.9
1961	622.5	125.7	26.6	5.8	464.3	24.2	440.1
1962	657.4	130.5	28.5	6.6	491.8	24.3	467.5
1963	684.9	134.0	29.9	7.0	514.0	25.4	488.6
1964	724.2	138.5	31.5	7.6	546.6	24.9	521.7
1965	770.9	143.7	33.5	7.9	585.9	26.1	559.8
1966	816.0	153.5	35.4	7.3	619.8	24.7	595.1
1967	836.4	162.0	37.5	7.4	629.5	25.8	603.7
1968	876.1	167.9	39.1	8.1	661.0	25.7	635.3
1969	899.5	172.7	41.1	7.9	677.8	26.1	651.7
1970	888.4	172.8	42.4	7.9	665.3	27.6	637.7
1971	911.8	174.3	43.7	9.5	684.2	29.0	655.2
1972	963.7	176.4	45.8	10.9	730.6	29.4	701.2
1973	1,023.5	178.5	48.3	15.1	781.6	29.2	752.4
1974	1,008.2	181.6	51.1	17.3	758.2	27.8	730.4
1975	986.7	185.3	52.4	13.9	735.1	29.6	705.5
1976	1,043.0	187.2	54.9	15.6	785.3	27.9	757.4
1977	1,105.4	189.2	58.7	16.9	840.6	29.7	810.9
1978	1,165.1	194.4	61.6	20.0	889.1	29.1	860.0
1979	1,194.8	197.6	64.3	26.3	906.6	30.5	876.1
1980	1,181.6	201.1	67.0	25.7	887.8	31.5	856.3
1981	1,212.6	202.4	71.3	25.6	913.0	36.1	876.9
1982	1,175.4	202.8	74.6	23.1	874.9	34.4	840.5

Sources: Column 1, NIPA, table 1.10, row 12; column 2, sum of NIPA, table 1.10, rows 19 and 20, and output of employees in the rest of the world, computed as the product of NIPA, table 1.10, row 21, and the ratio of row 49 to row 48 in NIPA, table 1.12; column 3, NIPA, table 1.21, row 15, reduced by the ratio of row 18 to row 17 in NIPA, table 1.20; column 4, NIPA, table 1.10, row 21, minus the output of employees in the rest of the world included in column 2; column 5, column 1 minus columns 2 through 4; column 6, sum of rows 13 and 18 in NIPA, table 1.19, the excess of row 14 over rows 17 and 23 in NIPA, table 1.10, and the excess of total government payments from U.S. Department of Agriculture, Economic Research Service, *Economic Indicators of the Farm Sector*, various issues, minus line 17 of NIPA, table 1.18, deflated by row 18 of NIPA, table 7.10; column 7, column 5 minus column 6.

a. Includes output of labor in the rest-of-the-world industry.
b. The small amount of labor in the dwellings industry is classified in nonfarm nonresidential business.
c. Includes output corresponding to net rent and government payments to nonoperator landlords. Excludes farm housing.
d. Includes output of persons on work relief.
e. Excludes output of persons on work relief; data from the Bureau of Economic Analysis.
f. See table 2-1, note e.

Table 2-7. Persons Employed, by Sector, Industrial Branch, and Type of Worker, and National Income per Person Employed and per Hour at Work, by Sector[a], 1929, 1940–41, and 1947–82

	Persons employed (thousands)							National income per person employed (1972 dollars)			National income per hour at work (1972 dollars)		
			Nonresidential business										
					Nonfarm[b]								
Year	Whole economy (1)	General government, households, and institutions (2)	Total[b] (3)	Farm (4)	Total (5)	Wage and salary workers (6)	Self-employed and unpaid family workers (7)	Whole economy (8)	General government, households, and institutions (9)	Nonresidential business[b] (10)	Whole economy (11)	General government, households, and institutions (12)	Nonresidential business[b] (13)
	Excluding Alaska and Hawaii												
1929	47,729	6,442	41,287	9,878	31,409	26,408	5,001	5,344	6,484	4,949	2.12	2.84	1.94
1940[c]	51,275	10,426	40,849	8,886	31,963	26,692	5,271	5,425	5,764	5,149	2.47	3.15	2.24
1940[d]	48,445	7,596	40,849	8,886	31,963	26,692	5,271	5,598	6,991	5,149	2.48	3.44	2.24
1941[c]	55,794	11,190	44,604	8,910	35,694	30,371	5,323	5,954	6,354	5,662	2.68	3.44	2.45
1941[d]	53,585	8,981	44,604	8,910	35,694	30,371	5,323	6,099	7,315	5,662	2.70	3.67	2.45
1947	59,601	9,536	50,065	7,927	42,138	36,066	6,072	6,539	7,776	6,068	3.02	4.15	2.74
1948	60,578	9,798	50,780	7,835	42,945	36,777	6,168	6,783	7,653	6,362	3.16	4.13	2.88
1949	59,258	10,194	49,064	7,659	41,405	35,281	6,124	6,864	7,817	6,383	3.24	4.22	2.93
1950	60,945	10,719	50,226	7,504	42,722	36,550	6,172	7,255	7,761	6,846	3.42	4.19	3.14
1951	64,769	12,546	52,223	7,079	45,144	38,958	6,186	7,404	7,786	6,986	3.50	4.17	3.21
1952	66,000	13,198	52,802	6,878	45,924	39,687	6,237	7,563	7,888	7,129	3.59	4.21	3.29
1953	66,830	13,260	53,570	6,637	46,933	40,731	6,202	7,732	7,858	7,558	3.68	4.20	3.40
1954	65,075	13,086	51,989	6,618	45,371	39,293	6,078	7,785	7,907	7,348	3.75	4.27	3.44
1955	66,534	13,415	53,119	6,498	46,621	40,523	6,098	8,165	7,888	7,806	3.92	4.30	3.64
1956	67,986	13,795	54,191	6,244	47,947	41,770	6,177	8,207	7,902	7,835	3.98	4.35	3.69
1957	68,126	14,054	54,072	5,928	48,144	41,869	6,275	8,296	7,978	7,897	4.08	4.40	3.77
1958	66,381	14,391	51,990	5,652	46,338	40,101	6,237	8,410	7,953	8,019	4.18	4.44	3.86
1959	67,868	14,631	53,237	5,540	47,697	41,518	6,179	8,784	7,981	8,468	4.34	4.49	4.05
1960	68,463	14,960	53,503	5,262	48,241	42,035	6,206	8,871	8,050	8,529	4.41	4.51	4.11
	Including Alaska and Hawaii												
1960	68,750	15,038	53,712	5,286	48,426	42,197	6,229	8,868	8,055	8,526	4.41	4.52	4.11
1961	68,781	15,609	53,172	5,139	48,033	41,792	6,241	9,050	8,053	8,733	4.53	4.56	4.23
1962	70,226	16,280	53,946	4,921	49,025	42,896	6,129	9,361	8,017	9,117	4.69	4.57	4.40
1963	70,830	16,585	54,245	4,638	49,607	43,612	5,995	9,669	8,078	9,475	4.85	4.61	4.59
1964	72,242	17,082	55,160	4,362	50,798	44,774	6,024	10,025	8,111	9,910	5.03	4.65	4.79
1965	74,485	17,678	56,807	4,151	52,656	46,662	5,994	10,349	8,129	10,313	5.19	4.69	4.98
1966	77,749	18,969	58,780	3,768	55,012	49,123	5,889	10,496	8,093	10,545	5.32	4.70	5.14
1967	79,502	19,900	59,602	3,633	55,969	50,146	5,823	10,521	8,142	10,561	5.40	4.70	5.22
1968	81,532	20,616	60,916	3,571	57,345	51,595	5,750	10,745	8,144	10,850	5.55	4.75	5.40
1969	83,774	20,965	62,809	3,439	59,370	53,414	5,956	10,737	8,237	10,792	5.57	4.81	5.40
1970	83,482	20,981	62,501	3,336	59,165	53,244	5,921	10,642	8,238	10,644	5.61	4.87	5.41
1971	83,322	21,044	62,278	3,259	59,019	53,000	6,019	10,943	8,285	10,987	5.80	4.94	5.61
1972	85,306	21,233	64,073	3,261	60,812	54,741	6,071	11,296	8,309	11,403	5.99	4.98	5.83
1973	88,561	21,484	67,077	3,243	63,834	57,661	6,173	11,557	8,308	11,653	6.15	4.98	5.98
1974	89,928	21,760	68,168	3,258	64,910	58,574	6,336	11,211	8,348	11,123	6.05	5.05	5.80
1975	88,380	22,303	66,077	3,199	62,878	56,533	6,345	11,164	8,310	11,125	6.10	5.06	5.86
1976	90,548	22,524	68,024	3,143	64,881	58,507	6,374	11,519	8,312	11,544	6.29	5.07	6.09
1977	93,727	22,912	70,815	3,012	67,803	61,062	6,741	11,794	8,256	11,870	6.46	5.07	6.28
1978	98,089	23,499	74,590	2,929	71,661	64,571	7,090	11,878	8,275	11,920	6.53	5.09	6.34
1979	101,219	23,795	77,424	2,887	74,537	67,102	7,435	11,804	8,303	11,710	6.52	5.13	6.27
1980	101,747	24,288	77,459	2,953	74,506	66,891	7,615	11,613	8,278	11,461	6.48	5.15	6.20
1981	102,517	24,299	78,218	2,837	75,381	67,688	7,693	11,828	8,329	11,672	6.63	5.17	6.35
1982	101,182	24,339	76,843	2,713	74,130	66,219	7,911	11,617	8,331	11,386	6.58	5.18	6.27

Sources: Columns 1–7, see "Derivations," table B-1, and *Slower Growth*, appendix B; columns 8–10, national income from table 2-6 divided by corresponding employment from columns 1–3 of this table; columns 11–13, national income from table 2-6 divided by (52 times total weekly hours). Total weekly hours for column 11 from table 2-1, column 9; for column 12, column 11 minus column 13; for column 13, table C-1, sum of columns 7 through 9.

a. No employment is classified in the "services of dwellings" and "international assets" sectors.
b. Includes persons employed in the dwellings sector.
c. Includes persons on work relief.
d. Excludes persons on work relief. Work relief data are from NIPA, table 6.7A, rows 80 and 86.

Table 2-8. Potential National Income in Constant Prices, Potential Employment, Potential Hours, and Potential National Income per Person Employed and per Hour at Work, by Sector, 1929, 1940–41, and 1947–82[a]

Year	Potential national income (billions of 1972 dollars)		Potential employment (thousands)		Potential national income per person employed (1972 dollars)		Total potential hours (millions per week)		Potential national income per hour at work (1972 dollars)	
	Whole economy (1)	Nonresidential business[b] (2)	Whole economy (3)	Nonresidential business[b] (4)	Whole economy (5)	Nonresidential business[b] (6)	Whole economy (7)	Nonresidential business[b] (8)	Whole economy (9)	Nonresidential business[b] (10)
				Excluding Alaska and Hawaii						
1929	250.6	199.8	46,990	40,548	5,333	4,927	2,268	1,985	2.12	1.94
1940	302.9	242.0	55,927	48,331	5,416	5,007	2,413	2,115	2.41	2.20
1941	331.6	257.4	57,306	48,325	5,786	5,326	2,461	2,117	2.59	2.34
1947	394.0	308.1	59,351	49,815	6,638	6,185	2,473	2,129	3.06	2.78
1948	406.0	318.1	60,211	50,413	6,743	6,310	2,483	2,134	3.14	2.87
1949	417.6	323.9	61,099	50,905	6,835	6,363	2,496	2,133	3.22	2.92
1950	438.9	340.5	62,143	51,424	7,063	6,621	2,527	2,145	3.34	3.05
1951	466.4	351.7	63,872	51,326	7,302	6,852	2,591	2,140	3.46	3.16
1952	493.8	371.1	64,766	51,568	7,624	7,196	2,625	2,149	3.62	3.32
1953	513.0	389.2	65,430	52,170	7,840	7,460	2,642	2,165	3.73	3.46
1954	522.4	397.8	66,433	53,347	7,864	7,457	2,665	2,198	3.77	3.48
1955	539.1	410.4	66,749	53,334	8,077	7,695	2,666	2,193	3.89	3.60
1956	564.7	431.3	67,953	54,158	8,310	7,964	2,707	2,225	4.01	3.73
1957	578.1	439.9	68,243	54,189	8,471	8,118	2,690	2,200	4.13	3.84
1958	598.9	457.7	69,240	54,849	8,650	8,341	2,717	2,221	4.24	3.96
1959	613.8	468.4	69,322	54,691	8,854	8,564	2,711	2,210	4.35	4.08
1960[c]	634.1	483.0	70,013	55,053	9,057	8,774	2,734	2,221	4.46	4.18
				Including Alaska and Hawaii						
1960[c]	636.5	484.7	70,306	55,268	9,053	8,770	2,745	2,230	4.46	4.18
1961	656.9	498.8	71,644	56,035	9,169	8,902	2,776	2,246	4.55	4.27
1962	673.6	508.0	71,836	55,556	9,377	9,144	2,769	2,221	4.68	4.40
1963	695.1	524.2	72,610	56,025	9,573	9,357	2,784	2,225	4.80	4.53
1964	725.8	548.2	73,506	56,424	9,874	9,716	2,809	2,237	4.97	4.71
1965	759.4	574.4	74,976	57,298	10,129	10,025	2,860	2,271	5.11	4.86
1966	799.5	603.4	77,309	58,340	10,342	10,343	2,919	2,290	5.27	5.07
1967	832.6	625.7	79,275	59,375	10,503	10,538	2,969	2,306	5.39	5.22
1968	869.9	654.7	80,956	60,340	10,745	10,850	3,010	2,330	5.56	5.40
1969	908.7	687.1	83,083	62,118	10,937	11,061	3,087	2,397	5.66	5.51
1970	932.0	708.8	84,754	63,773	10,997	11,114	3,112	2,430	5.76	5.61
1971	957.0	729.5	86,027	64,983	11,124	11,226	3,133	2,453	5.88	5.72
1972	1,004.9	771.8	87,615	66,382	11,470	11,627	3,184	2,503	6.07	5.93
1973	1,057.8	815.9	89,792	68,308	11,781	11,944	3,256	2,567	6.25	6.11
1974	1,087.8	837.9	92,277	70,517	11,788	11,882	3,326	2,634	6.29	6.12
1975	1,081.5	829.9	95,149	72,846	11,366	11,393	3,373	2,669	6.17	5.99
1976	1,123.8	866.1	96,289	73,765	11,671	11,741	3,408	2,698	6.34	6.17
1977	1,170.2	905.4	98,564	75,652	11,872	11,968	3,471	2,754	6.48	6.32
1978	1,218.1	942.1	101,364	77,865	12,017	12,099	3,557	2,824	6.58	6.42
1979	1,263.7	975.6	104,153	80,358	12,133	12,141	3,645	2,904	6.67	6.46
1980	1,296.0	1,002.1	106,920	82,632	12,121	12,127	3,723	2,972	6.69	6.48
1981	1,319.1	1,019.4	108,571	84,272	12,150	12,097	3,761	3,008	6.75	6.52
1982	1,333.9	1,033.4	110,875	86,536	12,031	11,942	3,825	3,073	6.71	6.47

Sources: Column 1, table 2-4, column 4; column 2, sum of table 2-6, column 5, and table 2-4, columns 2 and 3; column 3, table 2-1, column 8; column 4, sum of table 2-7, column 3, and table L-4, column 10; column 5, column 1 divided by column 3; column 6, column 2 divided by column 4; column 7, table 2-1, column 10; column 8, table C-1, sum of columns 7 through 9, plus table L-3, column 12; column 9, column 1 divided by (column 7 times 52 weeks); column 10, column 2 divided by (column 8 times 52 weeks).

a. In "general government, households, and institutions," "services of dwellings," and "international assets," potential national income is the same as actual national income (excluding work relief in 1940 and 1941). Employment, national income per person employed, and national income per hour at work (in "general government, households, and institutions"), farm employment, and the number of self-employed and unpaid family workers are also the same on a potential basis as on an actual basis. See table 2-7 for data. No employment is classified in "services of dwellings" and "international assets."

b. The small amount of labor in the dwellings industry and its output are classified in nonresidential business.

c. See table 2-1, note e.

Table 2-9. Growth Rates of Potential and Actual National Income, National Income per Person Employed, and National Income per Hour at Work in the Whole Economy and Nonresidential Business, Selected Periods, 1929–82

Item	Longer periods				Shorter periods						
	1929–1982	1929–1948	1948–1973	1973–1982	1929–1941	1941–1948	1948–1953	1953–1964	1964–1973	1973–1979	1979–1982
Whole economy											
Total potential national income	3.20	2.57	3.89	2.61	2.36	2.93	4.79	3.17	4.27	3.01	1.82
Per person potentially employed	1.55	1.24	2.26	0.23	0.68	2.21	3.06	2.12	1.98	0.49	−0.28
Per potential hour	2.19	2.09	2.79	0.79	1.67	2.81	3.50	2.63	2.58	1.09	0.19
Total actual national income	2.92	2.54	3.70	1.55	2.09[a]	3.33[a]	4.69	3.08	3.92	2.61	−0.54
Per person employed	1.48	1.26	2.16	0.06	1.11[a]	1.53[a]	2.65	2.39	1.59	0.36	−0.54
Per hour	2.16	2.11	2.70	0.75	2.02[a]	2.26[a]	3.13	2.89	2.25	0.98	0.28
Nonresidential business											
Total potential national income	3.14	2.48	3.82	2.66	2.13	3.07	4.12	3.13	4.52	3.02	1.94
Per person potentially employed	1.68	1.31	2.59	0.00	0.65	2.45	3.41	2.43	2.32	0.27	−0.55
Per potential hour	2.30	2.09	3.08	0.63	1.59	2.96	3.82	2.86	2.93	0.93	0.03
Total actual national income	2.77	2.44	3.58	1.26	1.78	3.58	4.00	3.01	4.05	2.50	−1.18
Per person employed	1.58	1.33	2.45	−0.26	1.13	1.68	2.89	2.78	1.82	0.08	−0.93
Per hour	2.24	2.11	2.96	0.51	1.96	2.37	3.36	3.17	2.50	0.77	0.00

Sources: Tables 2-2, 2-6, 2-7, and 2-8.

a. Based on data excluding work relief employees. When based on data including work relief employees, the growth rates of total actual national income are 2.23 percent in 1929–41 and 3.08 percent in 1941–48, the growth rates of actual national income per person employed are 0.90 percent in 1929–41 and 1.88 percent in 1941–48, and the growth rates of actual national income per hour are 1.97 percent in 1929–41 and 2.35 percent in 1941–48.

Table 3-1. Nonresidential Business: Indexes of Sector Labor Input, 1929, 1940–41, and 1947–82[a]
1972 = 100

Year	Employment (1)	Average weekly hours (2)	Total weekly hours (3)	Age-sex composition of total hours (4)	Efficiency of an hour's work as affected by changes in hours due to: Intra-group changes (5)	Specified intergroup shifts (6)	Amount of education (7)	Labor input (8)	Addendum: Effect of changes in hours (9)
1929	64.69	130.49	84.41	104.30	92.40	94.54	76.64	58.94	113.98
1940	64.00	117.34	75.10	105.91	98.04	94.53	82.79	61.03	108.75
1941	69.89	118.24	82.64	105.05	97.78	95.31	83.08	67.21	110.19
1947	78.44	113.39	88.95	104.78	98.63	96.57	85.42	75.83	108.00
1948	79.56	112.79	89.74	104.55	98.43	96.63	85.94	76.69	107.28
1949	76.87	111.38	85.62	104.50	98.98	96.35	86.69	73.97	106.22
1950	78.69	111.41	87.68	104.50	98.81	96.58	87.17	76.22	106.32
1951	81.82	111.36	91.12	104.70	98.66	97.08	87.48	79.94	106.66
1952	82.73	110.83	91.69	104.90	99.24	97.24	87.98	81.66	106.95
1953	83.93	110.22	92.51	105.10	99.29	97.47	88.45	83.23	106.67
1954	81.46	109.12	88.89	105.46	99.14	97.30	89.18	80.64	105.26
1955	83.23	109.56	91.18	105.13	99.30	97.57	89.55	83.17	106.15
1956	84.91	108.67	92.27	104.64	99.13	97.82	90.01	84.27	105.38
1957	84.72	107.03	90.68	104.56	99.53	97.96	90.60	83.75	104.35
1958	81.46	106.13	86.45	104.80	99.54	97.85	91.57	80.80	103.37
1959	83.41	106.78	89.07	104.54	99.55	98.11	92.10	83.76	104.29
1960	83.83	106.18	89.01	104.19	99.44	98.22	92.74	84.00	103.71
1961	82.99	105.60	87.63	104.28	99.58	98.25	93.50	83.59	103.32
1962	84.19	105.88	89.15	104.04	99.22	98.49	93.94	85.15	103.47
1963	84.66	105.66	89.45	104.13	98.94	98.80	94.34	85.90	103.29
1964	86.09	105.74	91.03	103.67	99.02	98.95	94.78	87.64	103.60
1965	88.66	105.97	93.95	102.97	98.78	99.18	95.36	90.38	103.82
1966	91.74	104.96	96.29	102.25	99.11	99.52	95.87	93.10	103.53
1967	93.02	103.38	96.17	102.24	99.52	99.66	96.54	94.15	102.53
1968	95.07	102.83	97.76	101.98	99.48	99.77	97.17	96.15	102.06
1969	98.03	102.19	100.17	101.22	99.55	99.86	97.72	98.50	101.59
1970	97.55	100.57	98.11	101.04	99.87	99.90	98.43	97.35	100.34
1971	97.20	100.11	97.30	100.87	99.85	99.93	99.30	97.25	99.89
1972	100.00	100.00	100.00	100.00	100.00	100.00	100.00	100.00	100.00
1973	104.69	99.57	104.23	99.16	100.19	100.09	100.83	104.50	99.85
1974	106.39	98.08	104.34	98.56	100.54	100.07	101.85	105.38	98.68
1975	103.13	97.02	100.05	99.03	100.57	99.97	103.02	102.62	97.54
1976	106.17	96.87	102.84	98.21	100.77	100.08	103.66	105.59	97.69
1977	110.52	96.58	106.74	97.56	100.85	100.13	104.20	109.57	97.53
1978	116.41	96.12	111.90	97.03	100.93	100.22	104.67	114.96	97.23
1979	120.84	95.55	115.46	96.77	101.02	100.22	105.40	119.23	96.74
1980	120.89	94.58	114.33	96.76	101.26	100.15	106.17	119.11	95.92
1981	122.08	94.05	114.81	96.78	101.45	100.25	106.72	120.60	95.65
1982	119.93	92.89	111.41	97.10	101.45	100.17	107.91	118.63	94.40

Sources: Column 1, table 2-7, column 3; column 2, table C-1, column 3; column 3, table C-1, columns 7–9; columns 4–6, see "Derivations" and *Slower Growth*; column 7, 1972–82, table F-5, column 5; column 7, 1929–71, *Slower Growth*, table F-5, column 5; column 8, product of columns 3, 4, 5, 6, and 7; column 9, product of columns 2, 5, and 6.

a. The series excluding and including Alaska and Hawaii were linked at 1960.

Table 3-2. Nonresidential Business: Indexes of Potential Sector Labor Input, 1929, 1940–41, and 1947–82[a]
Actual, 1972 = 100

| Year | Employment (1) | Average weekly hours (2) | Total weekly hours (3) | Age-sex composition of total hours (4) | Efficiency of an hour's work as affected by changes in hours due to: | | Amount of education (7) | Labor input (8) | Addendum: Effect of changes in hours (9) |
					Intra-group changes (5)	Specified intergroup shifts (6)			
1929	63.53	130.16	82.69	104.71	92.46	94.39	76.75	58.00	113.59
1940	75.73	116.36	88.12	103.75	98.04	95.78	82.23	70.59	109.27
1941	75.72	116.48	88.20	104.25	98.05	95.86	82.71	71.48	109.48
1947	78.05	113.65	88.70	105.00	98.53	96.52	85.42	75.66	108.08
1948	78.99	112.52	88.88	104.83	98.52	96.57	85.96	76.20	107.05
1949	79.76	111.41	88.86	104.05	99.02	96.61	86.50	76.51	106.58
1950	80.57	110.91	89.36	104.23	99.04	96.75	87.05	77.69	106.28
1951	80.42	110.87	89.16	105.15	98.79	96.97	87.52	78.60	106.21
1952	80.80	110.79	89.52	105.50	99.18	97.09	88.06	80.08	106.68
1953	81.74	110.31	90.17	105.75	99.20	97.30	88.55	81.50	106.47
1954	83.58	109.55	91.56	105.22	99.08	97.46	89.03	82.82	105.79
1955	83.56	109.33	91.36	105.20	99.44	97.62	89.51	83.51	106.13
1956	84.86	109.23	92.69	104.82	99.07	97.86	90.00	84.77	105.90
1957	84.90	107.95	91.65	104.70	99.40	98.00	90.56	84.65	105.16
1958	85.94	107.67	92.53	104.14	99.35	98.22	91.28	85.83	105.07
1959	85.69	107.45	92.07	104.26	99.49	98.28	91.95	86.30	105.06
1960	86.26	107.26	92.52	103.89	99.29	98.40	92.57	86.93	104.79
1961	87.45	106.56	93.19	103.61	99.48	98.54	93.22	88.23	104.46
1962	86.71	106.27	92.15	103.71	99.22	98.62	93.78	87.70	103.99
1963	87.44	105.60	92.34	103.71	99.05	98.94	94.17	88.38	103.49
1964	88.06	105.41	92.82	103.40	99.17	99.05	94.66	89.24	103.54
1965	89.43	105.36	94.22	102.91	98.97	99.21	95.30	90.73	103.45
1966	91.05	104.36	95.02	102.36	99.27	99.48	95.89	92.10	103.06
1967	92.67	103.26	95.69	102.29	99.56	99.65	96.56	93.77	102.45
1968	94.17	102.64	96.66	102.12	99.55	99.72	97.21	95.26	101.89
1969	96.95	102.58	99.45	101.44	99.47	99.81	97.76	97.91	101.84
1970	99.53	101.30	100.82	100.71	99.66	99.96	98.38	99.51	100.92
1971	101.42	100.38	101.81	100.10	99.69	100.06	99.20	100.84	100.13
1972	103.60	100.24	103.85	99.32	99.88	100.11	99.87	103.00	100.23
1973	106.61	99.91	106.51	98.83	100.06	100.15	100.73	106.26	100.12
1974	110.06	99.30	109.29	98.00	100.27	100.19	101.67	109.39	99.76
1975	113.69	97.41	110.74	97.46	100.45	100.33	102.48	111.47	98.17
1976	115.13	97.23	111.94	96.88	100.67	100.37	103.22	113.11	98.24
1977	118.07	96.78	114.27	96.43	100.82	100.37	103.83	115.78	97.93
1978	121.53	96.40	117.16	96.26	100.90	100.38	104.43	119.29	97.64
1979	125.42	96.06	120.48	96.14	100.95	100.36	105.19	123.44	97.32
1980	128.97	95.61	123.31	95.82	101.16	100.40	105.78	126.94	97.11
1981	131.52	94.89	124.80	95.67	101.41	100.52	106.27	129.34	96.73
1982	135.06	94.40	127.50	95.54	101.35	100.63	107.19	133.17	96.28

Sources: See "Derivations" and Slower Growth.
a. The series excluding and including Alaska and Hawaii were linked at 1960.

Table 3-4. Growth Rates of Potential and Actual Labor Input and Components, Nonresidential Business, Selected Periods, 1929–82

Percent a year

Basis and period	Employ-ment (1)	Average weekly hours (2)	Total weekly hours (3)	Age-sex composition of total hours (4)	Efficiency of an hour's work as affected by changes in hours due to: Intra-group changes (5)	Specified inter-group shifts (6)	Amount of educa-tion (7)	Labor input (8)	Addendum: Effect of changes in hours (9)
Potential labor input									
Longer periods									
1929–82	1.43	−0.60	0.82	−0.17	0.17	0.12	0.63	1.58	−0.31
1929–48	1.15	−0.76	0.38	0.01	0.33	0.12	0.60	1.45	−0.31
1948–73	1.21	−0.47	0.73	−0.24	0.06	0.15	0.64	1.34	−0.27
1973–82	2.66	−0.63	2.02	−0.38	0.14	0.05	0.69	2.54	−0.43
Shorter periods									
1929–41	1.47	−0.92	0.54	−0.04	0.49	0.13	0.63	1.76	−0.31
1941–48	0.61	−0.49	0.11	0.08	0.07	0.11	0.55	0.92	−0.32
1948–53	0.69	−0.40	0.29	0.17	0.14	0.15	0.60	1.35	−0.11
1953–64	0.68	−0.41	0.26	−0.20	0.00	0.16	0.61	0.83	−0.25
1964–73	2.15	−0.59	1.54	−0.50	0.10	0.12	0.69	1.96	−0.37
1973–79	2.75	−0.65	2.08	−0.46	0.15	0.03	0.72	2.53	−0.47
1979–82	2.50	−0.58	1.91	−0.21	0.13	0.09	0.63	2.56	−0.36
Actual labor input									
Longer periods									
1929–82	1.17	−0.64	0.53	−0.13	0.18	0.11	0.65	1.33	−0.35
1929–48	1.09	−0.76	0.32	0.01	0.33	0.12	0.60	1.40	−0.32
1948–73	1.10	−0.50	0.60	−0.21	0.07	0.14	0.64	1.25	−0.29
1973–82	1.52	−0.77	1.74	−0.23	0.14	0.01	0.76	1.42	−0.62
Shorter periods									
1929–41	0.64	−0.82	−0.18	0.06	0.47	0.07	0.67	1.10	−0.28
1941–48	1.87	−0.67	1.18	−0.07	0.09	0.20	0.48	1.90	−0.38
1948–53	1.08	−0.46	0.61	0.10	0.17	0.17	0.58	1.65	−0.11
1953–64	0.23	−0.38	−0.15	−0.12	−0.02	0.14	0.63	0.47	−0.27
1964–73	2.20	−0.67	1.52	−0.49	0.13	0.13	0.69	1.97	−0.41
1973–79	2.42	−0.68	1.72	−0.41	0.14	0.02	0.74	2.22	−0.53
1979–82	−0.25	−0.94	−1.18	0.11	0.14	−0.02	0.79	−0.17	−0.81

Sources: Computed from tables 3-1 and 3-2.

Table 3-5. Nonresidential Business: Average Hourly Earnings and Percentage Distribution of Total Hours and Earnings, by Sex and Age, Selected Years, 1929–82

Sex and age group	Hourly earnings as percentage of earnings of males 35–64			Percentage of total hours worked			Percentage of total earnings		
	1929–70[a] (1)	1970–75[a] (2)	1975–82[a] (3)	1948[b] (4)	1973[b] (5)	1982 (6)	1948[b] (7)	1973[b] (8)	1982 (9)
Male									
14–19	30	29	31	4.04	4.61	2.94	1.52	1.80	1.26
20–24	61	56	56	8.20	8.65	8.25	6.28	6.54	6.38
25–34	89	85	82	19.37	17.49	19.00	21.65	20.04	21.52
35–64	100	100	100	42.62	36.72	31.61	53.60	49.53	43.65
65 and over	66	66	75	3.52	1.83	1.51	2.92	1.63	1.56
Female									
14–19	29	26	28	2.08	2.74	2.21	0.76	0.96	0.85
20–24	47	44	44	3.84	5.31	6.16	2.27	3.15	3.74
25–34	54	54	54	5.33	6.55	10.84	3.62	4.77	8.08
35–64	54	54	54	10.42	15.31	16.76	7.08	11.14	12.51
65 and over	41	41	45	0.58	0.79	0.72	0.30	0.44	0.45
Total	. . .	. . .	. . .	100.00	100.00	100.00	100.00	100.00	100.00

Sources: See "Derivations" and *Slower Growth*, appendix D.
a. Refers to periods during which these percentages are used as weights.
b. Percentages adjusted to comparability with 1982 by use of 1966 and 1981 overlaps. See table 3-6.

Table 3-6. Nonresidential Business: Percentage Distribution of Total Hours Worked, by Sex and Age, Selected Years, 1929–82[a]

Year[b]	Males (by age group)						Females (by age group)					
	Total	14–19	20–24	25–34	35–64	65 and over	Total	14–19	20–24	25–34	35–64	65 and over
1929	83.48	6.15	10.89	20.63	42.41	3.40	16.52	2.56	3.74	3.99	5.88	0.35
1941	80.82	4.35	10.10	20.55	42.47	3.35	19.18	1.63	4.13	5.23	7.80	0.39
1948	77.75	4.01	8.04	19.06	43.04	3.59	22.25	2.01	3.71	5.25	10.73	0.55
1953	75.71	3.61	5.34	19.22	43.92	3.62	24.29	1.86	3.25	5.45	13.04	0.70
1964	73.33	3.57	7.18	15.92	44.11	2.56	26.67	1.84	3.64	4.48	15.89	0.82
1966[c]	72.04	4.19	7.12	15.60	42.66	2.47	27.96	2.30	3.96	4.74	16.15	0.81
1966[d]	72.00	4.24	7.14	15.58	42.64	2.41	28.00	2.40	4.03	4.70	16.03	0.84
1973	69.27	4.63	8.51	17.16	37.12	1.84	30.73	2.77	5.25	6.43	15.48	0.79
1974	68.63	4.63	8.71	17.43	36.04	1.82	31.37	2.86	5.46	6.90	15.46	0.69
1975	68.48	4.43	8.24	17.36	36.67	1.77	31.52	2.66	5.51	7.30	15.33	0.72
1976	67.66	4.20	8.76	18.24	34.79	1.68	32.34	2.75	5.68	7.79	15.42	0.69
1977	67.01	4.37	8.92	18.10	34.03	1.59	32.99	2.85	5.89	8.29	15.27	0.68
1978	66.15	4.32	8.92	18.10	33.20	1.61	33.85	2.88	6.05	8.71	15.54	0.67
1979	65.55	4.12	9.01	18.23	32.61	1.59	34.45	2.85	6.17	9.10	15.66	0.68
1980	64.54	3.83	8.53	18.28	32.37	1.54	35.46	2.71	6.20	9.72	16.14	0.69
1981[e]	64.07	3.46	8.49	18.77	31.83	1.52	35.93	2.48	6.23	10.18	16.33	0.71
1981[f]	64.11	3.44	8.63	19.10	31.43	1.51	35.89	2.45	6.29	10.30	16.15	0.71
1982	63.31	2.94	8.25	19.00	31.61	1.51	36.69	2.21	6.16	10.84	16.76	0.72

Sources: See "Derivations" and *Slower Growth*, appendix D.
a. Distributions are based on hours worked by civilians other than wage and salary workers employed in government or private households.
b. See *Accounting for Growth*, table F-5, for comparable estimates for 1940, 1947, 1949–52, and 1954–60. See *Slower Growth* for comparable estimates for 1961–63, 1965, and 1967–72.
c. Distributions comparable to preceding years.
d. Distributions comparable to 1967–81.
e. Distributions comparable to 1966–80.
f. Distributions comparable to 1982.

Table 3-7. Wage and Salary Workers in Nonfarm Business: Employment and Hours by Sex and Full-Time or Part-Time Status, 1966–82[a]

Year[b]	Employment (thousands)				Total weekly hours (millions)				Average weekly hours			
	Males		Females		Males		Females		Males		Females	
	Full-time (1)	Part-time (2)	Full-time (3)	Part-time (4)	Full-time (5)	Part-time (6)	Full-time (7)	Part-time (8)	Full-time (9)	Part-time (10)	Full-time (11)	Part-time (12)
1966	29,626	2,882	13,038	3,577	1,264.50	48.22	499.96	66.53	42.7	16.7	38.3	18.6
1967	29,936	2,945	13.360	3,904	1,263.41	49.07	504.65	72.28	42.2	16.7	37.8	18.5
1968	30,560	2,983	13,818	4,234	1,284.46	49.65	519.52	77.41	42.0	16.6	37.6	18.3
1969	30,984	3,236	14,584	4,610	1,301.69	55.06	548.77	84.24	42.0	17.0	37.6	18.3
1970	30,461	3,417	14,375	4,991	1,264.02	61.70	536.18	89.46	41.5	18.1	37.3	17.9
1971	30,259	3,486	14,145	5,111	1,251.36	62.25	525.09	93.19	41.4	17.9	37.1	18.2
1972	31,118	3,561	14,745	5,317	1,293.38	60.62	549.70	95.92	41.6	17.0	37.3	18.0
1973	32,582	3,672	15,671	5,736	1,351.48	63.09	582.15	102.54	41.5	17.2	37.2	17.9
1974	32,548	3,807	16,121	6,097	1,329.10	67.46	593.70	110.82	40.8	17.7	36.8	18.2
1975	30,684	4,009	15,549	6,291	1,244.31	74.21	570.58	114.22	40.5	18.5	36.6	18.1
1976	31,702	3,938	16,383	6,484	1,285.99	69.06	601.57	117.12	40.6	17.5	36.7	18.1
1977	32,839	4,123	17,388	6,712	1,326.16	73.28	635.02	121.87	40.4	17.8	36.5	18.2
1978	34,428	4,136	18,845	7,162	1,376.93	72.82	691.20	127.78	40.0	17.6	36.7	17.8
1979	35,422	4,221	19,953	7,505	1,410.48	76.00	722.17	133.63	39.8	18.0	36.2	17.8
1980	34,421	4,497	20,157	7,816	1,363.86	79.09	729.21	141.11	39.6	17.6	36.2	18.1
1981	34,946	4,060	20,605	8,077	1,363.06	79.76	741.34	146.78	39.0	19.6	36.0	18.2
1982	32,812	4,827	20,191	8,388	1,288.51	88.93	726.54	149.81	39.3	18.4	36.0	17.9

Sources: See "Derivations" and *Slower Growth*, appendix E.
a. Tables 2-7 and C-1 provide combined data for the four groups of workers.
b. See *Slower Growth*, table 3-7, for earlier years and "Derivations" for comment on comparability.

Table 3-8. Nonfarm Self-Employed and Unpaid Family Workers: Employment and Hours by Sex and Full-Time or Part-Time Status, 1966–82[a]

	Employment (thousands)				Total weekly hours (millions)				Average weekly hours			
	Males		Females		Males		Females		Males		Females	
	Full-time	Part-time	Full-time	Part-time	Full-time	Part-time	Full-time	Part-time	Full-time	Part-time	Full-time	Part-time
Year[b]	(1)	(2)	(3)	(4)	(5)	(6)	(7)	(8)	(9)	(10)	(11)	(12)
1966	3,578	523	1,080	709	194.87	8.41	55.06	12.76	54.5	16.1	51.0	18.0
1967	3,538	522	1,053	710	189.46	8.35	54.34	12.62	53.6	16.0	51.6	17.8
1968	3,525	519	1,032	674	189.08	8.56	54.09	11.68	53.6	16.5	52.4	17.3
1969	3,601	567	1,072	716	192.29	9.51	54.92	12.32	53.4	16.8	51.2	17.2
1970	3,513	625	1,047	735	185.94	10.48	53.36	12.83	52.9	16.8	51.0	17.5
1971	3,525	661	1,062	772	186.90	10.86	54.76	13.31	53.0	16.4	51.6	17.3
1972	3,529	670	1,063	809	185.20	11.38	54.34	14.05	52.5	17.0	51.1	17.4
1973	3,597	641	1,106	828	187.60	11.13	55.91	14.00	52.2	17.4	50.6	16.9
1974	3,658	733	1,101	844	188.06	12.44	55.34	14.46	51.4	17.0	50.3	17.1
1975	3,577	828	1,078	863	183.14	14.66	53.78	14.78	51.2	17.7	49.9	17.1
1976	3,621	768	1,099	886	185.16	13.11	53.26	15.25	51.1	17.1	48.5	17.2
1977	3,810	768	1,209	955	193.38	13.38	58.94	16.84	50.8	17.4	48.8	17.6
1978	4,016	774	1,300	1,000	203.61	13.54	63.96	16.70	50.7	17.5	49.2	16.7
1979	4,169	809	1,373	1,083	209.67	14.43	66.09	18.46	50.3	17.8	48.1	17.0
1980	4,165	937	1,424	1,088	205.85	17.59	68.95	18.53	49.4	18.8	48.4	17.0
1981	4,144	952	1,416	1,181	204.05	17.69	68.15	19.74	49.2	18.6	48.1	16.7
1982	4,078	1,091	1,437	1,304	202.06	19.95	69.19	21.49	49.5	18.3	48.1	16.5

Sources: See "Derivations" and *Slower Growth*, appendix G.
a. Tables 2-7 and C-1 provide combined data for the four groups of workers.
b. See *Slower Growth*, table 3-8, for earlier years and "Derivations" for comment on comparability.

Table 3-9. Farm Workers: Employment and Hours by Sex and Full-Time or Part-Time Status, 1966–82[a]

	Employment (thousands)				Total weekly hours (millions)				Average weekly hours			
	Males		Females		Males		Females		Males		Females	
	Full-time	Part-time	Full-time	Part-time	Full-time	Part-time	Full-time	Part-time	Full-time	Part-time	Full-time	Part-time
Year[b]	(1)	(2)	(3)	(4)	(5)	(6)	(7)	(8)	(9)	(10)	(11)	(12)
1966	2,448	626	351	343	136.28	11.06	16.80	6.83	55.7	17.7	47.9	19.9
1967	2,340	653	313	328	130.45	11.48	14.91	6.56	55.8	17.6	47.6	20.0
1968	2,308	646	317	301	129.38	10.84	15.25	6.21	56.1	16.8	48.1	20.6
1969	2,189	632	309	309	123.05	10.70	15.24	6.34	56.2	16.9	49.3	20.5
1970	2,108	647	299	282	118.80	10.82	14.85	5.88	56.4	16.7	49.7	20.9
1971	2,025	657	290	287	115.95	11.23	14.13	5.93	57.3	17.1	48.7	20.7
1972	2.057	609	291	304	115.18	10.30	13.73	6.18	56.0	16.9	47.2	20.4
1973	2,071	587	303	281	114.06	9.77	14.59	5.72	55.1	16.6	48.1	20.4
1974	2,092	608	291	265	113.50	10.47	13.96	5.33	54.3	17.2	48.0	20.1
1975	2,037	612	296	254	111.67	10.34	14.42	5.13	54.8	16.9	48.7	20.2
1976	1,983	609	292	259	108.80	10.33	13.52	5.16	54.9	17.0	46.3	19.9
1977	1,910	537	296	269	105.02	9.06	14.06	5.44	55.0	16.9	47.5	20.2
1978	1,842	505	326	256	100.89	8.59	15.81	4.97	54.8	17.0	48.5	19.4
1979	1,870	450	334	233	103.54	7.73	15.72	4.62	55.4	17.2	47.1	19.8
1980	1,874	503	319	258	102.02	8.76	15.27	5.19	54.4	17.4	47.9	20.1
1981	1,808	467	322	240	98.23	8.43	14.92	4.74	54.3	18.0	46.3	19.7
1982	1,694	488	301	231	91.14	8.53	14.32	4.46	53.8	17.5	47.6	19.3

Sources: See "Derivations" and *Slower Growth*, appendix E.
a. Tables 2-7 and C-1 provide combined data for the four groups of workers.
b. See *Slower Growth*, table 3-9, for earlier years and "Derivations" for comment on comparability.

Table 3-10. Percentage Distribution of Persons Employed in the Business Sector, by Sex and Years of School Completed, Full-Time Equivalent Basis, Survey Dates, 1976–83[a]

Years of school completed	March 1976 (1)	March 1977 (2)	March 1978 (3)	March 1979 (4)	March 1980[b] (5)	March 1981[b] (6)	March 1982 (7)	March 1983 (8)
Males								
Total	100.00	100.00	100.00	100.00	100.00	100.00	100.00	100.00
No school years completed	0.32	0.32	0.30	0.27	0.24	0.24	0.22	0.22
Elementary, 1–4	1.65	1.62	1.54	1.36	1.27	1.25	1.13	1.16
Elementary, 5–7	4.65	4.24	4.21	3.73	3.44	3.43	3.40	2.90
Elementary, 8	6.36	6.15	5.67	5.45	5.12	4.67	4.05	3.88
High school, 1–3	15.68	15.55	15.30	14.36	14.14	13.50	12.75	12.00
High school, 4	38.80	38.58	38.43	39.22	39.08	39.55	39.68	38.71
College, 1–3	15.69	16.16	16.96	17.30	17.55	17.49	17.57	18.11
College, 4	10.00	10.10	10.21	10.52	10.91	11.53	11.95	12.44
College, 5 or more	6.85	7.28	7.38	7.79	8.25	8.34	9.25	10.58
Females								
Total	100.00	100.00	100.00	100.00	100.00	100.00	100.00	100.00
No school years completed	0.26	0.23	0.25	0.23	0.18	0.20	0.16	0.17
Elementary, 1–4	0.72	0.67	0.68	0.62	0.52	0.55	0.48	0.48
Elementary, 5–7	2.75	2.72	2.51	2.44	2.18	2.09	1.92	1.67
Elementary, 8	4.92	4.24	4.25	3.63	3.44	3.01	2.79	2.55
High school, 1–3	15.97	15.56	15.16	14.29	13.40	12.59	12.32	10.90
High school, 4	49.88	49.94	49.56	49.59	49.92	50.00	49.54	48.82
College, 1–3	16.28	16.71	17.60	18.59	18.68	19.56	19.71	20.85
College, 4	6.42	6.84	6.80	7.08	7.77	8.14	8.68	9.52
College, 5 or more	2.80	3.09	3.19	3.53	3.91	3.86	4.40	5.04

Sources: See "Derivations" and *Slower Growth*.
Note: Similar distributions for seventeen earlier dates appear in *Accounting for Growth*, table I-15, p. 244, and *Slower Growth*, table 3-10, p. 43.
a. Distributions are for persons 16 years of age and over.
b. There is a slight incomparability between 1980 and 1981 data. See "Derivations."

Table 4-1. Nonresidential Business: Capital Stock Values in Constant Prices and Indexes, 1929, 1940–41, and 1947–82[a]
Values in billions of 1972 dollars; indexes, 1972 = 100

| | Inventories | | Nonresidential structures and equipment | | | | | |
| | | | Values | | Ratio of net stock to gross stock | Indexes | | |
Year	Value (1)	Index (2)	Gross stock (3)	Net stock (4)	(5)	Gross stock (6)	Net stock (7)	Weighted average (8)
1929	91.6	33.66	599.8	319.1	0.532	42.15	38.49	41.19
1940	90.2	33.15	555.9	258.9	0.466	39.07	31.23	36.94
1941	99.2	36.44	557.2	261.8	0.470	39.16	31.58	37.11
1947	116.2	42.70	581.7	283.7	0.488	40.88	34.22	39.10
1948	118.8	43.68	612.1	310.3	0.507	43.02	37.42	41.55
1949	119.4	43.88	635.7	329.9	0.519	44.68	39.80	43.40
1950	122.4	45.00	656.9	345.4	0.526	46.17	41.66	45.00
1951	134.6	49.45	681.3	362.1	0.531	47.88	43.67	46.79
1952	144.0	52.94	706.1	377.7	0.535	49.62	45.55	48.58
1953	147.0	54.01	731.0	392.8	0.537	51.37	47.38	50.34
1954	146.1	53.69	755.6	407.3	0.539	53.10	49.12	52.08
1955	148.9	54.72	781.1	422.0	0.540	54.90	50.91	53.87
1956	155.7	57.22	808.9	439.8	0.544	56.85	53.05	55.88
1957	159.4	58.56	836.7	452.9	0.541	58.80	54.63	57.74
1958	159.2	58.51	859.6	467.3	0.544	60.41	56.36	59.38
1959	161.8	59.46	879.6	481.8	0.548	61.82	58.11	60.88
1960	167.0	61.39	902.4	494.9	0.548	63.42	59.69	62.48
1961	170.3	62.59	925.4	508.2	0.549	65.04	61.29	64.09
1962	175.8	64.59	948.5	522.4	0.551	66.66	63.01	65.74
1963	183.4	67.42	976.5	539.2	0.552	68.63	65.02	67.72
1964	190.8	70.10	1,007.4	559.5	0.555	70.80	67.48	69.96
1965	200.2	73.58	1,047.3	588.1	0.562	73.60	70.93	72.94
1966	214.5	78.83	1,097.5	625.4	0.570	77.13	75.43	76.71
1967	229.0	84.16	1,150.2	663.1	0.576	80.83	79.97	80.63
1968	239.6	88.06	1,202.8	698.2	0.580	84.53	84.21	84.46
1969	249.6	91.73	1,260.0	735.3	0.584	88.55	88.69	88.60
1970	257.0	94.45	1,317.6	770.8	0.585	92.60	97.97	92.70
1971	263.0	96.64	1,369.9	799.9	0.584	96.27	96.48	96.33
1972	272.1	100.00	1,422.9	829.1	0.583	100.00	100.00	100.00
1973	285.8	105.03	1,487.4	868.0	0.584	104.53	104.70	104.57
1974	300.2	110.33	1,557.9	911.0	0.585	109.49	109.88	109.59
1975	302.6	111.21	1,617.2	941.4	0.582	113.66	113.54	113.63
1976	303.1	111.39	1,668.2	962.9	0.577	117.24	116.13	116.96
1977	313.6	115.27	1,726.0	989.9	0.574	121.30	119.40	120.82
1978	328.3	120.65	1,797.2	1,028.3	0.572	126.30	124.03	125.73
1979	340.0	124.94	1,878.9	1,075.2	0.572	132.04	129.68	131.45
1980	341.4	125.47	1,959.7	1.119.8	0.571	137.72	135.06	137.06
1981	343.4	126.22	2,039.5	1,162.0	0.570	143.33	140.16	142.53
1982	343.0	126.06	2,114.5	1,198.4	0.567	148.60	144.54	147.58

Sources: Column 1, NIPA, table 5.11, except that 1929–41 was extrapolated from 1947 by corresponding data in *Slower Growth* (see "Derivations"); column 2, computed from column 1; columns 3 and 4, which include private nonhousekeeping residential capital and exclude capital of nonprofit institutions, provided by the Bureau of Economic Analysis; column 5, the ratio of column 4 to column 3; columns 6 and 7, computed from columns 3 and 4; column 8, derived from annual percentage changes in column 3 (weighted 3) and column 4 (weighted 1).

a. Indexes are computed from capital stock data in millions of dollars. The values have been rounded to a tenth of a billion. All data are averages of values at the start and end of the year.

Table 4-2. Growth Rates of Capital Input in the Nonresidential Business Sector, Selected Periods, 1929–82

Percent a year

Period	Total capital input		Capital input per person employed		Capital input per person potentially employed	
	Inventories (1)	Nonresidential structures and equipment (2)	Inventories (3)	Nonresidential structures and equipment (4)	Inventories (5)	Nonresidential structures and equipment (6)
Longer						
1929–82	2.52	2.44	1.34	1.25	1.07	0.99
1929–48	1.38	0.05	0.28	−1.04	−0.23	−1.10
1948–73	3.71	3.76	2.44	2.63	2.34	2.57
1973–82	2.05	3.90	0.52	2.34	−0.60	1.21
Shorter						
1929–41	0.66	−0.87	0.02	−1.50	−0.80	−2.31
1941–48	2.62	1.63	0.74	−0.24	2.01	1.01
1948–53	4.34	3.91	3.23	2.81	3.63	3.21
1953–64	2.40	3.04	2.16	2.80	1.71	2.34
1964–73	4.59	4.57	2.35	2.32	2.40	2.37
1973–79	2.94	3.89	0.50	1.43	0.19	1.11
1979–82	0.30	3.93	0.55	4.20	−2.15	1.40

Sources: Computed from tables 2-6, 2-7, and 4-1.

Table 4-3. U.S. Aggregate Saving and Investment Ratios, 1948–83[a]

	Percent of gross national product			Percent of net national product					Real net private domestic investment as percent of real net national product (1972 prices)
Year	Gross private saving (1)	Government surplus (2)	Gross national saving and gross private investment[b] (3)	Net private saving (4)	Government surplus (5)	Net national saving and net national investment[b] (6)	Net foreign investment (7)	Net private domestic investment (8)	(9)
1948	15.6	3.2	18.8	8.5	3.5	12.0	1.0	11.0	9.9
1949	15.2	−1.3	13.9	7.4	−1.4	6.0	0.4	5.6	5.4
1950	15.2	2.8	18.0	7.6	3.1	10.6	−0.7	11.3	10.1
1951	15.9	1.8	17.8	8.4	2.0	10.4	0.3	10.1	8.7
1952	16.0	−1.1	14.9	8.3	−1.2	7.1	0.2	6.9	6.2
1953	15.8	−1.9	13.9	8.0	−2.1	6.0	−0.4	6.3	5.9
1954	16.1	−2.0	14.2	7.9	−2.1	5.8	0.1	5.7	5.3
1955	16.3	0.8	17.1	8.3	0.9	9.2	0.1	9.0	8.1
1956	16.5	1.2	17.7	8.1	1.4	9.4	0.7	8.7	7.7
1957	16.6	0.2	16.8	7.9	0.2	8.2	1.2	7.0	6.3
1958	16.8	−2.8	14.0	7.8	−3.1	4.7	0.2	4.5	4.4
1959	16.2	−0.3	15.9	7.7	−0.4	7.4	−0.3	7.6	7.2
1960	15.1	0.6	15.7	6.6	0.7	7.3	0.6	6.7	6.4
1961	15.8	−0.8	15.0	7.4	−0.9	6.5	0.8	5.7	5.6
1962	16.2	−0.7	15.6	8.3	−0.7	7.5	0.7	6.9	6.7
1963	15.7	0.1	15.9	7.9	0.1	8.0	0.8	7.2	7.2
1964	16.7	−0.4	16.3	9.1	−0.4	8.8	1.2	7.6	7.6
1965	17.2	0.1	17.3	9.9	0.1	10.0	0.9	9.1	9.1
1966	17.1	−0.2	17.0	9.9	−0.2	9.7	0.4	9.3	9.2
1967	17.5	−1.8	15.7	10.1	−1.9	8.1	0.4	7.8	7.8
1968	16.1	−0.7	15.4	8.6	−0.7	7.8	0.1	7.8	7.8
1969	15.0	1.1	16.0	7.1	1.1	8.3	0.0	8.2	8.2
1970	15.9	−1.1	14.9	7.7	−1.2	6.6	0.4	6.3	6.4
1971	17.0	−1.8	15.2	8.8	−2.0	6.9	−0.1	6.9	7.0
1972	16.1	−0.3	15.9	7.8	−0.3	7.6	−0.5	8.1	8.1
1973	17.2	0.6	17.8	9.2	0.6	9.9	0.5	9.3	9.3
1974	16.5	−0.3	16.0	7.7	−0.4	7.2	0.2	7.0	6.9
1975	18.5	−4.1	14.3	9.1	−4.6	4.5	1.3	3.2	2.9
1976	17.3	−2.1	15.2	7.9	−2.4	5.5	0.3	5.2	4.9
1977	17.1	−0.9	16.2	7.7	−1.0	6.7	−0.8	7.4	6.8
1978	17.2	0.0	17.3	7.7	0.0	7.8	−0.7	8.5	7.8
1979	16.8	0.6	17.4	7.0	0.7	7.7	−0.1	7.8	7.0
1980	16.6	−1.2	15.5	6.1	−1.3	4.9	0.3	4.6	4.4
1981	17.4	−0.9	16.5	7.0	−1.0	6.0	0.2	5.8	5.4
1982	17.1	−3.8	13.3	6.1	−4.3	1.8	−0.2	2.1	2.5
1983	17.3	−4.1	13.2	6.7	−4.6	2.1	−1.2	3.2	3.9

Sources: Computed from NIPA, tables 1.1, 1.2, 1.7, 1.8, and 5.1. Incorporates data from July 1984 *Survey of Current Business*.

a. Ratios computed from data in which gross and net national product, gross and net investment, and net private domestic investment have been reduced, and gross and net private saving raised, by half the value of the statistical discrepancy in the NIPA.

b. Percentages shown are for gross and net investment. Percentages for gross and net saving are the same except in 1970–72, 1974, and 1979–81, when there is a difference, never exceeding 0.2 percentage points, because total saving includes capital grants received by the United States (net), which are not shown.

Table 4-4. Derivation of the Effect of Changes in Average Age on the Growth Rate of National Income in Nonresidential Business According to an Extreme Vintage Model, Selected Periods, 1948–82

	Longer periods		Shorter periods				
Item	1948–73	1973–82	1948–53	1953–64	1964–73	1973–79	1979–82
1. Change in ratio of net stock to gross stock, in percentage points	0.077	−0.017	0.030	0.018	0.028	−0.011	−0.006
2. Decline in average age of capital, in years (with composition held constant)	1.84	−0.41	0.73	0.43	0.68	−0.27	−0.13
3. Annual decline in average age of capital, in years	0.07	−0.04	0.15	0.04	0.08	−0.04	−0.04
4. Effect on growth rate of output, in percentage points	0.10	−0.06	0.20	0.05	0.11	−0.06	−0.06

Sources: Row 1, calculated from table 4-1, column 5 (based on unrounded ratios); row 2, row 1 times 24-year service life; row 3, row 2 divided by length of period; row 4 equals row 3 times the contribution of advances in knowledge and determinants not elsewhere classified (n.e.c.) to the nonresidential business growth rate in 1948–73, estimated at 1.4 percent a year.

Table 4-6. Nonresidential Business: Indexes of Sector National Income, Sector Inputs, and Sector National Income per Unit of Total Factor Input, 1929, 1940–41, and 1947–82, Actual and Potential Basis[a]
Actual, 1972 = 100

Year	Actual sector national income in 1972 prices (1)	Potential sector national income in 1972 prices (2)	Actual labor (3)	Potential labor (4)	Inventories (5)	Nonresidential structures and equipment (6)	All reproducible capital (7)	Land (8)	Actual total factor input (9)	Potential total factor input (10)	Actual sector national income per unit of input (11)	Potential sector national income per unit of input (12)	Potential discrepancy factor (13)
1929	28.07	27.43	58.94	58.00	33.66	41.19	38.48	100.00	56.27	55.51	49.88	49.24	100.35
1940	28.89	33.22	61.03	70.59	33.15	36.94	35.49	100.00	57.12	64.08	50.58	52.81	98.17
1941	34.69	35.34	67.21	71.48	36.44	37.11	36.70	100.00	62.00	65.09	55.95	54.94	98.82
1947	41.73	42.30	75.83	75.66	42.70	39.10	40.12	100.00	69.20	69.08	60.26	61.16	100.12
1948	44.37	43.67	76.69	76.20	43.68	41.55	42.07	100.00	70.37	70.03	63.05	62.38	99.97
1949	43.02	44.47	73.97	76.51	43.88	43.40	43.39	100.00	68.80	70.63	62.53	63.34	99.40
1950	47.23	46.75	76.22	77.69	45.00	45.00	44.84	100.00	70.84	71.89	66.67	65.32	99.56
1951	50.11	48.28	79.94	78.60	49.45	46.79	47.45	100.00	74.27	73.28	67.47	65.85	100.05
1952	51.70	50.95	81.66	80.08	52.94	48.58	49.76	100.00	76.13	74.96	67.91	67.82	100.22
1953	53.97	53.43	83.23	81.50	54.01	50.34	51.32	100.00	77.69	76.40	69.47	69.79	100.21
1954	52.47	54.61	80.64	82.82	53.69	52.08	52.48	100.00	76.03	77.67	69.01	70.53	99.69
1955	56.95	56.34	83.17	83.51	54.72	53.87	54.05	100.00	78.31	78.56	72.72	71.84	99.83
1956	58.32	59.21	84.27	84.77	57.22	55.88	56.20	100.00	79.63	80.01	73.24	74.10	99.87
1957	58.65	60.39	83.75	84.65	58.56	57.74	57.91	100.00	79.61	80.29	73.67	75.31	99.87
1958	57.26	62.81	80.80	85.83	58.51	59.38	59.10	100.00	77.56	81.45	73.83	77.54	99.45
1959	61.92	64.31	83.76	86.30	59.46	60.88	60.46	100.00	80.16	82.09	77.25	78.58	99.70
1960	62.68	66.31	84.00	86.93	61.39	62.48	62.14	100.00	80.68	82.92	77.69	80.21	99.70
1961	63.56	68.24	83.59	88.23	62.59	64.09	63.65	100.00	80.65	84.23	78.81	81.41	99.52
1962	67.32	69.50	85.15	87.70	64.59	65.74	65.39	100.00	82.20	84.17	81.90	82.85	99.66
1963	70.35	71.71	85.90	88.38	67.42	67.72	67.59	100.00	83.22	85.14	84.53	84.52	99.65
1964	74.82	75.00	87.64	89.24	70.10	69.96	69.95	100.00	85.03	86.28	87.99	87.22	99.66
1965	80.19	78.58	90.38	90.73	73.58	72.94	73.05	100.00	87.77	88.06	91.36	89.45	99.75
1966	84.84	82.55	93.10	92.10	78.83	76.71	77.21	100.00	90.69	89.95	93.55	91.81	99.96
1967	86.16	85.60	94.15	93.77	84.16	80.63	81.49	100.00	92.33	92.06	93.32	93.01	99.97
1968	90.47	89.57	96.15	95.26	88.06	84.46	85.34	100.00	94.60	93.93	95.63	95.34	100.02
1969	92.78	94.00	98.50	97.91	91.73	88.60	89.36	100.00	97.15	96.72	95.50	97.16	100.03
1970	91.06	96.97	97.35	99.51	94.45	92.70	93.12	100.00	96.83	98.61	94.04	98.46	99.87
1971	93.65	99.80	97.25	100.84	96.64	96.33	96.41	100.00	97.23	100.19	96.32	99.81	99.88
1972	100.00	105.59	100.00	103.00	100.00	100.00	100.00	100.00	100.00	102.47	100.00	103.18	99.87
1973	106.99	111.62	104.50	106.26	105.03	104.57	104.69	100.00	104.34	105.79	102.54	105.65	99.87
1974	103.78	114.63	105.38	109.39	110.33	109.59	109.78	100.00	105.74	109.05	98.15	105.18	99.94
1975	100.61	113.54	102.62	111.47	111.21	113.63	113.01	100.00	103.86	111.19	96.87	102.46	99.66
1976	107.49	118.49	105.59	113.11	111.39	116.96	115.55	100.00	106.66	112.88	100.78	105.28	99.71
1977	115.05	123.87	109.57	115.78	115.27	120.82	119.42	100.00	110.47	115.60	104.15	107.44	99.73
1978	121.70	128.89	114.96	119.29	120.65	125.73	124.45	100.00	115.60	119.16	105.28	108.31	99.87
1979	124.09	133.47	119.23	123.44	124.94	131.45	129.81	100.00	119.83	123.28	103.56	108.38	99.89
1980	121.51	137.09	119.11	126.94	125.47	137.06	134.09	100.00	120.26	126.73	101.04	108.33	99.86
1981	124.96	139.46	120.60	129.34	126.22	142.53	138.41	100.00	122.02	129.26	102.41	108.03	99.87
1982	119.75	141.38	118.63	133.17	126.06	147.58	142.08	100.00	120.79	132.90	99.14	106.53	99.86

Sources: Column 1, table 2-6, column 5; column 2, table 2-8, column 2; column 3, table 3-1, column 8; column 4, table 3-2, column 8; columns 5 and 6, table 4-1, columns 2 and 8; columns 7–10, see *Slower Growth;* column 11, quotient of columns 1 and 9; column 12, table 5-2, column 1; column 13, column 2 divided by (columns 10 times 12).

a. Series excluding and including Alaska and Hawaii are linked at 1960.

Table 4-7. Nonresidential Business: Growth Rates on Actual and Potential Basis of National Income, Inputs, and National Income per Unit of Total Factor Input, Selected Periods, 1929–82
Percent a year

| Period | Actual sector national income in 1972 prices (1) | Potential sector national income in 1972 prices (2) | Indexes of inputs | | | | | | | | Actual sector national income per unit of input (11) | Potential sector national income per unit of input (12) | Potential discrepancy factor (13) |
			Actual labor (3)	Potential labor (4)	Inventories (5)	Nonresidential structures and equipment (6)	All reproducible capital (7)	Land (8)	Actual total factor input (9)	Potential total factor input (10)			
Longer													
1929–82	2.77	3.14	1.33	1.58	2.52	2.44	2.50	0.00	1.45	1.66	1.30	1.47	−0.01
1929–48	2.44	2.48	1.40	1.45	1.38	0.05	0.47	0.00	1.18	1.23	1.24	1.25	−0.02
1948–73	3.58	3.82	1.25	1.34	3.71	3.76	3.71	0.00	1.59	1.66	1.96	2.13	0.00
1973–82	1.26	2.66	1.42	2.54	2.05	3.90	3.45	0.00	1.64	2.57	−0.37	0.09	0.00
Shorter													
1929–48	1.78	2.13	1.10	1.76	0.66	−0.87	−0.39	0.00	0.81	1.34	0.96	0.92	−0.13
1941–48	3.58	3.07	1.90	0.92	2.62	1.63	1.97	0.00	1.83	1.05	1.72	1.83	0.17
1948–53	4.00	4.12	1.65	1.35	4.34	3.91	4.05	0.00	2.00	1.76	1.96	2.27	0.03
1953–64	3.01	3.13	0.47	0.83	2.40	3.04	2.86	0.00	0.82	1.11	2.17	2.05	−0.05
1964–73	4.05	4.52	1.97	1.96	4.59	4.57	4.58	0.00	2.30	2.29	1.71	2.15	0.02
1973–79	2.50	3.02	2.22	2.53	2.94	3.89	3.65	0.00	2.33	2.58	0.17	0.43	0.00
1979–82	−1.18	1.94	−0.17	2.56	0.30	3.93	3.06	0.00	0.27	2.54	−1.44	−0.57	−0.01

Source: Computed from table 4-6.

Table 5-1. Nonresidential Business: Indexes of Sector Output per Unit of Input, 1929, 1940–41, and 1947–82

1972 = 100

| | | | | | | | | Effects of irregular factors | | | | |
| | | Gains from reallocation of resources from: | | Effects of changes in legal and human environment | | | | Changes in intensity of utilization of employed resources resulting from: | | Other determinants | | |
Year	Output per unit of input (1)	Farming (2)	Nonfarm self employment (3)	Pollution abatement (4)	Employee safety and health (5)	Dishonesty and crime (6)	Effect of weather on farm output (7)	Work stoppages (8)	Fluctuations in intensity of demand[a] (9)	Total (semiresidual) (10)	Economies of scale (11)	Advances in knowledge and miscellaneous (residual) (12)
1929	49.88	88.37	97.12	100.49	100.12	100.33	100.15	100.04	103.57	55.49	86.38	64.24
1940	50.58	89.22	96.63	100.49	100.12	100.33	99.32	100.03	102.52	57.06	87.64	65.11
1941	55.95	90.76	97.45	100.49	100.12	100.33	99.88	99.99	106.56	58.89	88.05	66.88
1947	60.26	93.70	97.49	100.49	100.12	100.33	99.56	99.96	101.22	64.87	90.58	71.62
1948	63.05	93.96	97.47	100.49	100.12	100.33	100.04	99.97	103.82	65.69	90.95	72.23
1949	62.53	93.75	97.16	100.49	100.12	100.33	99.85	99.92	102.27	66.65	91.25	73.04
1950	66.67	94.21	97.31	100.49	100.12	100.33	100.22	99.95	105.46	68.20	91.48	74.55
1951	67.47	95.12	97.76	100.49	100.12	100.33	99.79	100.00	105.06	68.56	91.95	74.56
1952	67.91	95.40	97.85	100.49	100.12	100.33	99.80	99.88	102.54	70.51	92.60	76.14
1953	69.47	95.80	98.05	100.49	100.12	100.33	100.04	99.98	101.91	71.88	93.14	77.18
1954	69.01	95.56	97.85	100.49	100.12	100.33	100.06	100.00	101.05	72.31	93.46	77.37
1955	72.72	95.98	98.08	100.49	100.12	100.33	100.16	99.98	104.19	73.35	93.62	78.35
1956	73.24	96.57	98.17	100.49	100.12	100.33	100.01	99.97	101.69	75.28	93.96	80.12
1957	73.67	96.85	98.20	100.49	100.12	100.33	99.85	100.01	100.72	76.30	94.32	80.89
1958	73.83	96.93	97.96	100.49	100.12	100.27	100.02	99.99	98.78	78.02	94.53	82.53
1959	77.25	97.18	98.28	100.49	100.12	100.28	99.75	99.84	101.54	79.28	94.79	83.64
1960	77.69	97.48	98.34	100.49	100.12	100.22	100.07	100.00	100.09	80.25	95.04	84.44
1961	78.81	97.55	98.29	100.49	100.12	100.20	99.99	100.02	100.33	81.26	95.30	85.27
1962	81.90	97.91	98.56	100.49	100.12	100.20	99.92	100.01	102.11	82.51	95.58	86.33
1963	84.53	98.27	98.83	100.49	100.12	100.17	100.06	100.01	103.29	83.55	95.89	87.13
1964	87.99	98.62	98.90	100.49	100.12	100.15	99.93	100.00	104.06	86.10	96.37	89.34
1965	91.36	98.90	99.24	100.49	100.12	100.16	100.08	100.00	105.19	87.74	96.99	90.46
1966	93.55	99.36	99.63	100.49	100.12	100.14	99.82	100.00	104.78	89.68	97.65	91.84
1967	93.32	99.52	99.78	100.49	100.12	100.09	100.05	99.97	103.20	90.41	98.16	92.10
1968	95.63	99.63	99.94	100.44	100.12	100.04	99.91	99.96	103.12	92.70	98.61	94.01
1969	95.50	99.83	99.92	100.37	100.10	99.98	99.85	99.97	101.04	94.50	99.15	95.31
1970	94.04	99.89	99.95	100.25	100.09	99.91	100.00	99.92	98.43	95.53	99.47	96.04
1971	96.32	99.94	99.88	100.13	100.05	99.89	100.17	99.96	99.63	96.66	99.58	97.07
1972	100.00	100.00	100.00	100.00	100.00	100.00	100.00	100.00	100.00	100.00	100.00	100.00
1973	102.54	100.10	100.16	99.92	99.94	99.96	99.90	100.00	100.01	102.55	100.76	101.78
1974	98.15	100.10	100.10	99.68	99.83	99.86	99.90	99.96	96.29	102.52	101.20	101.30
1975	96.87	100.05	99.90	99.53	99.72	99.70	100.14	99.99	98.02	99.79	101.26	98.55
1976	100.78	100.17	100.04	99.44	99.70	99.40	99.91	99.98	99.12	103.07	101.29	101.76
1977	104.15	100.34	99.96	99.39	99.68	99.48	99.98	99.99	100.28	105.10	101.63	103.41
1978	105.28	100.50	99.98	99.34	99.69	99.50	99.89	99.99	100.34	106.10	102.28	103.73
1979	103.56	100.56	99.93	99.22	99.64	99.45	99.87	100.00	98.62	106.42	102.83	103.49
1980	101.04	100.52	99.75	99.03	99.61	99.34	99.84	100.00	96.49	106.74	103.06	103.57
1981	102.41	100.60	99.86	99.00	99.64	99.36	100.34	100.01	98.13	105.62	103.10	102.44
1982	99.14	100.62	99.59	(98.85)[b]	(99.64)[b]	99.36	100.08	100.03	96.70	104.43	103.22	101.17

Sources: Column 1, table 4-6, column 11. Columns 2–3, see "Derivations," table H-1, and *Slower Growth*. Columns 4–6, see table 5-4, row 14, table 5-5, column 4, table 5-6, column 3; *Slower Growth*, table 5-6, column 4; "Derivations"; and Edward F. Denison, "Effects of Selected Changes in the Institutional and Human Environment upon Output per Unit of Input," *Survey of Current Business*, vol. 58 (January 1978) (Brookings Reprint 335). Columns 7–12, see "Derivations," tables I-1 to I-5, and *Slower Growth*.

a. Includes changes in intensity of utilization due to materials shortages and miscellaneous causes.

b. Assumed values.

Table 5-2. Nonresidential Business: Indexes of Potential Sector Output per Unit of Input, 1929, 1940–41, and 1947–82
Actual, 1972 = 100

		Gains from reallocation of resources from:		Effects of changes in legal and human environment			Effects of irregular factors			Other determinants		
								Changes in intensity of utilization of employed resources resulting from:				
Year	Output per unit of input (1)	Farming (2)	Nonfarm self-employment (3)	Pollution abatement (4)	Employee safety and health (5)	Dishonesty and crime (6)	Effect of weather on farm output (7)	Work stoppages (8)	Fluctuations in intensity of demand[a] (9)	Total (semiresidual) (10)	Economies of scale (11)	Advances in knowledge and miscellaneous (residual) (12)
1929	49.24	87.98	96.90	100.49	100.12	100.33	100.15	100.04	102.91	55.49	86.38	64.24
1940	52.81	91.34	98.18	100.49	100.12	100.33	99.32	100.03	102.91	57.06	87.64	65.11
1941	54.94	91.66	98.11	100.49	100.12	100.33	99.88	99.99	102.91	58.89	88.05	66.88
1947	61.16	93.60	97.44	100.49	100.12	100.33	99.56	99.96	102.91	64.87	90.58	71.62
1948	62.38	93.84	97.40	100.49	100.12	100.33	100.04	99.97	102.91	65.69	90.95	72.23
1949	63.34	94.04	97.50	100.49	100.12	100.33	99.85	99.92	102.91	66.65	91.25	73.04
1950	65.32	94.37	97.53	100.49	100.12	100.33	100.22	99.95	102.91	68.20	91.48	74.55
1951	65.85	94.92	97.61	100.49	100.12	100.33	99.79	100.00	102.91	68.56	91.95	74.56
1952	67.82	95.15	97.63	100.49	100.12	100.33	99.80	99.88	102.91	70.51	92.60	76.14
1953	69.79	95.53	97.82	100.49	100.12	100.33	100.04	99.98	102.91	71.88	93.14	77.18
1954	70.53	95.69	98.07	100.49	100.12	100.33	100.06	100.00	102.91	72.31	93.46	77.37
1955	71.84	95.95	98.12	100.49	100.12	100.33	100.16	99.98	102.91	73.35	93.62	78.35
1956	74.10	96.53	98.18	100.49	100.12	100.33	100.01	99.97	102.91	75.28	93.96	80.12
1957	75.31	96.84	98.25	100.49	100.12	100.33	99.85	100.01	102.91	76.30	94.32	80.89
1958	77.54	97.23	98.45	100.49	100.12	100.27	100.02	99.99	102.91	78.02	94.53	82.53
1959	78.58	97.31	98.51	100.49	100.12	100.28	99.75	99.84	102.91	79.28	94.79	83.64
1960	80.21	97.63	98.59	100.49	100.12	100.22	100.07	100.00	102.91	80.25	95.04	84.44
1961	81.41	97.81	98.72	100.49	100.12	100.20	99.99	100.02	102.91	81.26	95.30	85.27
1962	82.85	98.04	98.79	100.49	100.12	100.20	99.92	100.01	102.91	82.51	95.58	86.33
1963	84.52	98.40	99.06	100.49	100.12	100.17	100.06	100.01	102.91	83.55	95.89	87.13
1964	87.22	98.69	99.06	100.49	100.12	100.15	99.93	100.00	102.91	86.10	96.37	89.34
1965	89.45	98.93	99.29	100.49	100.12	100.16	100.08	100.00	102.91	87.74	96.99	90.46
1966	91.81	99.33	99.58	100.49	100.12	100.14	99.82	100.00	102.91	89.68	97.65	91.84
1967	93.01	99.50	99.75	100.49	100.12	100.09	100.05	99.97	102.91	90.41	98.16	92.10
1968	95.34	99.59	99.88	100.44	100.12	100.04	99.91	99.96	102.91	92.70	98.61	94.01
1969	97.16	99.79	99.85	100.37	100.10	99.98	99.85	99.97	102.91	94.50	99.15	95.31
1970	98.46	99.92	100.06	100.25	100.09	99.91	100.00	99.92	102.91	95.53	99.47	96.04
1971	99.81	100.03	100.11	100.13	100.05	99.89	100.17	99.96	102.91	96.66	99.58	97.07
1972	103.18	100.07	100.19	100.00	100.00	100.00	100.00	100.00	102.91	100.00	100.00	100.00
1973	105.65	100.14	100.25	99.92	99.94	99.96	99.90	100.00	102.91	102.55	100.76	101.78
1974	105.18	100.17	100.29	99.68	99.83	99.86	99.90	99.96	102.91	102.52	101.20	101.30
1975	102.46	100.26	100.44	99.53	99.72	99.70	100.14	99.99	102.91	99.79	101.26	98.55
1976	105.28	100.34	100.49	99.44	99.70	99.40	99.91	99.98	102.91	103.07	101.29	101.76
1977	107.44	100.48	100.34	99.39	99.68	99.48	99.98	99.99	102.91	105.10	101.63	103.41
1978	108.31	100.58	100.21	99.34	99.69	99.50	99.89	99.99	102.91	106.10	102.28	103.73
1979	108.38	100.64	100.14	99.22	99.64	99.45	99.87	100.00	102.91	106.42	102.83	103.49
1980	108.33	100.65	100.15	99.03	99.61	99.34	99.84	100.00	102.91	106.74	103.06	103.57
1981	108.03	100.74	100.31	99.00	99.64	99.36	100.34	100.01	102.91	105.62	103.10	102.44
1982	106.53	100.83	100.35	(98.85)[b]	(99.64)[b]	99.36	100.08	100.03	102.91	104.43	103.22	101.17

Sources: Column 1, product of columns 2 through 10; columns 2–3, see "Derivations" and *Slower Growth;* columns 4–8, table 5-1; column 9, see "Derivations"; columns 10–12, table 5-1.

a. Includes changes in intensity of utilization due to materials shortages and miscellaneous causes.

b. Assumed values.

Table 5-3. Nonresidential Business: Growth Rates of Potential and Actual Output per Unit of Input and Components, Selected Periods, 1929–82

Percent a year

| | | Gains from reallocation of resources from: | | Effects of changes in legal and human environment | | | Effects of irregular factors | | | Other determinants | | |
| | | | | | | | | Changes in intensity of utilization of employed resources resulting from: | | | | |
Basis and period	Output per unit of input (1)	Farming (2)	Nonfarm self-employment (3)	Pollution abatement (4)	Employee safety and health (5)	Dishonesty and crime (6)	Effect of weather on farm output (7)	Work stoppages (8)	Fluctuations in intensity of demand[a] (9)	Total (semiresidual) (10)	Economies of scale (11)	Advances in knowledge and miscellaneous (residual) (12)
Potential												
Longer periods												
1929–82	1.47	0.26	0.07	−0.03	−0.01	−0.02	0.00	0.00	0.00	1.20	0.34	0.86
1929–48	1.25	0.34	0.03	0.00	0.00	0.00	−0.01	0.00	0.00	0.89	0.27	0.62
1948–73	2.13	0.26	0.12	−0.02	−0.01	−0.01	−0.01	0.00	0.00	1.80	0.41	1.38
1973–82	0.09	0.08	0.01	−0.12	−0.03	−0.07	0.02	0.00	0.00	0.20	0.27	−0.07
Shorter periods												
1929–41	0.92	0.34	0.10	0.00	0.00	0.00	−0.02	0.00	0.00	0.50	0.16	0.34
1941–48	1.83	0.34	−0.10	0.00	0.00	0.00	0.02	0.00	0.00	1.57	0.46	1.11
1948–53	2.27	0.36	0.09	0.00	0.00	0.00	0.00	0.00	0.00	1.82	0.48	1.33
1953–64	2.05	0.30	0.11	0.00	0.00	−0.02	−0.01	0.00	0.00	1.65	0.31	1.34
1964–73	2.15	0.16	0.13	−0.06	−0.02	−0.02	0.00	0.00	0.00	1.96	0.50	1.46
1973–79	0.43	0.08	−0.02	−0.12	−0.05	−0.09	−0.01	0.00	0.00	0.62	0.34	0.28
1979–82	−0.57	0.06	0.07	−0.12	0.00	−0.03	0.07	0.01	0.00	−0.63	0.13	−0.75
Actual												
Longer periods												
1929–82	1.30	0.25	0.05	−0.03	−0.01	−0.02	0.00	0.00	−0.13	1.20	0.34	0.86
1929–48	1.24	0.32	0.02	0.00	0.00	0.00	−0.01	0.00	0.01	0.89	0.27	0.62
1948–73	1.96	0.25	0.11	−0.02	−0.01	−0.01	−0.01	0.00	−0.15	1.80	0.41	1.38
1973–82	−0.37	0.06	−0.06	−0.12	−0.03	−0.07	0.02	0.00	−0.37	0.20	0.27	−0.07
Shorter periods												
1929–41	0.96	0.22	0.03	0.00	0.00	0.00	−0.02	0.00	0.24	0.50	0.16	0.34
1941–48	1.72	0.50	0.00	0.00	0.00	0.00	0.02	0.00	−0.37	1.57	0.46	1.11
1948–53	1.96	0.39	0.12	0.00	0.00	0.00	0.00	0.00	−0.37	1.82	0.48	1.33
1953–64	2.17	0.26	0.08	0.00	0.00	−0.02	−0.01	0.00	0.19	1.65	0.31	1.34
1964–73	1.71	0.17	0.14	−0.06	−0.02	−0.02	0.00	0.00	−0.44	1.96	0.50	1.46
1973–79	0.17	0.08	−0.04	−0.12	−0.05	−0.09	−0.01	0.00	−0.23	0.62	0.34	0.28
1979–82	−1.44	0.02	−0.11	−0.12	0.00	−0.03	0.07	0.01	−0.65	−0.63	0.13	−0.75

Sources: Computed from tables 5-1 and 5-2.

a. Includes changes in intensity of utilization due to materials shortages and miscellaneous causes.

Table 5-4. Incremental Pollution Abatement Costs That Reduce National Income per Unit of Input in Nonresidential Business, 1967–81

Item	1967	1968	1969	1970	1971	1972	1973	1974	1975	1976	1977	1978	1979	1980	1981
							Costs (millions of dollars)								
Current Costs															
1. Motor vehicle emission abatement[a]	0	68	140	200	309	435	610	1,060	1,294	1,492	1,659	1,912	2,640	3,804	4,523
2. Air and water pollution abatement except motor vehicle emissions	0	74	200	439	718	1,367	1,597	2,246	2,806	3,476	4,271	5,142	6,341	7,529	8,269
3. Payments to use public sewerage systems	0	0	34	74	106	145	186	237	298	336	381	496	603	708	779
4. Solid waste disposal	0	49	123	260	378	503	567	900	999	1,287	1,397	1,629	2,091	2,629	3,058
5. Research and development	0	4	12	28	45	99	98	125	153	160	217	226	266	221	197
Depreciation															
6. Motor vehicle emission abatement[a]	0	4	10	17	29	45	68	103	159	234	322	436	577	754	971
7. Air and water pollution abatement except motor vehicle emissions	0	30	87	192	315	454	647	1,036	1,464	1,819	2,197	2,592	3,145	3,799	4,534
8. Solid waste disposal	0	0	1	2	4	8	14	24	37	49	66	89	120	162	209
Net opportunity cost of invested capital															
9. Motor vehicle emission abatement[a]	0	4	10	16	26	39	58	85	129	186	249	325	414	520	648
10. Air and water pollution abatement except motor vehicle emissions	0	70	186	405	657	946	1,425	2,050	2,688	3,223	3,763	4,370	5,124	6,015	6,760
11. Solid waste disposal	0	0	1	3	6	12	20	33	49	63	81	106	138	180	223
Less															
12. Value of materials and energy reclaimed	0	13	34	75	123	274	299	356	498	668	718	794	1,048	1,274	1,412
13. Total incremental cost	0	290	769	1,562	2,470	3,779	4,991	7,545	9,578	11,656	13,885	16,528	20,411	25,047	28,760
							Percent of input diverted to pollution abatement								
14. Total incremental cost	0.000	0.049	0.120	0.237	0.350	0.484	0.565	0.801	0.953	1.037	1.090	1.140	1.262	1.448	1.481

Sources: Unpublished estimates provided by the Bureau of Economic Analysis; see "Derivations" and *Slower Growth* for the methodology.

a. Business vehicles only.

Table 5-5. Incremental Costs for Protection of Employee Safety and Health That Reduce National Income per Unit of Input in Nonresidential Business, 1967–82

Percent of input diverted to protection

Year	Safety equipment on motor vehicles[a] (1)	Mining (except oil and gas)[b] (2)	Other industries[b] (3)	Total incremental cost (4)
1967	0.00	0.00	0.00	0.00
1968	*	0.00	0.00	*
1969	0.01	0.01	0.00	0.02
1970	0.02	0.01	0.00	0.03
1971	0.03	0.03	0.01	0.07
1972	0.04	0.05	0.03	0.12
1973	0.05	0.07	0.06	0.18
1974	0.07	0.12	0.10	0.29
1975	0.09	0.17	0.14	0.40
1976	0.11	0.18	0.13	0.42
1977	0.12	0.19	0.13	0.44
1978	0.14	0.16	0.13	0.43
1979	0.15	0.18	0.15	0.48
1980	0.15	0.21	0.15	0.51
1981	0.14	0.20	0.14	0.48
1982	0.15	0.20	0.13	0.48

Sources: See "Derivations" and *Slower Growth*.
* Less than 0.005 percent.
a. Depreciation and net opportunity cost of invested capital. Business vehicles only.
b. Current costs, depreciation, and net opportunity cost of invested capital. Excludes costs of safety equipment on motor vehicles.

Table 5-6. Indexes of Effects of Changes in Costs of Dishonesty and Crime on Output per Unit of Input in Nonresidential Business, 1972–82[a]

1972 = 100

Year	Type of Cost		
	Protection (1)	Losses (2)	Total (3)
1972	100.00	100.00	100.00
1973	100.00	99.96	99.96
1974	99.96	99.90	99.86
1975	99.95	99.75	99.70
1976	99.96	99.44	99.40
1977	99.97	99.51	99.48
1978	99.97	99.53	99.50
1979	99.96	99.49	99.45
1980	99.93	99.41	99.34
1981	(99.93)[b]	99.43	99.36
1982	n.a.	n.a.	(99.36)[b]

Sources: See "Derivations" and *Slower Growth*.
n.a. Not available.
a. For earlier years, see *Slower Growth*, table 5-6.
b. Assumed to be unchanged from previous year.

Table 5-7. Composition of the Year, 1929, 1940–41, and 1947–84

Days in addition to 52 weeks[a]	Years
Sunday	1950, 1961, 1967, 1978
Saturday	1949, 1955, 1966, 1977, 1983
Saturday and Sunday	1972
Weekday	1929, 1941, 1947, 1951, 1953, 1957, 1958, 1959, 1962, 1963, 1969, 1970, 1973, 1974, 1975, 1979, 1981
Weekday and Sunday	1956, 1984
Friday	1954, 1965, 1971, 1982
Friday and Saturday	1960
Two weekdays	1940, 1952, 1964, 1968, 1980
Friday and weekday	1948, 1976

a. "Weekday" is used to denote Monday through Thursday.

Table 6-1. General Government (Excluding Work Relief), Households, and Institutions: Indexes of Sector Labor Input and Components, 1929, 1940–41, and 1947–82[a]
1972 = 100

Year	Employment (1)	Total (2)	Effect of changes in hours on a year's work			Other labor character-istics (6)	Total labor input (7)
			Average hours (3)	Implied efficiency offset (4)	Inclusion of military re-serves on inactive duty (5)		
1929	30.5	112.9	137.6	82.4	99.5	69.2	23.8
1940	36.0	113.9	122.2	93.4	99.8	73.9	30.3
1941	42.5	112.4	120.2	94.2	99.3	78.4	37.5
1947	45.1	111.1	112.6	99.0	99.6	84.3	42.3
1948	46.4	110.2	110.8	99.3	100.1	83.6	42.8
1949	48.3	110.0	110.3	99.3	100.5	85.6	45.4
1950	50.7	110.1	110.5	99.1	100.5	84.9	47.4
1951	59.4	110.9	111.9	99.2	100.0	84.6	55.7
1952	62.5	111.3	112.4	99.1	99.9	85.4	59.4
1953	62.8	110.9	112.2	99.0	99.9	85.3	59.4
1954	62.0	109.8	110.9	98.8	100.1	86.9	59.0
1955	63.5	108.4	109.6	98.6	100.3	87.6	60.3
1956	65.3	107.3	108.3	98.6	100.4	88.7	62.2
1957	66.5	107.2	107.8	98.8	100.7	89.6	63.9
1958	68.1	106.0	106.7	98.8	100.5	90.3	65.2
1959	69.3	105.2	106.0	98.8	100.5	91.4	66.6
1960	70.8	105.3	106.2	98.7	100.5	92.0	68.7
1961	73.5	104.3	105.3	98.6	100.5	92.9	71.3
1962	76.7	103.3	104.8	98.3	100.3	93.4	74.0
1963	78.1	103.5	104.7	98.6	100.3	93.9	76.0
1964	80.5	103.1	104.0	98.8	100.4	94.7	78.5
1965	83.3	102.7	103.7	98.9	100.2	95.3	81.5
1966	89.3	102.3	103.1	99.1	100.2	95.2	87.0
1967	93.7	103.2	103.4	99.5	100.3	95.0	91.8
1968	97.1	102.4	102.8	99.6	100.0	95.7	95.2
1969	98.7	102.2	102.5	99.6	100.1	97.1	97.9
1970	98.8	101.0	101.1	99.7	100.2	98.1	98.0
1971	99.1	100.4	100.4	99.9	100.1	99.3	98.8
1972	100.0	100.0	100.0	100.0	100.0	100.0	100.0
1973	101.2	99.9	99.9	100.1	100.0	100.1	101.2
1974	102.5	99.3	99.1	100.3	99.9	101.1	102.9
1975	105.0	98.1	98.4	99.8	99.9	101.9	105.0
1976	106.1	98.3	98.4	100.0	99.9	101.8	106.1
1977	107.9	97.7	97.6	100.2	99.9	101.8	107.3
1978	110.7	97.7	.97.4	100.4	99.8	101.9	110.2
1979	112.1	97.7	97.2	100.6	99.8	102.3	112.0
1980	114.4	97.1	96.5	100.8	99.8	102.7	114.0
1981	114.4	97.3	96.6	100.8	99.9	103.1	114.7
1982	114.6	97.0	96.4	100.8	99.9	103.4	115.0

Sources: Column 1, table 2-7, column 2; column 2, product of columns 3, 4, and 5; column 3, table C-1, column 2; columns 4 and 5, see "Derivations" and *Slower Growth;* column 6, column 7 divided by (column 1 times 2), expressed with 1972 = 100; column 7, table 2-6, column 2.
   a. A change in the method of measuring labor input and output affects the comparability of changes in data before 1947 with those in later years; columns 2, 4, 6, and 7 are affected. Columns 1, 3, 4, and 6 exclude military reserves on inactive duty in all years.

Table 6-2. Full-Time Equivalent Employment in the Government, Households, and Institutions Sector, by Major Component, Selected Periods, 1948–82
Thousands

Employment	Full-time equivalent employment						Average annual increase				
	1948	1953	1964	1973	1979	1982	1948–1953	1953–1964	1964–1973	1973–1979	1979–1982
Federal civilian government	1,378	1,751	1,752	1,911	2,020	2,016	75	0	18	18	−1
Federal military[a]	1,544	3,630	2,896	2,439	2,189	2,293	417	−67	−51	−42	35
Public education	1,418	1,732	3,076	4,757	5,354	5,414	63	122	187	100	20
State and local government nonschool	1,723	2,082	3,034	4,305	5,003	4,935	72	87	141	116	−23
Rest of the world	7	−78	−56	−15	−20	−25	−17	2	5	−1	−2
Nonprofit institutions, total	1,543	1,824	3,015	4,445	5,304	5,719	56	108	159	143	138
Amusement and other recreation	53	52	65	99	125	139	0	1	4	4	5
Health services	499	625	983	1,675	2,216	2,555	25	33	77	90	113
Educational services	383	424	626	919	1,026	1,055	8	18	33	18	10
Social services	574	674	1,195	1,552	724	765	20	47	40	34	14
Membership organizations					1,034	1,013					−7
Miscellaneous professional services	28	36	50	99	103	108	2	1	5	1	2
Other industries	6	13	96	101	76	84	1	8	1	−4	3
Private households	1,574	1,483	1,513	978	803	727	−18	3	−59	−29	−25
Sector total	9,187	12,424	15,230	18,820	20,653	21,079	647	255	399	306	142

Sources: NIPA, table 6.8B, except for nonprofit institutions, for which estimates were provided by the Bureau of Economic Analysis.
a. Includes military reserves on inactive duty, who are excluded from other employment tables.

Table 6-3. National Income by Sector and Output Determinants in the Smaller Sectors: Growth Rate and Contributions to Growth Rate of Sector and Total National Income, Selected Periods, 1929–82

Growth rates and contributions in percentage points

Sector and determinant	Longer periods				Shorter periods						
	1929– 1982	1929– 1948	1948– 1973	1973– 1982	1929– 1941[a]	1941– 1948[a]	1948– 1953	1953– 1964	1964– 1973	1973– 1979	1979– 1982
	Growth rate of sector national income, or contribution of determinant to it										
Whole economy	2.92	2.54	3.70	1.55	2.09	3.33	4.69	3.08	3.92	2.61	−0.54
General government, households, institutions[b]	3.01	3.12	3.51	1.43	3.84	1.91	6.80	2.57	2.86	1.71	0.87
Employment	2.53	2.23	3.17	1.39	2.80	1.26	6.24	2.28	2.58	1.72	0.76
Effect of changes in hours	−0.29	−0.13	−0.39	−0.33	−0.04	−0.28	0.13	−0.66	−0.35	−0.38	−0.23
Average hours	−0.67	−1.13	−0.41	−0.40	−1.12	−1.16	0.25	−0.69	−0.45	−0.45	−0.29
Implied efficiency offset	0.38	0.99	−0.02	0.08	1.12	0.76	−0.06	−0.02	0.15	0.10	0.03
Inclusion of military reserves	0.01	0.05	0.00	−0.01	−0.02	0.11	−0.04	0.05	−0.04	−0.03	0.03
Other labor characteristics	0.76	1.00	0.72	0.36	1.05	0.92	0.40	0.95	0.62	0.37	0.34
Services of dwellings	4.71	2.29	6.50	4.95	0.42	5.51	9.58	6.44	4.87	4.88	5.09
Quantity of housing	4.52	1.60	6.71	4.74	0.05	4.32	10.48	6.64	4.76	4.50	5.21
Occupancy ratio	0.17	0.66	−0.21	0.20	0.37	1.16	−0.81	−0.19	0.10	0.36	−0.11
International assets	4.36	0.81	6.97	4.84	−2.83	7.39	6.30	6.50	7.93	9.69	−4.23
Nonresidential business	2.77	2.44	3.58	1.26	1.78	3.58	4.00	3.01	4.05	2.50	−1.18
	Weights for calculation of contributions										
Whole economy	1.0000	1.0000	1.0000	1.0000	1.0000	1.0000	1.0000	1.0000	1.0000	1.0000	1.0000
General government, households, institutions	0.1683	0.1727	0.1788	0.1736	0.1809	0.1931	0.1902	0.1971	0.1838	0.1706	0.1678
Services of dwellings	0.0441	0.0249	0.0353	0.0544	0.0235	0.0225	0.0268	0.0364	0.0451	0.0500	0.0570
International assets	0.0144	0.0082	0.0106	0.0169	0.0075	0.0059	0.0070	0.0088	0.0124	0.0178	0.0212
Nonresidential business	0.7732	0.7942	0.7753	0.7551	0.7881	0.7785	0.7759	0.7577	0.7587	0.7616	0.7540
	Contributions to growth rate of whole economy										
Whole economy	2.92	2.54	3.70	1.55	2.09	3.33	4.69	3.08	3.92	2.61	−0.54
General government, households, institutions	0.51	0.54	0.62	0.25	0.70	0.37	1.29	0.51	0.52	0.29	0.15
Employment	0.43	0.39	0.57	0.24	0.51	0.24	1.19	0.45	0.47	0.29	0.13
Effect of changes in hours	−0.05	−0.02	−0.07	−0.06	0.00	−0.05	0.02	−0.13	−0.06	−0.06	−0.04
Average hours	−0.11	−0.20	−0.07	−0.07	−0.20	−0.22	0.05	−0.14	−0.08	−0.08	−0.05
Implied efficiency offset	0.06	0.17	0.00	0.01	0.20	0.15	−0.02	0.00	0.03	0.02	0.01
Inclusion of military reserves	0.00	0.01	0.00	0.00	0.00	0.02	−0.01	0.01	−0.01	0.00	0.00
Other labor characteristics	0.13	0.17	0.12	0.07	0.19	0.18	0.08	0.19	0.11	0.06	0.06
Services of dwellings	0.21	0.06	0.23	0.27	0.01	0.12	0.26	0.23	0.22	0.24	0.29
Quantity of housing	0.20	0.04	0.24	0.26	0.00	0.10	0.28	0.24	0.21	0.22	0.30
Occupancy ratio	0.01	0.02	−0.01	0.01	0.01	0.02	−0.02	−0.01	0.01	0.02	−0.01
International assets	0.06	0.01	0.07	0.08	−0.02	0.05	0.04	0.06	0.10	0.17	−0.09
Nonresidential business	2.14	1.93	2.78	0.95	1.40	2.79	3.10	2.28	3.08	1.91	−0.89

Sources: Upper panel computed from tables 2-6, 6-1, and 6-4. Middle panel computed from table 2-5; the percentage distributions of national income among the sectors were calculated for the first and last years of the period, these percentages were interpolated to obtain a synthetic interpolated percentage for the next to last year, and the distributions for the first and next to last year were averaged; see *Accounting for Growth*, p. 22. Lower panel is the product of the corresponding series in the upper panel and the sector weight from the middle panel.

a. Based on data excluding work relief employees.

b. Growth rates refer to both national income and labor input.

Table 6-4. Services of Dwellings: Indexes of Sector Output and Its Determinants, 1929, 1940–41, and 1947–82
Indexes, 1972 = 100

Year	Sector national income (1)	Sector national income at constant (1972) occupancy ratio (2)	Effect of changes in occupancy ratio (3)
1929	14.3	15.4	92.7
1940	14.0	14.7	95.1
1941	15.0	15.5	96.9
1947	20.6	19.4	106.1
1948	21.9	20.9	105.1
1949	24.6	23.8	103.6
1950	26.8	25.8	104.0
1951	29.2	28.8	101.4
1952	32.1	31.7	101.1
1953	34.6	34.3	100.9
1954	37.3	37.0	100.8
1955	39.7	39.5	100.5
1956	41.8	41.8	100.1
1957	44.8	45.0	99.7
1958	48.4	48.7	99.4
1959	51.6	51.9	99.4
1960	55.0	55.3	99.4
1961	58.1	58.4	99.4
1962	62.2	62.6	99.3
1963	65.4	65.9	99.1
1964	68.8	69.7	98.8
1965	73.1	74.3	98.4
1966	77.4	78.4	98.6
1967	81.9	82.7	99.1
1968	85.6	86.1	99.4
1969	89.9	90.3	99.6
1970	92.6	92.7	99.8
1971	95.5	95.6	99.9
1972	100.0	100.0	100.0
1973	105.5	105.9	99.7
1974	111.6	111.1	100.4
1975	114.6	113.9	100.6
1976	120.0	118.8	101.0
1977	128.3	126.5	101.4
1978	134.5	132.0	101.9
1979	140.5	137.9	101.9
1980	146.5	144.1	101.6
1981	155.9	152.9	101.9
1982	163.0	160.6	101.5

Sources: Column 1, table 2-6, column 3; column 2, column 1 divided by column 3; column 3, see "Derivations" and *Slower Growth*, appendix K.

Table 7-1. Nonresidential Business: Sources of Growth of Actual Sector National Income, Selected Periods, 1929–82
Contributions to sector growth rates in percentage points

Item	Longer periods				Shorter periods						
	1929–1982	1929–1948	1948–1973	1973–1982	1929–1941	1941–1948	1948–1953	1953–1964	1964–1973	1973–1979	1979–1982
Sector national income	2.77	2.44	3.58	1.26	1.78	3.58	4.00	3.01	4.05	2.50	−1.18
Total factor input	1.46	1.19	1.60	1.63	0.81	1.84	2.02	0.83	2.32	2.33	0.27
Labor	1.08	1.11	1.01	1.17	0.87	1.51	1.32	0.39	1.61	1.84	−0.14
Employment	0.95	0.87	0.89	1.25	0.51	1.48	0.86	0.19	1.78	2.00	−0.21
Hours	−0.29	−0.25	−0.23	−0.51	−0.22	−0.30	−0.09	−0.22	−0.33	−0.43	−0.67
Average hours	−0.52	−0.61	−0.40	−0.63	−0.64	−0.53	−0.37	−0.31	−0.54	−0.56	−0.78
Efficiency offset	0.14	0.27	0.06	0.11	0.37	0.07	0.14	−0.02	0.11	0.11	0.12
Intergroup shift offset	0.09	0.09	0.11	0.01	0.05	0.16	0.14	0.11	0.10	0.02	−0.01
Age-sex composition	−0.11	0.01	−0.17	−0.19	0.05	−0.05	0.09	−0.10	−0.40	−0.34	0.09
Education	0.53	0.48	0.52	0.62	0.53	0.38	0.46	0.52	0.56	0.61	0.65
Capital	0.38	0.08	0.59	0.46	−0.06	0.33	0.70	0.44	0.71	0.49	0.41
Inventories	0.11	0.07	0.16	0.07	0.03	0.15	0.24	0.10	0.18	0.10	0.01
Nonresidential structures and equipment	0.27	0.01	0.43	0.39	−0.09	0.18	0.46	0.34	0.53	0.39	0.40
Land	0.00	0.00	0.00	0.00	0.00	0.00	0.00	0.00	0.00	0.00	0.00
Output per unit of input	1.31	1.25	1.98	−0.37	0.97	1.74	1.98	2.18	1.73	0.17	−1.45
Advances in knowledge and n.e.c.	0.86	0.63	1.40	−0.07	0.34	1.12	1.35	1.35	1.46	0.28	−0.75
Improved resource allocation	0.30	0.35	0.37	0.00	0.26	0.50	0.51	0.35	0.31	0.04	−0.10
Farm	0.25	0.33	0.26	0.06	0.23	0.50	0.39	0.27	0.17	0.08	0.02
Nonfarm self-employment	0.05	0.02	0.11	−0.06	0.03	0.00	0.12	0.08	0.14	−0.04	−0.12
Legal and human environment	−0.06	0.00	−0.05	−0.22	0.00	0.00	0.00	−0.01	−0.10	−0.25	−0.16
Pollution abatement	−0.03	0.00	−0.02	−0.12	0.00	0.00	0.00	0.00	−0.06	−0.12	−0.13
Worker safety and health	−0.01	0.00	−0.01	−0.03	0.00	0.00	0.00	0.00	−0.02	−0.05	0.00
Dishonesty and crime	−0.02	0.00	−0.02	−0.07	0.00	0.00	0.00	−0.01	−0.02	−0.08	−0.03
Economies of scale	0.34	0.27	0.42	0.27	0.16	0.47	0.49	0.31	0.50	0.34	0.13
Irregular factors	−0.13	0.00	−0.16	−0.35	0.21	−0.35	−0.37	0.18	−0.44	−0.24	−0.57
Weather in farming	0.00	−0.01	−0.01	0.02	−0.02	0.02	0.00	−0.01	0.00	−0.01	0.07
Labor disputes	0.00	0.00	0.00	0.00	−0.01	0.00	0.00	0.00	0.00	0.00	0.01
Intensity of demand	−0.13	0.01	−0.15	−0.37	0.24	−0.37	−0.37	0.19	−0.44	−0.23	−0.65

Sources: Derived from tables 2-9, 3-4, 4-7, 5-3, and G-2.
n.e.c. Not elsewhere classified.

Table 7-2. Nonresidential Business: Sources of Growth of Potential Sector National Income, Selected Periods, 1929–82
Contributions to sector growth rates in percentage points

Item	Longer periods				Shorter periods						
	1929–1982	1929–1948	1948–1973	1973–1982	1929–1941	1941–1948	1948–1953	1953–1964	1964–1973	1973–1979	1979–1982
Sector national income	**3.14**	**2.48**	**3.82**	**2.66**	**2.13**	**3.07**	**4.12**	**3.13**	**4.52**	**3.02**	**1.94**
Total factor input	**1.67**	**1.23**	**1.68**	**2.57**	**1.20**	**1.21**	**1.80**	**1.10**	**2.33**	**2.59**	**2.51**
Labor	1.29	1.15	1.09	2.11	1.27	0.84	1.10	0.66	1.62	2.10	2.11
Employment	1.17	0.92	0.98	2.21	1.07	0.56	0.56	0.54	1.77	2.27	2.06
Hours	−0.25	−0.24	−0.22	−0.36	−0.22	−0.29	−0.09	−0.20	−0.31	−0.39	−0.30
Average hours	−0.49	−0.61	−0.39	−0.52	−0.66	−0.45	−0.32	−0.33	−0.49	−0.54	−0.48
Efficiency offset	0.14	0.27	0.05	0.12	0.35	0.06	0.11	0.00	0.08	0.12	0.11
Intergroup shift offset	0.10	0.10	0.12	0.04	0.09	0.10	0.12	0.13	0.10	0.03	0.07
Age-sex composition	−0.14	0.00	−0.19	−0.31	−0.03	0.07	0.14	−0.16	−0.41	−0.38	−0.17
Education	0.51	0.47	0.52	0.57	0.45	0.50	0.49	0.48	0.57	0.60	0.52
Capital	0.38	0.08	0.59	0.46	−0.07	0.37	0.70	0.44	0.71	0.49	0.40
Inventories	0.11	0.07	0.16	0.07	0.03	0.17	0.24	0.10	0.18	0.10	0.01
Nonresidential structures and equipment	0.27	0.01	0.43	0.39	−0.10	0.20	0.46	0.34	0.53	0.39	0.39
Land	0.00	0.00	0.00	0.00	0.00	0.00	0.00	0.00	0.00	0.00	0.00
Output per unit of input	**1.47**	**1.25**	**2.14**	**0.09**	**0.93**	**1.86**	**2.32**	**2.03**	**2.19**	**0.43**	**−0.57**
Advances in knowledge and n.e.c.	0.86	0.62	1.40	−0.07	0.34	1.13	1.37	1.34	1.49	0.28	−0.75
Improved resource allocation	0.33	0.37	0.38	0.09	0.45	0.24	0.46	0.41	0.30	0.06	0.13
Farm	0.26	0.34	0.26	0.08	0.35	0.34	0.37	0.30	0.16	0.08	0.06
Nonfarm self-employment	0.07	0.03	0.12	0.01	0.10	−0.10	0.09	0.11	0.14	−0.02	0.07
Legal and human environment	−0.06	0.00	−0.05	−0.22	0.00	0.00	0.00	−0.02	−0.10	−0.25	−0.16
Pollution abatement	−0.03	0.00	−0.02	−0.12	0.00	0.00	0.00	0.00	−0.06	−0.12	−0.13
Worker safety and health	−0.01	0.00	−0.01	−0.03	0.00	0.00	0.00	0.00	−0.02	−0.05	0.00
Dishonesty and crime	−0.02	0.00	−0.02	−0.07	0.00	0.00	0.00	−0.02	−0.02	−0.08	−0.03
Economies of scale	0.34	0.27	0.42	0.27	0.16	0.47	0.49	0.31	0.50	0.34	0.13
Irregular factors	0.00	−0.01	−0.01	0.02	−0.02	0.02	0.00	−0.01	0.00	0.00	0.08
Weather in farming	0.00	−0.01	−0.01	0.02	−0.02	0.02	0.00	−0.01	0.00	0.00	0.07
Labor disputes	0.00	0.00	0.00	0.00	0.00	0.00	0.00	0.00	0.00	0.00	0.01

Sources: Derived from tables 2-9, 3-4, 4-7, 5-3, and G-2.
n.e.c. Not elsewhere classified.

Table 7-3. Nonresidential Business: Sources of Growth of Actual Sector National Income per Person Employed, Selected Periods, 1929–82

Contributions to sector growth rates in percentage points

Item	Longer periods				Shorter periods						
	1929–1982	1929–1948	1948–1973	1973–1982	1929–1941	1941–1948	1948–1953	1953–1964	1964–1973	1973–1979	1979–1982
Sector national income	**1.58**	**1.33**	**2.45**	**−0.26**	**1.13**	**1.68**	**2.89**	**2.78**	**1.82**	**0.08**	**−0.93**
Total factor input	**0.28**	**0.09**	**0.48**	**0.12**	**0.16**	**−0.04**	**0.92**	**0.59**	**0.10**	**−0.09**	**0.52**
Labor	0.13	0.24	0.11	−0.08	0.36	0.03	0.46	0.19	−0.17	−0.16	0.07
Hours	−0.29	−0.25	−0.24	−0.51	−0.22	−0.30	−0.09	−0.22	−0.33	−0.43	−0.67
Average hours	−0.52	−0.61	−0.40	−0.63	−0.64	−0.53	−0.37	−0.31	−0.54	−0.56	−0.78
Efficiency offset	0.14	0.27	0.05	0.11	0.37	0.07	0.14	−0.02	0.11	0.11	0.12
Intergroup shift offset	0.09	0.09	0.11	0.01	0.05	0.16	0.14	0.11	0.10	0.02	−0.01
Age-sex composition	−0.11	0.01	−0.17	−0.19	0.05	−0.05	0.09	−0.10	−0.40	−0.34	0.09
Education	0.53	0.48	0.52	0.62	0.53	0.38	0.46	0.51	0.56	0.61	0.65
Capital	0.20	−0.10	0.41	0.26	−0.17	0.02	0.51	0.41	0.36	0.16	0.44
Inventories	0.06	0.01	0.11	0.02	0.00	0.04	0.18	0.09	0.09	0.02	0.02
Nonresidential structures and equipment	0.14	−0.11	0.30	0.24	−0.17	−0.02	0.33	0.32	0.27	0.14	0.42
Land	−0.05	−0.05	−0.04	−0.06	−0.03	−0.09	−0.05	−0.01	−0.09	−0.09	0.01
Output per unit of input	**1.30**	**1.24**	**1.97**	**−0.38**	**0.97**	**1.72**	**1.97**	**2.19**	**1.72**	**0.17**	**−1.45**
Advances in knowledge and n.e.c.	0.86	0.62	1.40	−0.07	0.34	1.11	1.35	1.36	1.46	0.28	−0.75
Improved resource allocation	0.29	0.35	0.36	0.00	0.26	0.50	0.51	0.35	0.31	0.04	−0.10
Farm	0.24	0.33	0.25	0.06	0.23	0.50	0.39	0.27	0.17	0.08	0.02
Nonfarm self-employment	0.05	0.02	0.11	−0.06	0.03	0.00	0.12	0.08	0.14	−0.04	−0.12
Legal and human environment	−0.06	0.00	−0.05	−0.22	0.00	0.00	0.00	−0.01	−0.10	−0.25	−0.16
Pollution abatement	−0.03	0.00	−0.02	−0.12	0.00	0.00	0.00	0.00	−0.06	−0.12	−0.13
Worker safety and health	−0.01	0.00	−0.01	−0.03	0.00	0.00	0.00	0.00	−0.02	−0.05	0.00
Dishonesty and crime	−0.02	0.00	−0.02	−0.07	0.00	0.00	0.00	−0.01	−0.02	−0.08	−0.03
Economies of scale	0.34	0.27	0.42	0.27	0.16	0.46	0.48	0.31	0.49	0.34	0.13
Irregular factors	−0.13	0.00	−0.16	−0.36	0.21	−0.35	−0.37	0.18	−0.44	−0.24	−0.57
Weather in farming	0.00	−0.01	−0.01	0.02	−0.02	0.02	0.00	−0.01	0.00	−0.01	0.07
Labor disputes	0.00	0.00	0.00	0.00	−0.01	0.00	0.00	0.00	0.00	0.00	0.01
Intensity of demand	−0.13	0.01	−0.15	−0.38	0.24	−0.37	−0.37	0.19	−0.44	−0.23	−0.65

Sources: Derived from tables 2-9, 3-1, 3-4, 4-6, 4-7, 5-3, and G-2.
n.e.c. Not elsewhere classified.

Table 7-4. Nonresidential Business: Sources of Growth of Potential Sector National Income per Person Potentially Employed, Selected Periods, 1929–82
Contributions to sector growth rates in percentage points

	Longer periods				Shorter periods						
Item	1929–1982	1929–1948	1948–1973	1973–1982	1929–1941	1941–1948	1948–1953	1953–1964	1964–1973	1973–1979	1979–1982
Sector national income	**1.68**	**1.31**	**2.59**	**0.00**	**0.65**	**2.45**	**3.41**	**2.43**	**2.32**	**0.27**	**−0.55**
Total factor input	**0.22**	**0.08**	**0.45**	**−0.09**	**−0.21**	**0.50**	**1.09**	**0.42**	**0.14**	**−0.16**	**0.04**
Labor	0.12	0.22	0.11	−0.10	0.18	0.29	0.56	0.12	−0.14	−0.18	0.05
Hours	−0.25	−0.25	−0.22	−0.36	−0.23	−0.28	−0.08	−0.20	−0.31	−0.39	−0.30
Average hours	−0.49	−0.62	−0.39	−0.52	−0.67	−0.44	−0.31	−0.33	−0.49	−0.54	−0.48
Efficiency offset	0.14	0.27	0.05	0.12	0.35	0.06	0.11	0.00	0.08	0.12	0.11
Intergroup shift offset	0.10	0.10	0.12	0.04	0.09	0.10	0.12	0.13	0.10	0.03	0.07
Age-sex composition	−0.14	0.00	−0.19	−0.31	−0.03	0.07	0.14	−0.16	−0.41	−0.38	−0.17
Education	0.51	0.47	0.52	0.57	0.44	0.50	0.50	0.48	0.58	0.59	0.52
Capital	0.16	−0.09	0.39	0.10	−0.32	0.24	0.56	0.33	0.36	0.12	0.07
Inventories	0.05	0.02	0.10	−0.02	−0.04	0.12	0.19	0.07	0.09	0.01	−0.07
Nonresidential structures and equipment	0.11	−0.11	0.29	0.12	−0.28	0.12	0.37	0.26	0.27	0.11	0.14
Land	−0.06	−0.05	−0.05	−0.09	−0.07	−0.03	−0.03	−0.03	−0.08	−0.10	−0.08
Output per unit of input	**1.46**	**1.23**	**2.14**	**0.09**	**0.86**	**1.95**	**2.32**	**2.01**	**2.18**	**0.43**	**−0.59**
Advances in knowledge and n.e.c.	0.86	0.61	1.40	−0.07	0.32	1.18	1.37	1.33	1.48	0.28	−0.77
Improved resource allocation	0.32	0.36	0.38	0.09	0.41	0.25	0.46	0.40	0.30	0.06	0.13
Farm	0.26	0.33	0.26	0.08	0.32	0.35	0.37	0.29	0.16	0.08	0.06
Nonfarm self-employment	0.06	0.03	0.12	0.01	0.09	−0.10	0.09	0.11	0.14	−0.02	0.07
Legal and human environment	−0.06	0.00	−0.05	−0.22	0.00	0.00	0.00	−0.02	−0.10	−0.25	−0.16
Pollution abatement	−0.03	0.00	−0.02	−0.12	0.00	0.00	0.00	0.00	−0.06	−0.12	−0.13
Worker safety and health	−0.01	0.00	−0.01	−0.03	0.00	0.00	0.00	0.00	−0.02	−0.05	0.00
Dishonesty and crime	−0.02	0.00	−0.02	−0.07	0.00	0.00	0.00	−0.02	−0.02	−0.08	−0.03
Economies of scale	0.34	0.27	0.42	0.27	0.15	0.50	0.49	0.31	0.50	0.34	0.13
Irregular factors	0.00	−0.01	−0.01	0.02	−0.02	0.02	0.00	−0.01	0.00	0.00	0.08
Weather in farming	0.00	−0.01	−0.01	0.02	−0.02	0.02	0.00	−0.01	0.00	0.00	0.07
Labor disputes	0.00	0.00	0.00	0.00	0.00	0.00	0.00	0.00	0.00	0.00	0.01

Sources: Derived from tables 2-9, 3-2, 3-4, 4-6, 4-7, 5-3, and G-2.
n.e.c. Not elsewhere classified.

Table 8-1. Sources of Growth of Total Actual National Income, Selected Periods, 1929–82
Contributions to growth rates in percentage points

Item	Longer periods				Shorter periods						
	1929–1982	1929–1948	1948–1973	1973–1982	1929–1941	1941–1948	1948–1953	1953–1964	1964–1973	1973–1979	1979–1982
National income	**2.92**	**2.54**	**3.70**	**1.55**	**2.09**ᵃ	**3.33**ᵃ	**4.69**	**3.08**	**3.92**	**2.61**	**−0.54**
Total factor input	**1.90**	**1.53**	**2.17**	**1.82**	**1.32**	**1.96**	**3.18**	**1.44**	**2.59**	**2.46**	**0.56**
Labor	1.34	1.42	1.40	1.13	1.39	1.55	2.32	0.80	1.74	1.69	0.04
Employment	1.12	1.01	1.22	1.19	0.78	1.42	1.59	0.55	1.82	1.80	−0.01
Hours	−0.27	−0.22	−0.25	−0.45	−0.17	−0.29	−0.05	−0.29	−0.31	−0.39	−0.55
Average hours	−0.51	−0.68	−0.38	−0.55	−0.71	−0.64	−0.24	−0.37	−0.49	−0.51	−0.64
Efficiency offset	0.17	0.39	0.04	0.09	0.50	0.23	0.08	0.00	0.10	0.11	0.10
Intergroup shift offset	0.07	0.07	0.09	0.01	0.04	0.12	0.11	0.08	0.08	0.01	−0.01
Age-sex composition	−0.08	0.01	−0.13	−0.14	0.04	−0.04	0.07	−0.08	−0.30	−0.26	0.07
Education	0.40	0.38	0.40	0.47	0.42	0.30	0.36	0.39	0.42	0.47	0.49
Unallocated	0.17	0.24	0.16	0.06	0.32	0.16	0.35	0.23	0.11	0.07	0.04
Capital	0.56	0.11	0.77	0.69	−0.07	0.41	0.86	0.64	0.85	0.77	0.52
Inventories	0.09	0.06	0.13	0.05	0.02	0.12	0.18	0.08	0.14	0.08	0.01
Nonresidential structures and equipment	0.21	0.00	0.33	0.30	−0.07	0.14	0.36	0.26	0.40	0.30	0.30
Dwellings	0.20	0.04	0.24	0.26	0.00	0.10	0.28	0.24	0.21	0.22	0.30
International assets	0.06	0.01	0.07	0.08	−0.02	0.05	0.04	0.06	0.10	0.17	−0.09
Land	0.00	0.00	0.00	0.00	0.00	0.00	0.00	0.00	0.00	0.00	0.00
Output per unit of input	**1.02**	**1.01**	**1.53**	**−0.27**	**0.77**	**1.37**	**1.51**	**1.64**	**1.33**	**0.15**	**−1.10**
Advances in knowledge and n.e.c.	0.66	0.50	1.09	−0.05	0.26	0.87	1.05	1.02	1.12	0.22	−0.57
Improved resource allocation	0.23	0.27	0.29	−0.01	0.20	0.39	0.40	0.26	0.24	0.03	−0.07
Farm	0.19	0.26	0.20	0.04	0.18	0.39	0.31	0.20	0.13	0.06	0.02
Nonfarm self-employment	0.04	0.01	0.09	−0.05	0.02	0.00	0.09	0.06	0.11	−0.03	−0.09
Legal and human environment	−0.04	0.00	−0.04	−0.16	0.00	0.00	0.00	−0.01	−0.08	−0.20	−0.11
Pollution abatement	−0.02	0.00	−0.02	−0.09	0.00	0.00	0.00	0.00	−0.05	−0.09	−0.09
Worker safety and health	−0.01	0.00	−0.01	−0.02	0.00	0.00	0.00	0.00	−0.01	−0.04	0.00
Dishonesty and crime	−0.01	0.00	−0.01	−0.05	0.00	0.00	0.00	−0.01	−0.02	−0.07	−0.02
Dwellings occupancy ratio	0.01	0.02	−0.01	0.01	0.01	0.02	−0.02	−0.01	0.01	0.02	−0.01
Economies of scale	0.26	0.22	0.32	0.20	0.13	0.36	0.37	0.24	0.38	0.26	0.09
Irregular factors	−0.10	0.00	−0.12	−0.26	0.17	−0.27	−0.29	0.14	−0.34	−0.18	−0.43
Weather in farming	0.00	−0.01	0.00	0.02	−0.02	0.02	0.00	−0.01	0.00	0.00	0.05
Labor disputes	0.00	0.00	0.00	0.00	0.00	0.00	0.00	0.00	0.00	0.00	0.01
Intensity of demand	−0.10	0.01	−0.12	−0.28	0.19	−0.29	−0.29	0.15	−0.34	−0.18	−0.49

Sources: Derived from tables 2-2, 2-9, 6-3, and 7-1.
n.e.c. Not elsewhere classified.
a. Based on data excluding work relief employees. When based on data including work relief employees, growth rates are 2.23 percent in 1929–41 and 3.08 percent in 1941–48.

Table 8-2. Sources of Growth of Total Potential National Income, Selected Periods, 1929–82
Contributions to growth rates in percentage points

Item	Longer periods				Shorter periods						
	1929–1982	1929–1948	1948–1973	1973–1982	1929–1941	1941–1948	1948–1953	1953–1964	1964–1973	1973–1979	1979–1982
National income	**3.20**	**2.57**	**3.89**	**2.61**	**2.36**	**2.93**	**4.79**	**3.17**	**4.27**	**3.01**	**1.82**
Total factor input	**2.03**	**1.56**	**2.23**	**2.53**	**1.62**	**1.46**	**3.02**	**1.64**	**2.60**	**2.66**	**2.27**
Labor	1.49	1.45	1.46	1.86	1.69	1.02	2.16	1.01	1.75	1.90	1.76
Employment	1.29	1.05	1.28	1.90	1.34	0.57	1.34	0.83	1.79	2.01	1.68
Hours	−0.25	−0.21	−0.24	−0.33	−0.17	−0.27	−0.03	−0.28	−0.29	−0.36	−0.27
Average hours	−0.50	−0.68	−0.37	−0.46	−0.72	−0.56	−0.20	−0.39	−0.45	−0.48	−0.41
Efficiency offset	0.17	0.39	0.04	0.10	0.48	0.22	0.07	0.01	0.08	0.10	0.08
Intergroup shift offset	0.08	0.08	0.09	0.03	0.07	0.07	0.10	0.10	0.08	0.02	0.06
Age-sex composition	−0.11	0.00	−0.15	−0.24	−0.02	0.05	0.11	−0.12	−0.31	−0.29	−0.13
Education	0.40	0.38	0.40	0.44	0.35	0.39	0.37	0.36	0.43	0.46	0.40
Unallocated	0.16	0.23	0.17	0.09	0.19	0.28	0.37	0.22	0.13	0.08	0.08
Capital	0.54	0.11	0.77	0.67	−0.07	0.44	0.86	0.63	0.85	0.76	0.51
Inventories	0.09	0.06	0.13	0.05	0.02	0.13	0.18	0.07	0.14	0.08	0.01
Nonresidential structures and equipment	0.21	0.00	0.33	0.31	−0.07	0.16	0.36	0.26	0.40	0.30	0.30
Dwellings	0.18	0.04	0.24	0.24	0.00	0.10	0.28	0.24	0.21	0.21	0.28
International assets	0.06	0.01	0.07	0.07	−0.02	0.05	0.04	0.06	0.10	0.17	−0.08
Land	0.00	0.00	0.00	0.00	0.00	0.00	0.00	0.00	0.00	0.00	0.00
Output per unit of input	**1.17**	**1.01**	**1.66**	**0.08**	**0.74**	**1.47**	**1.77**	**1.53**	**1.67**	**0.35**	**−0.45**
Advances in knowledge and n.e.c.	0.68	0.49	1.09	−0.05	0.27	0.88	1.06	1.01	1.14	0.22	−0.58
Improved resource allocation	0.25	0.29	0.30	0.07	0.35	0.18	0.35	0.31	0.23	0.05	0.10
Farm	0.20	0.27	0.21	0.06	0.27	0.27	0.28	0.22	0.13	0.06	0.05
Nonfarm self-employment	0.05	0.02	0.09	0.01	0.08	−0.09	0.07	0.09	0.10	−0.01	0.05
Legal and human environment	−0.04	0.00	−0.04	−0.17	0.00	0.00	0.00	−0.01	−0.09	−0.20	−0.12
Pollution abatement	−0.02	0.00	−0.02	−0.09	0.00	0.00	0.00	0.00	−0.05	−0.09	−0.10
Worker safety and health	−0.01	0.00	−0.01	−0.03	0.00	0.00	0.00	0.00	−0.02	−0.04	0.00
Dishonesty and crime	−0.01	0.00	−0.01	−0.05	0.00	0.00	0.00	−0.01	−0.02	−0.07	−0.02
Dwellings occupancy ratio	0.01	0.02	−0.01	0.01	0.01	0.02	−0.02	−0.01	0.00	0.02	−0.01
Economies of scale	0.27	0.22	0.32	0.21	0.13	0.37	0.38	0.24	0.39	0.26	0.10
Irregular factors	0.00	−0.01	0.00	0.01	−0.02	0.02	0.00	−0.01	0.00	0.00	0.06
Weather in farming	0.00	−0.01	0.00	0.01	−0.02	0.02	0.00	−0.01	0.00	0.00	0.05
Labor disputes	0.00	0.00	0.00	0.00	0.00	0.00	0.00	0.00	0.00	0.00	0.01

Sources: Derived from tables 2-2, 2-8, 6-3, and 7-2.
n.e.c. Not elsewhere classified.

Table 8-3. Sources of Growth of Actual National Income per Person Employed, Selected Periods, 1929–82
Contributions to growth rates in percentage points

	Longer periods				Shorter periods						
Item	1929–1982	1929–1948	1948–1973	1973–1982	1929–1941	1941–1948	1948–1953	1953–1964	1964–1973	1973–1979	1979–1982
National income per person employed	**1.48**	**1.26**	**2.16**	**0.06**	**1.11**[a]	**1.53**[a]	**2.66**	**2.39**	**1.59**	**0.36**	**−0.54**
Total factor input	**0.47**	**0.26**	**0.63**	**0.33**	**0.34**	**0.16**	**1.16**	**0.75**	**0.26**	**0.21**	**0.56**
Labor	0.22	0.41	0.18	−0.06	0.61	0.13	0.73	0.25	−0.08	−0.11	0.05
Hours	−0.27	−0.22	−0.25	−0.45	−0.17	−0.29	−0.05	−0.29	−0.31	−0.39	−0.55
Average hours	−0.51	−0.68	−0.38	−0.55	−0.71	−0.64	−0.24	−0.37	−0.49	−0.51	−0.64
Efficiency offset	0.17	0.39	0.04	0.09	0.50	0.23	0.08	0.00	0.10	0.11	0.10
Intergroup shift offset	0.07	0.07	0.09	0.01	0.04	0.12	0.11	0.08	0.08	0.01	−0.01
Age-sex composition	−0.08	0.01	−0.13	−0.14	0.04	−0.04	0.07	−0.08	−0.30	−0.26	0.07
Education	0.40	0.38	0.40	0.47	0.42	0.30	0.36	0.39	0.42	0.47	0.49
Unallocated	0.17	0.24	0.16	0.06	0.32	0.16	0.35	0.23	0.11	0.07	0.04
Capital	0.30	−0.12	0.50	0.43	−0.23	0.09	0.50	0.52	0.41	0.38	0.51
Inventories	0.04	−0.01	0.07	0.02	−0.01	0.00	0.09	0.05	0.06	0.02	0.01
Nonresidential structures and equipment	0.09	−0.10	0.19	0.18	−0.17	−0.01	0.17	0.20	0.19	0.12	0.29
Dwellings	0.13	0.01	0.18	0.17	−0.02	0.06	0.22	0.22	0.10	0.11	0.30
International assets	0.04	−0.02	0.06	0.06	−0.03	0.04	0.02	0.05	0.06	0.13	−0.09
Land	−0.05	−0.03	−0.05	−0.04	−0.04	−0.06	−0.07	−0.02	−0.07	−0.06	0.00
Output per unit of input	**1.01**	**1.00**	**1.53**	**−0.27**	**0.77**	**1.37**	**1.50**	**1.64**	**1.33**	**0.15**	**−1.10**
Advances in knowledge and n.e.c.	0.65	0.49	1.09	−0.05	0.26	0.87	1.05	1.02	1.12	0.22	−0.57
Improved resource allocation	0.23	0.27	0.29	−0.01	0.20	0.39	0.40	0.26	0.24	0.03	−0.07
Farm	0.19	0.26	0.20	0.04	0.18	0.39	0.31	0.20	0.13	0.06	0.02
Nonfarm self-employment	0.04	0.01	0.09	−0.05	0.02	0.00	0.09	0.06	0.11	−0.03	−0.09
Legal and human environment	−0.04	0.00	−0.04	−0.16	0.00	0.00	0.00	−0.01	−0.08	−0.20	−0.11
Pollution abatement	−0.02	0.00	−0.02	−0.09	0.00	0.00	0.00	0.00	−0.05	−0.09	−0.09
Worker safety and health	−0.01	0.00	−0.01	−0.02	0.00	0.00	0.00	0.00	−0.01	−0.04	0.00
Dishonesty and crime	−0.01	0.00	−0.01	−0.05	0.00	0.00	0.00	−0.01	−0.02	−0.07	−0.02
Dwellings occupancy ratio	0.01	0.02	−0.01	0.01	0.01	0.02	−0.02	−0.01	0.01	0.02	−0.01
Economies of scale	0.26	0.22	0.32	0.20	0.13	0.36	0.37	0.24	0.38	0.26	0.09
Irregular factors	−0.10	0.00	−0.12	−0.26	0.17	−0.27	−0.30	0.14	−0.34	−0.18	−0.43
Weather in farming	0.00	−0.01	0.00	0.02	−0.02	0.02	0.00	−0.01	0.00	0.00	0.05
Labor disputes	0.00	0.00	0.00	0.00	0.00	0.00	0.00	0.00	0.00	0.00	0.01
Intensity of demand	−0.10	0.01	−0.12	−0.28	0.19	−0.29	−0.30	0.15	−0.34	−0.18	−0.49

Sources: Derived from tables 2-2, 2-6, 2-9, 3-1, 4-1, 6-3, 6-4, 7-1, and G-2.
n.e.c. Not elsewhere classified.
a. Based on data excluding work relief employees. When based on data including work relief employees, growth rates are 0.90 percent in 1929–41 and 1.88 percent in 1941–48.

Table 8-4. Sources of Growth of Potential National Income per Person Potentially Employed, Selected Periods, 1929–82

Contributions to growth rates in percentage points

Item	Longer periods				Shorter periods						
	1929–1982	1929–1948	1948–1973	1973–1982	1929–1941	1941–1948	1948–1953	1953–1964	1964–1973	1973–1979	1979–1982
National income per person potentially employed	**1.55**	**1.24**	**2.26**	**0.23**	**0.68**	**2.21**	**3.06**	**2.12**	**1.98**	**0.49**	**−0.28**
Total factor input	**0.38**	**0.23**	**0.61**	**0.15**	**−0.06**	**0.74**	**1.30**	**0.59**	**0.32**	**0.14**	**0.17**
Labor	0.20	0.40	0.18	−0.04	0.35	0.45	0.82	0.18	−0.04	−0.11	0.08
Hours	−0.25	−0.21	−0.24	−0.33	−0.17	−0.27	−0.03	−0.28	−0.29	−0.36	−0.27
Average hours	−0.50	−0.68	−0.37	−0.46	−0.72	−0.56	−0.20	−0.39	−0.45	−0.48	−0.41
Efficiency offset	0.17	0.39	0.04	0.10	0.48	0.22	0.07	0.01	0.08	0.10	0.08
Intergroup shift offset	0.08	0.08	0.09	0.03	0.07	0.07	0.10	0.10	0.08	0.02	0.06
Age-sex composition	−0.11	0.00	−0.15	−0.24	−0.02	0.05	0.11	−0.12	−0.31	−0.29	−0.13
Education	0.40	0.38	0.40	0.44	0.35	0.39	0.37	0.36	0.43	0.46	0.40
Unallocated	0.16	0.23	0.17	0.09	0.19	0.28	0.37	0.22	0.13	0.08	0.08
Capital	0.23	−0.12	0.48	0.26	−0.34	0.31	0.54	0.44	0.43	0.32	0.14
Inventories	0.03	0.00	0.07	−0.01	−0.04	0.09	0.10	0.04	0.07	0.01	−0.04
Nonresidential structures and equipment	0.06	−0.12	0.19	0.11	−0.22	0.08	0.19	0.16	0.19	0.10	0.14
Dwellings	0.11	0.01	0.17	0.12	−0.04	0.09	0.22	0.20	0.10	0.09	0.16
International assets	0.03	−0.01	0.05	0.04	−0.04	0.05	0.03	0.04	0.07	0.12	−0.12
Land	−0.05	−0.05	−0.05	−0.07	−0.07	−0.02	−0.06	−0.03	−0.07	−0.07	−0.05
Output per unit of input	**1.17**	**1.01**	**1.65**	**0.08**	**0.74**	**1.47**	**1.76**	**1.53**	**1.66**	**0.35**	**−0.45**
Advances in knowledge and n.e.c.	0.68	0.49	1.08	−0.05	0.27	0.88	1.05	1.01	1.13	0.22	−0.58
Improved resource allocation	0.25	0.29	0.30	0.07	0.35	0.18	0.35	0.31	0.23	0.05	0.10
Farm	0.20	0.27	0.21	0.06	0.27	0.27	0.28	0.22	0.13	0.06	0.05
Nonfarm self-employment	0.05	0.02	0.09	0.01	0.08	−0.09	0.07	0.09	0.10	−0.01	0.05
Legal and human environment	−0.04	0.00	−0.04	−0.17	0.00	0.00	0.00	−0.01	−0.09	−0.20	−0.12
Pollution abatement	−0.02	0.00	−0.02	−0.09	0.00	0.00	0.00	0.00	−0.05	−0.09	−0.10
Worker safety and health	−0.01	0.00	−0.01	−0.03	0.00	0.00	0.00	0.00	−0.02	−0.04	0.00
Dishonesty and crime	−0.01	0.00	−0.01	−0.05	0.00	0.00	0.00	−0.01	−0.02	−0.07	−0.02
Dwellings occupancy ratio	0.01	0.02	−0.01	0.01	0.01	0.02	−0.02	−0.01	0.00	0.02	−0.01
Economies of scale	0.27	0.22	0.32	0.21	0.13	0.37	0.38	0.24	0.39	0.26	0.10
Irregular factors	0.00	−0.01	0.00	0.01	−0.02	0.02	0.00	−0.01	0.00	0.00	0.06
Weather in farming	0.00	−0.01	0.00	0.01	−0.02	0.02	0.00	−0.01	0.00	0.00	0.05
Labor disputes	0.00	0.00	0.00	0.00	0.00	0.00	0.00	0.00	0.00	0.00	0.01

Sources: Derived from tables 2-2, 2-8, 2-9, 3-2, 4-1, 6-3, 6-4, and G-2.
n.e.c. Not elsewhere classified.

Table 8-7. Composition of the Gap between Total Actual and Potential National Income, and Potential GNP and GNP Gap, 1929, 1940–41, and 1947–82[a]

Actual less potential, in billions of 1972 dollars; column 12, billions of 1972 dollars

Year	Total national income gap (1)	Intensity of demand, effect on output per unit of input (2)	Total labor input, resource allocation, and unallocated (3)	Labor input — Employment (4)	Hours (5)	Age-sex composition (6)	Education (7)	Resource allocation — Farm (8)	Nonfarm self-employment (9)	Unallocated (10)	GNP data — Total GNP gap (11)	Total potential GNP (12)
1929	4.5	1.3	3.2	2.9	0.5	−0.7	−0.2	0.9	0.5	−0.7	5.0	310.7
1940[b]	−24.7	−0.8	−30.9	−30.0	−0.8	3.3	1.1	−4.9	−3.4	3.8	−28.3	372.4
1941[b]	0.6	8.7	−13.5	−15.9	1.3	1.4	0.7	−2.3	−1.6	2.9	0.7	399.7
1947	−4.3	−5.1	0.8	1.2	−0.2	−0.5	0.0	0.4	0.2	−0.3	−4.9	475.2
1948	4.9	2.8	2.1	1.7	0.4	−0.7	−0.1	0.4	0.3	0.1	5.4	484.4
1949	−10.8	−2.0	−8.8	−9.2	−0.8	1.0	0.5	−0.9	−1.1	1.7	−12.2	504.4
1950	3.3	8.3	−5.0	−6.2	0.1	0.6	0.3	−0.5	−0.7	1.4	3.7	531.1
1951	13.1	7.5	5.6	4.8	1.1	−1.3	−0.2	0.8	0.6	−0.2	14.8	564.6
1952	5.3	−1.4	6.7	7.0	0.6	−1.7	−0.3	1.0	0.8	−0.7	6.0	594.8
1953	3.7	−3.9	7.6	8.2	0.5	−2.0	−0.4	1.1	1.0	−0.8	4.2	619.4
1954	−15.8	−7.0	−8.8	−8.1	−1.6	0.7	0.5	−0.5	−0.9	1.1	−17.9	634.0
1955	4.2	5.1	−0.9	−1.3	−0.1	−0.3	0.1	0.2	−0.1	0.6	4.7	652.8
1956	−6.7	−5.1	−1.6	0.2	−1.9	−0.7	0.0	0.3	0.0	0.5	−7.5	679.1
1957	−12.9	−9.3	−3.6	−0.8	−2.9	−0.5	0.2	0.1	−0.2	0.5	−14.4	698.2
1958	−40.6	−17.4	−23.2	−19.5	−6.0	2.2	1.1	−1.2	−2.1	2.3	−45.7	726.6
1959	−17.6	−6.1	−11.5	−10.2	−2.8	1.0	0.6	−0.5	−1.0	1.4	−19.7	741.4
1960	−26.8	−12.9	−13.9	−11.2	−4.2	1.1	0.7	−0.6	−1.2	1.4	−29.9	767.1
1961	−34.4	−11.9	−22.5	−20.9	−4.1	2.4	1.1	−1.2	−2.0	2.2	−38.6	795.2
1962	−16.2	−3.9	−12.3	−12.1	−2.0	1.2	0.7	−0.6	−1.1	1.6	−18.3	818.6
1963	−10.2	1.9	−12.1	−13.5	−0.9	1.6	0.7	−0.6	−1.1	1.7	−11.5	844.0
1964	−1.6	6.0	−7.6	−9.9	0.2	1.1	0.5	−0.4	−0.9	1.8	−1.8	878.2
1965	11.5	12.7	−1.2	−3.9	1.5	0.2	0.3	−0.2	−0.3	1.2	12.8	916.5
1966	16.5	11.1	5.4	3.3	2.0	−0.5	−0.1	0.2	0.3	0.2	18.5	966.3
1967	3.8	1.8	2.0	1.5	0.3	−0.2	−0.1	0.1	0.2	0.2	4.2	1,007.2
1968	6.2	1.3	4.9	4.5	0.8	−0.7	−0.2	0.2	0.4	−0.1	6.9	1,051.2
1969	−9.2	−12.5	3.3	5.9	−1.4	−1.2	−0.2	0.3	0.5	0.0	−10.2	1,097.8
1970	−43.6	−30.3	−13.3	−12.0	−3.4	1.9	0.3	−0.2	−0.8	0.9	−48.9	1,134.5
1971	−45.2	−22.5	−22.7	−25.1	−1.4	4.5	0.6	−0.6	−1.6	0.9	−51.1	1,173.5
1972	−41.2	−21.3	−19.9	−22.4	−1.4	4.2	0.8	−0.5	−1.5	0.9	−46.5	1,232.4
1973	−34.3	−22.7	−11.6	−12.5	−1.9	2.2	0.6	−0.3	−0.7	1.0	−38.5	1,292.8
1974	−79.6	−52.1	−27.5	−23.3	−7.4	3.8	1.2	−0.6	−1.6	0.4	−89.8	1,336.1
1975	−94.8	−36.7	−58.1	−64.6	−4.1	10.2	3.4	−1.6	−4.1	2.7	−107.5	1,339.1
1976	−80.8	−30.0	−50.8	−56.7	−3.8	9.2	2.9	−1.3	−3.6	2.5	−91.5	1,389.7
1977	−64.8	−22.0	−42.8	−48.7	−2.9	8.3	2.6	−1.2	−3.3	2.4	−73.0	1,442.7
1978	−53.0	−22.8	−30.2	−33.2	−3.2	6.0	1.7	−0.7	−2.1	1.3	−59.4	1,498.0
1979	−68.9	−39.4	−29.5	−29.7	−4.7	5.1	1.6	−0.8	−2.0	1.0	−77.3	1,556.7
1980	−114.4	−59.1	−55.3	−52.5	−9.7	7.6	2.9	−1.2	−3.8	1.4	−128.7	1,603.7
1981	−106.5	−44.5	−62.0	−61.4	−8.9	9.2	3.4	−3.8	−4.3	1.3	−119.4	1,633.2
1982	−158.5	−56.2	−102.3	−97.1	−15.4	12.6	5.2	1.4	−7.1	1.4	−178.6	1,664.0

Sources: Column 1, table 2-4, column 5; column 2, table 2-4, column 2, sign reversed; column 3, table 2-4, column 3, sign reversed; column 4, table L-5, product of columns 20 and 21 times (ratio of column 1 in table 3-2 to column 1 in table 3-1, minus 1), sign reversed; columns 5, 6, and 7, same as column 4 except that column 9, 4, or 7, respectively, of tables 3-2 and 3-1 is substituted for column 1; column 8, table L-5, column 21 times (ratio of column 2 in table 5-2 to column 2 in table 5-1, minus 1), sign reversed; column 9, same as column 8 except that column 3 of tables 5-2 and 5-1 is substituted for column 2; column 10, table L-5, column 21 times (ratio of column 13 of table 4-6 to 100.00 minus 1), sign reversed; column 11, column 1 of this table times the ratio of "net domestic business product less housing" to "domestic business income less housing," both in 1972 dollars and both from NIPA, table 1.10; column 12, actual GNP in constant dollars from NIPA, table 1.2, less column 11.

a. Column 1 equals the sum of columns 2 and 3 (except in 1940–41; see note b). Column 3 equals the sum of columns 4–10; detail is adjusted to equal total. Data for 1929–59 exclude Alaska and Hawaii.

b. The output of employees on work relief ($7.0 billion in 1940 and $5.4 billion in 1941) is not offset against the gap in nonresidential business in column 3 but is added to column 1. See table 2-4.

Table B-1. Derivation of Total Employment, 1959–82
Thousands

	Civilian employment, based mainly on establishment reports							Estimated employment			
Year[a]	Full-time and part-time employment (1)	Active proprietors of unincorporated enterprises[b] (2)	Unpaid family workers[b] (3)	Civilian employment overseas (4)	Total domestic (5)	CPS civilian employment[b] (6)	Ratio, column 6 to column 5 (7)	Domestic civilian (8)	Total civilian (9)	Military (10)	Total (11)
				Excluding Alaska and Hawaii							
1959	57,872	8,428	1,633	76	67,857	65,636	0.96727	65,249	65,325	2,543	67,868
1960	. . .	. . .	. . .	64	. . .	66,448	. . .	65,883[c]	65,947	2,516	68,463
				Including Alaska and Hawaii							
1960	58,988	8,305	1,586	64	68,815	66,737	0.96980	66,170	66,234	2,516	68,750
1961	59,083	8,177	1,565	65	68,760	66,852	0.97255	66,118	66,183	2,598	68,781
1962	60,657	8,009	1,452	65	70,053	67,903	0.96931	67,361	67,426	2,800	70,226
1963	61,754	7,722	1,350	66	70,760	68,867	0.97325	68,041	68,107	2,723	70,830
1964	63,309	7,652	1,337	64	72,234	70,416	0.97483	69,458	69,522	2,720	72,242
1965	65,760	7,526	1,332	65	74,553	72,239	0.96896	71,688	71,753	2,732	74,485
1966	69,097	7,271	1,203	68	77,503	74,127	0.95644	74,525	74,593	3,156	77,749
1967	70,757	7,188	1,174	72	79,047	75,608	0.95649	76,009	76,081	3,421	79,502
1968	72,862	7,115	1,153	71	81,059	77,209	0.95250	77,944	78,015	3,517	81,532
1969	75,159	7,199	1,160	72	83,446	79,221	0.94937	80,239	80,311	3,463	83,774
1970	75,398	7,093	1,105	70	83,526	79,989	0.95765	80,316	80,386	3,096	83,482
1971	75,575	7,117	1,110	64	83,738	80,501	0.96134	80,520	80,584	2,738	83,322
1972	77,928	7,198	1,088	62	86,152	83,116	0.96476	82,841	82,903	2,403	85,306
1973	81,384	7,264	1,063	64	89,647	85,886	0.95805	86,202	86,266	2,295	88,561
1974	82,810	7,458	961	68	91,161	87,408	0.95883	87,658	87,726	2,202	89,928
1975	81,306	7,420	942	65	89,603	86,172	0.96171	86,160	86,225	2,155	88,380
1976	83,686	7,392	879	64	91,893	88,844	0.96682	88,362	88,426	2,122	90,548
1977	86,693	7,669	914	65	95,211	92,019	0.96647	91,552	91,617	2,110	93,727
1978	90,918	8,063	849	64	99,766	95,853	0.96078	95,932	95,996	2,093	98,089
1979	93,905	8,394	815	64	103,050	98,317	0.95407	99,090	99,154	2,065	101,219
1980	94,229	8,665	754	68	103,580	98,448	0.95045	99,599	99,667	2,080	101,747
1981	94,956	8,759	697	70	104,342	99,376	0.95257	100,332	100,402	2,115	102,517
1982	93,368	8,927	696	70	102,921	. . .	. . .	98,966	99,036	2,146	101,182

Sources: Column 1, NIPA, table 6.7, total minus military, federal government work relief, and state and local government work relief; column 2, NIPA, table 6.10; column 3, Bureau of Labor Statistics, *Employment and Earnings*, January 1982 and earlier issues; column 4, sum of (1) U.S. citizens employed abroad by the U.S. government, for which the BEA provided data based on the Civil Service Commission series, and (2) U.S. citizens employed abroad by private enterprises, which is a component of the NIPA series for employment in the rest-of-the-world industry and was supplied by the BEA from worksheets; column 5, sum of columns 1, 2, and 3 minus column 4; column 6, same as column 3; column 8, column 5 times 0.96157 (see "Derivations"); column 9, column 4 plus column 8; column 10, the NIPA military employment series excluding reserve personnel, provided by the BEA; column 11, column 9 plus column 10.

a. Comparable data for 1929, 1940–41, and 1947–58 appear in *Slower Growth*, table B-1.

b. Data are before adjustment to agree with the 1980 Census of Population; see "Derivations" for explanation.

c. The ratio to the following row is assumed to be the same as in column 6.

Table C-1. Weekly Hours at Work per Person Employed and Total Weekly Hours, 1929, 1940–41, and 1947–82[a]

| | | | Weekly hours at work per person employed[b] | | | | Total weekly hours at work in nonresidential business (millions) | | |
| | | | | Nonresidential business | | | | | |
Year	Whole economy (1)	General government, households, and institutions (2)	Total (3)	Farms (4)	Nonfarm self-employed and unpaid family workers (5)	Wage and salary workers in nonfarm business (6)	Farms (7)	Nonfarm self-employed and unpaid family workers (8)	Wage and salary workers in nonfarm business (9)
			Excluding Alaska and Hawaii						
1929	48.4	43.9	49.08	54.6	53.9	46.1	539.18	269.60	1,217.64
1940[c]	42.3	35.1	44.14	53.1	47.8	40.4	471.86	251.82	1,079.26
1940[d]	43.3	38.9	44.14	53.1	47.8	40.4	471.86	251.82	1,079.26
1941[c]	42.7	35.5	44.47	52.5	48.9	41.3	467.84	260.25	1,255.59
1941[d]	43.4	38.3	44.47	52.5	48.9	41.3	467.84	260.25	1,255.59
1947	41.6	35.9	42.65	50.1	47.8	40.1	397.04	290.36	1,447.87
1948	41.3	35.3	42.42	50.1	47.9	39.9	392.36	295.29	1,466.67
1949	40.8	35.2	41.89	49.1	47.9	39.3	376.01	293.30	1,386.15
1950	40.8	35.2	41.91	48.4	47.9	39.6	363.12	295.40	1,446.26
1951	40.7	35.6	41.89	49.0	47.8	39.6	346.96	295.95	1,544.50
1952	40.6	35.8	41.69	48.6	47.8	39.5	334.37	297.87	1,568.89
1953	40.4	35.7	41.46	49.1	47.8	39.2	325.88	296.40	1,598.61
1954	40.0	35.3	41.04	48.3	47.8	38.8	319.72	290.63	1,523.48
1955	40.0	34.9	41.21	47.6	48.0	39.2	309.10	292.57	1,587.18
1956	39.7	34.5	40.87	46.5	48.7	38.9	290.15	301.12	1,623.68
1957	39.1	34.3	40.26	45.4	47.7	38.4	269.06	299.43	1,608.27
1958	38.7	34.0	39.92	45.0	47.0	38.1	254.59	293.31	1,527.42
1959	38.9	33.8	40.16	45.2	46.8	38.5	250.66	288.88	1,598.68
1960	38.7	33.8	39.94	45.2	46.8	38.3	238.09	290.58	1,608.05
			Including Alaska and Hawaii						
1960	38.7	33.8	39.94	45.2	46.8	38.3	239.18	291.65	1,614.24
1961	38.4	33.5	39.72	44.7	46.2	38.1	229.71	288.28	1,593.90
1962	38.4	33.4	39.83	45.4	46.4	38.3	223.33	284.08	1,641.02
1963	38.3	33.3	39.74	45.6	45.9	38.3	211.72	275.06	1,668.98
1964	38.3	33.1	39.77	44.8	45.9	38.5	195.54	276.75	1,721.56
1965	38.3	33.0	39.86	45.5	46.0	38.6	188.87	275.82	1,799.50
1966	37.9	32.8	39.48	45.4	46.0	38.2	170.98	271.09	1,878.42
1967	37.5	32.9	38.88	45.0	45.5	37.7	163.40	264.77	1,889.40
1968	37.2	32.7	38.68	45.3	45.8	37.4	161.68	263.41	1,931.03
1969	37.1	32.6	38.44	45.2	45.2	37.3	155.34	269.04	1,989.77
1970	36.5	32.2	37.83	45.1	44.4	36.6	150.35	262.62	1,951.36
1971	36.3	32.0	37.65	45.2	44.2	36.5	147.24	265.86	1,931.88
1972	36.2	31.8	37.61	44.6	43.6	36.5	145.40	264.98	1,999.62
1973	36.1	31.8	37.45	44.4	43.5	36.4	144.14	268.64	2,099.26
1974	35.7	31.6	36.89	44.0	42.7	35.9	143.25	270.31	2,101.08
1975	35.2	31.3	36.49	44.2	42.0	35.4	141.56	266.36	2,003.32
1976	35.2	31.3	36.43	43.9	41.9	35.4	137.85	266.78	2,073.74
1977	35.1	31.1	36.33	44.3	41.9	35.3	133.58	282.54	2,156.33
1978	35.0	31.0	36.16	44.5	42.0	35.1	130.26	297.81	2,268.74
1979	34.8	31.0	35.94	45.6	41.5	34.9	131.61	308.65	2,342.28
1980	34.5	30.7	35.57	44.4	40.8	34.6	131.24	310.92	2,313.27
1981	34.3	30.7	35.37	44.5	40.2	34.4	126.32	309.64	2,330.94
1982	34.0	30.7	34.94	43.7	39.5	34.1	118.45	312.68	2,253.79

Sources: See "Derivations" and *Slower Growth,* appendix C.

a. See table 2-1 for total hours at work in the whole economy.

b. Hours worked by military reservists not on full-time active duty are included in the numerator in the computation of hours per person in the whole economy but are excluded in the computation of columns 2–6.

c. Including persons on work relief.

d. Excluding persons on work relief.

Table E-1. 1960 Efficiency Equivalents to Average Weekly Hours of Nonfarm Wage and Salary Workers Used in Construction of "Intragroup" Efficiency Indexes

Males		Females	
Average weekly hours	Efficiency equivalents	Average weekly hours	Efficiency equivalents
Postwar values		Postwar values	
38.3	38.90	. . .	. . .
39.0	39.57	. . .	. . .
40.0	40.48	36.0	36.52
41.0	41.32	37.0	37.38
42.0	42.08	38.0	38.18
42.3[a]	42.30	38.7[a]	38.70
43.0	42.76	39.0	38.90
43.1	42.83	40.0	39.54
Prewar values		Prewar values	
43.6	43.14	40.4	39.78
44.1	43.43	40.7	39.96
48.8	45.29	45.1	41.67

Source: See *Slower Growth*, pp. 36–39.
a. 1960 level.

Table F-2. Mean Income of Year-Round Full-Time Workers, by Years of School Completed[a]
Mean income of men with 8 years of education = 100 percent

Years of school completed	1971–75 average (1)	1976–79 average (2)
Elementary		
0–7 years	84.0	81.9
8 years	100.0	100.0
High school		
1–3 years	112.1	109.5
4 years	131.4	130.8
College		
1–3 years	156.1	151.4
4 years	192.2	193.8
5 and more years	218.7	219.9

Sources: Column 1, *Slower Growth*, table F-2; column 2, U.S. Bureau of the Census, "Money Income in . . . of Families and Persons in the United States," annually.
a. Percentages shown are averages of percentages for each of four ten-year age groups of men 25–64 years of age.

Table F-3. Civilians 16 Years of Age and Over: Unemployment Rates and Education Quality Indexes, Based on Years of Education, by Sex, Survey Dates, 1976–83
Weight of persons with 8 years of education = 100
Based on 1969 weights for education groups

Sex and date	Percent unemployed (1)	Education quality indexes based on years of education			Percent by which column 3 exceeds column 2 (5)	Ratio of column 4 to column 3 (6)
		Civilian labor force (2)	Civilian employment (3)	FTE business employment (4)		
Males						
March 1976	7.82	133.44	134.44	132.28	0.75	0.9839
March 1977	7.46	134.00	134.96	132.98	0.72	0.9853
March 1978	6.27	134.43	135.27	133.46	0.62	0.9866
March 1979	5.75	135.39	136.19	134.40	0.59	0.9869
March 1980[a]	6.59	135.84	136.84	135.29	0.74	0.9887
March 1981[a]	8.09	136.16	137.47	135.92	0.96	0.9887
March 1982	10.30	137.18	138.67	137.24	1.09	0.9897
March 1983	11.92	138.33	140.28	139.02	1.41	0.9910
Females						
March 1976	8.48	131.10	131.86	127.79	0.58	0.9691
March 1977	8.48	131.58	132.30	128.61	0.55	0.9721
March 1978	7.01	131.86	132.51	128.93	0.49	0.9730
March 1979	6.57	132.70	133.36	129.87	0.50	0.9738
March 1980[a]	6.61	133.66	134.39	130.89	0.55	0.9740
March 1981[a]	7.60	133.81	134.66	131.44	0.64	0.9761
March 1982	8.92	134.63	135.69	132.42	0.79	0.9759
March 1983	9.65	135.94	137.42	133.98	1.09	0.9750

Sources: See "Derivations" and *Slower Growth*.
FTE: Full-time equivalent.
a. There is a slight incomparability between 1980 and 1981 data. See "Derivations."

Table F-4. Derivation of Education Quality Indexes for the Business Sector, Based on Years of Education, by Sex, Annually, 1972–82

Based on 1969 weights for education groups. Data refer to persons 16 years of age and over.

Sex, census of population year on which labor force weights are based, and year[a]	Index for civilian labor force[b] (1)	Percent of civilian labor force unemployed (2)	Index for civilian employment[b] (3)	Estimated ratio of index for FTE business employment to index for civilian employment (4)	Index for FTE business employment[b] (5)
Males					
1970 census weights					
1972	129.58	4.95	130.15	.9843	128.11
1973	130.58	4.13	131.02	.9851	129.07
1974	131.62	4.83	132.18	.9855	130.26
1975	132.70	7.88	133.78	.9845	131.71
1976	133.59	7.04	134.53	.9844	132.43
1977	134.12	6.25	134.93	.9857	133.00
1978	134.72	5.21	135.35	.9867	133.55
1979	135.51	5.07	136.12	.9875	134.42
1980	135.92	6.91	136.85	.9887	135.30
1980 census weights					
1980	135.95	6.94	136.89	.9887	135.34
1981	136.47	7.39	137.49	.9890	135.98
1982	137.52	9.89	138.99	.9901	137.61
Females					
1970 census weights					
1972	127.88	6.63	128.48	.9691	124.51
1973	128.83	5.97	129.35	.9684	125.26
1974	129.77	6.71	130.38	.9689	126.33
1975	130.46	9.29	131.38	.9695	127.37
1976	131.23	8.64	132.08	.9701	128.13
1977	131.66	8.18	132.46	.9723	128.79
1978	132.12	7.15	132.80	.9732	129.24
1979	132.98	6.79	133.62	.9739	130.13
1980	133.68	7.38	134.39	.9747	130.99
1980 census weights					
1980	133.72	7.41	134.44	.9747	131.04
1981	134.06	7.92	134.84	.9760	131.60
1982	135.02	9.42	135.99	.9756	132.67

Sources: Column 1, straight-line interpolation of data from table F-3, column 2, or similar data; column 2, BLS, *Employment and Earnings*, various issues; column 3, column 1 raised by a percentage equal to −0.1928 plus (column 2 times 0.1274) for males, and −0.1287 plus (column 2 times 0.0896) for females; column 4, straight-line interpolation of data from table F-3, column 6, or similar data; column 5, column 3 times column 4.

FTE: Full-time equivalent.

a. See "Derivations" for explanation of census of population year.

b. Weight of persons with 8 years of education = 100.

Table F-5. Indexes of the Effect of Amount of Education on Labor Input in the Business Sector, 1972–82
1972 = 100

| Year[a] | Before allowance for change in days per year of school | | Final indexes | | | Female share of earnings |
	Males (1)	Females (2)	Males (3)	Females (4)	Both sexes (5)	(6)
1972	100.00	100.00	100.00	100.00	100.00	20.11
1973	100.75	100.60	100.86	100.73	100.83	20.46
1974	101.68	101.46	101.89	101.70	101.85	21.01
1975	102.81	102.30	103.12	102.66	103.02	21.09
1976	103.37	102.91	103.75	103.34	103.66	21.97
1977	103.82	103.44	104.26	103.94	104.20	22.54
1978	104.25	103.80	104.75	104.37	104.67	23.28
1979	104.93	104.51	105.46	105.14	105.40	23.79
1980	105.61	105.20	106.24	105.90	106.17	24.59
1981	106.11	105.65	106.80	106.40	106.72	25.01
1982	107.38	106.51	108.10	107.26	107.91	25.63

Sources: Columns 1 and 2, table F-4, column 5; columns 3–6, see "Derivations" and *Slower Growth*, appendix F.
a. For earlier years, see *Slower Growth*, table F-5.

Table G-1. Nonresidential Business: Percentage Distribution of Earnings in the Sector, by Type of Input, 1967–82ᵃ

			Earnings (percent)		
Year	Total (1)	Labor (2)	Nonresidential structures and equipment (3)	Inventories (4)	Land (5)
1967	100.00	79.16	12.26	4.36	4.22
1968	100.00	79.58	12.11	4.22	4.09
1969	100.00	81.38	11.03	3.78	3.81
1970	100.00	83.99	9.52	3.15	3.34
1971	100.00	82.98	10.22	3.25	3.55
1972	100.00	82.33	10.48	3.36	3.83
1973	100.00	81.90	10.13	3.50	4.47
1974	100.00	84.70	8.65	3.05	3.60
1975	100.00	83.13	9.76	3.29	3.82
1976	100.00	82.87	10.20	3.29	3.64
1977	100.00	81.83	10.87	3.53	3.77
1978	100.00	81.60	10.87	3.57	3.96
1979	100.00	82.98	9.82	3.33	3.81
1980	100.00	84.86	8.98	3.02	3.14
1981	100.00	83.30	9.93	3.24	3.54
1982	100.00	85.54	8.63	2.78	3.05

Sources: See "Derivations" and *Slower Growth*, appendix G.
a. Including Alaska and Hawaii.

Table G-2. Nonresidential Business: Weights Used for Inputs in the Sector

Period ending[a]	Total (1)	Labor (2)	Nonresidential structures and equipment (3)	Inventories (4)	Land (5)
1940	100.00	79.33	11.10	4.70	4.87
1941	100.00	78.90	11.41	5.22	4.47
1947	100.00	78.62	10.90	5.72	4.76
1948	100.00	78.31	10.82	5.95	4.92
1949	100.00	78.16	11.56	5.66	4.62
1950	100.00	78.08	12.09	5.43	4.40
1951	100.00	78.60	11.78	5.38	4.25
1952	100.00	79.35	11.27	5.24	4.14
1953	100.00	79.75	11.28	5.03	3.94
1954	100.00	80.31	11.29	4.74	3.66
1955	100.00	80.94	11.15	4.46	3.45
1956	100.00	81.20	11.14	4.31	3.35
1957	100.00	81.31	11.18	4.20	3.31
1958	100.00	81.71	11.00	4.00	3.29
1959	100.00	82.04	10.89	3.85	3.22
1960	100.00	81.88	11.01	3.85	3.26
1961	100.00	81.61	11.05	3.88	3.46
1962	100.00	81.25	11.19	3.94	3.62
1963	100.00	80.62	11.50	4.08	3.80
1964	100.00	79.78	11.99	4.26	3.97
1965	100.00	79.24	12.26	4.37	4.13
1966	100.00	79.06	12.26	4.40	4.28
1967	100.00	79.24	12.16	4.36	4.24
1968	100.00	79.85	11.90	4.19	4.06
1969	100.00	80.70	11.44	3.96	3.90
1970	100.00	81.46	11.02	3.70	3.82
1971	100.00	82.00	10.75	3.49	3.76
1972	100.00	82.32	10.55	3.37	3.76
1973	100.00	82.48	10.10	3.36	4.06
1974	100.00	82.66	9.75	3.40	4.19
1975	100.00	82.69	9.89	3.42	4.00
1976	100.00	82.61	10.20	3.37	3.82
1977	100.00	82.66	10.35	3.35	3.64
1978	100.00	82.78	10.24	3.34	3.64
1979	100.00	82.83	10.06	3.34	3.77
1980	100.00	82.96	10.00	3.36	3.68
1981	100.00	83.21	9.99	3.28	3.52
1982	100.00	83.35	9.93	3.20	3.52

Sources: See "Derivations" and *Slower Growth*, appendix G.
a. Entries for 1940 refer to the 1929–40 period and those for 1947 to the 1941–47 period. All others refer to the pair of years ending in the year shown.

Table G-3. Nonresidential Business: National Income Originating in the Sector, and Distribution among Types of Income, 1967–82
Billions of dollars

| Year | Total (1) | Compensation of employees (2) | Income, except compensation of employees | | |
			Originating in nonfarm corporations (3)	Earnings of farm proprietors and property used on farms (4)	Earnings of non-farm proprietors and noncorporate nonfarm property (5)
1967	514.4	362.8	82.2	16.3	53.1
1968	560.0	398.6	88.3	16.6	56.4
1969	601.9	438.9	86.1	18.6	58.2
1970	616.8	463.8	75.6	18.6	58.8
1971	659.4	490.8	86.4	19.6	62.6
1972	730.6	541.5	97.9	24.9	66.3
1973	828.2	609.5	105.9	42.3	70.5
1974	876.8	669.5	97.7	35.3	74.4
1975	932.1	701.2	117.8	33.6	79.5
1976	1,042.1	786.1	138.5	27.9	89.7
1977	1,181.5	881.2	169.1	29.6	101.6
1978	1,347.7	1,004.1	192.7	38.9	112.1
1979	1,502.0	1,135.1	193.9	46.7	126.3
1980	1,597.1	1,241.5	189.9	38.3	127.4
1981	1,789.1	1,373.8	235.1	49.5	130.7
1982	1,812.3	1,434.6	203.5	41.0	133.2

Sources: See "Derivations" and *Slower Growth*, appendix G.

Table G-4. Nonresidential Business: Estimated Value of Tangible Assets Owned by the Sector, Excluding Dwellings and Sites, 1967–81[a]

Billions of dollars

	Nonfarm corporate				Nonfarm noncorporate				Farm			
Year	Total (1)	Nonresidential structures and equipment (2)	Inventories (3)	Land (4)	Total (5)	Nonresidential structures and equipment (6)	Inventories (7)	Land (8)	Total (9)	Nonresidential structures and equipment (10)	Inventories (11)	Land (12)
1967	631.3	400.7	147.6	83.1	128.2	77.9	16.3	34.0	221.6	40.5	29.6	151.6
1968	690.8	440.4	159.6	90.7	137.1	83.2	16.8	37.2	234.0	43.5	30.0	160.4
1969	766.6	490.6	174.5	101.5	153.2	94.3	17.6	41.3	247.0	47.3	32.0	167.8
1970	849.6	547.6	188.0	114.0	171.9	105.6	18.4	47.8	258.6	51.3	32.8	174.5
1971	923.4	599.6	197.8	126.0	188.8	115.7	20.1	53.0	274.0	54.6	34.5	184.9
1972	997.2	648.4	211.2	137.6	206.9	125.9	22.4	58.5	303.9	58.8	41.2	204.0
1973	1,116.9	719.6	242.0	155.3	231.0	141.5	25.1	64.3	361.2	65.4	56.1	239.8
1974	1,349.3	857.7	303.9	187.7	274.8	168.8	27.6	78.3	419.3	78.3	64.5	276.5
1975	1,555.9	995.0	345.8	215.1	307.3	189.7	27.6	90.0	468.2	91.1	63.4	313.6
1976	1,674.5	1,079.0	367.3	228.2	317.4	198.5	26.7	92.2	532.0	100.1	62.6	369.3
1977	1,838.6	1,182.4	408.6	247.5	345.1	217.0	27.7	100.4	597.6	112.3	60.2	425.1
1978	2,061.6	1,323.5	463.8	274.3	399.8	252.1	30.2	117.5	687.2	129.8	66.9	490.4
1979	2,347.5	1,498.5	542.1	306.9	472.7	299.5	33.7	139.5	801.9	150.1	77.9	573.9
1980	2,667.7	1,702.7	619.3	345.6	553.7	351.5	36.8	165.4	900.9	169.4	84.4	647.1
1981	2,989.8	1,929.8	675.2	384.8	638.1	405.6	39.6	193.0	948.9	186.9	84.4	677.6

Sources: See "Derivations" and *Slower Growth*, appendix G.

a. Classified by ownership except that property used on farms is classified in "farm" regardless of ownership. Data are averages of values at the beginning and end of the year.

Table G-5. Proprietors' and Property Earnings: Ratio of Actual Earnings to Unadjusted Imputed Earnings, Farm and Unincorporated Nonfarm Subsectors of Nonresidential Business

Year	Farm	Nonfarm noncorporate
1967	0.365	0.929
1968	0.355	0.935
1969	0.414	0.904
1970	0.463	0.905
1971	0.452	0.877
1972	0.507	0.844
1973	0.767	0.822
1974	0.677	0.822
1975	0.564	0.788
1976	0.406	0.811
1977	0.374	0.801
1978	0.441	0.777
1979	0.512	0.785
1980	0.392	0.734
1981	0.486	0.656

Sources: See "Derivations" and *Slower Growth*, appendix G.

Table H-1. Series Used in Estimation of Gains from Reallocation of Resources and Related Series, 1966–82

Year[a]	Farm percentages of nonresidential business sector					Nonfarm self-employed and unpaid family workers: share of full-time equivalent employment, weighted by sex, in nonfarm nonresidential business[b] (6)
	National income measured in		Employment			
	Constant 1972 prices (1)	Current prices (2)	Full-time and part-time (3)	Full-time equiv-alent, weighted by sex (4)	Labor input (5)	
1966	3.99	4.33	6.41	6.51	5.77	10.51
1967	4.10	3.88	6.10	6.19	5.49	10.25
1968	3.89	3.65	5.86	5.98	5.30	9.98
1969	3.85	3.76	5.48	5.58	4.95	10.00
1970	4.15	3.71	5.34	5.46[c]	4.84	9.95
1971	4.24	3.63	5.23	5.34	4.73	10.08
1972	4.02	4.03	5.09	5.22	4.62	9.87
1973	3.74	5.76	4.83	5.00	4.43	9.59
1974	3.67	4.73	4.78	5.00	4.43	9.69
1975	4.03	4.32	4.84	5.10	4.51[c]	10.03[c]
1976	3.55	3.40	4.62	4.84	4.28	9.78
1977	3.53	3.22	4.25	4.47	3.95	9.92
1978	3.27	3.55	3.93	4.13	3.65	9.89
1979	3.36	3.78	3.73	4.00	3.53	9.97
1980	3.55	2.97	3.81	4.08	3.61	10.26
1981	3.95	3.41	3.63	3.89	3.44	10.09
1982	3.93	2.92	3.53	3.82	3.38	10.53

Sources: Column 1, table 2-6; column 2, table 2-5; column 3, table 2-7; other columns, see "Derivations" and *Slower Growth*. The 1966 figure in column 1 in *Slower Growth* was erroneously shown as 4.86; it should have been 3.86, based on estimates at the time.

a. See *Slower Growth*, table H-1, for 1929–66 data based on slightly different Census Bureau definitions.

b. Percentages also used for labor input.

c. Comparable to later years. The number comparable to earlier years is 0.01 percentage point larger.

Table I-1. Series Used in Analyzing the Effect of Changes in Intensity of Utilization on Output per Unit of Input in Nonresidential Business, 1929, 1940–41, and 1947–82

	Nonfinancial corporations				Nonresidential business	
	Nonlabor share of national income (percent) (1)	Implicit deflator for national income (1972 = 100) (2)	Compensation per hour worked (1972 = 100) (3)	Ratio of hourly compensation index to implicit deflator (4)	Adjusted output per unit of input with the effect of work stoppages:	
Year					Not removed (1972 = 100) (5)	Removed (1972 = 100) (6)
1929	21.60	n.a.	n.a.	n.a.	57.49	57.47
1940	22.00	n.a.	n.a.	n.a.	58.52	58.50
1941	26.02	n.a.	n.a.	n.a.	62.74	62.75
1947	20.58	n.a.	n.a.	n.a.	65.64	65.67
1948	23.18	62.89	30.21	0.4804	68.17	68.20
1949	21.89	64.09	31.35	0.4892	68.11	68.16
1950	24.36	64.33	33.07	0.5141	71.89	71.92
1951	23.84	67.25	35.74	0.5314	72.03	72.03
1952	20.98	68.75	37.85	0.5505	72.21	72.30
1953	19.56	69.06	40.15	0.5814	73.24	73.25
1954	19.22	70.81	41.68	0.5886	73.07	73.07
1955	22.37	71.51	43.21	0.6043	76.41	76.42
1956	19.89	73.93	45.89	0.6207	76.53	76.55
1957	18.87	76.21	48.75	0.6397	76.85	76.84
1958	17.43	78.45	50.66	0.6458	77.06	77.07
1959	20.11	79.15	52.53	0.6637	80.37	80.50
1960	18.39	79.29	54.78	0.6909	80.32	80.32
1961	18.57	79.49	56.60	0.7120	81.54	81.52
1962	20.05	79.57	58.80	0.7390	84.25	84.25
1963	21.03	79.25	60.57	0.7643	86.31	86.30
1964	21.78	79.94	62.80	0.7856	89.59	89.59
1965	23.05	80.67	64.81	0.8034	92.30	92.30
1966	22.52	82.69	68.57	0.8292	93.97	93.97
1967	21.00	85.09	72.39	0.8507	93.28	93.30
1968	20.51	87.80	77.72	0.8852	95.56	95.59
1969	18.36	91.07	83.05	0.9119	95.45	95.48
1970	15.55	94.54	88.82	0.9395	93.96	94.03
1971	16.61	97.21	94.54	0.9725	96.26	96.30
1972	17.02	100.00	100.00	1.0000	100.00	100.00
1973	16.73	103.85	107.75	1.0376	102.56	102.56
1974	13.62[a]	116.08	118.20	1.0183	98.67	98.71
1975	16.03[a]	128.85	129.73	1.0068	97.81	97.82
1976	16.37[a]	134.89	140.21	1.0394	102.14	102.16
1977	17.28[a]	143.08	151.05	1.0557	105.38	105.39
1978	16.90[a]	152.28	164.05	1.0773	106.45	106.46
1979	14.69[a]	163.41	179.71	1.0997	104.95	104.95
1980	12.76[a]	181.06	198.47	1.0962	103.00	103.00
1981	14.36[a]	196.67	217.95	1.1082	103.66	103.65
1982	12.55[a]	208.82	235.32	1.1269	101.01	100.98

Sources: Column 1, NIPA, table 1.13, one minus row 24 divided by row 23; column 2, NIPA, table 1.13, row 23 divided by row 40, converted to 1972 = 100; column 3, see "Derivations"; column 4, column 3 divided by column 2; column 5, table 5-1, column 1 divided by the product of columns 2 through 7; column 6, column 5 divided by table 5-1, column 8.

n.a. Not available.

a. Adjusted for oil and gas; see "Derivations." Unadjusted percentages beginning with 1974 are 14.35, 16.74, 17.29, 17.95, 17.49, 15.71, 14.43, 15.71, and 13.63.

Table I-2. Deviations of Selected Variables from Trend Values, and Alternative Estimates of the Effect of Intensity of Utilization on Output per Unit of Input, 1948–73

	Deviations of actual values from trend values						Estimated ratio of actual output per unit of input to output per unit of input if intensity of utilization were at average level, based on:[a]			
	Nonlabor share, trends based on:		Ratio of employee compensation to price, trends based on:		Adjusted output per unit of input, trends based on:					
	1947–69	1947–73	1948–69	1948–73	1947–69	1947–73			*(N₁ and*	*(N₂ and*
	Deviation in percentage points		Deviation in percentage of trend value		Deviation in percentage of trend value					
	(N_1)	(N_2)	(W_1)	(W_2)	(P_1)	(P_2)	(N_1)	(N_2)	$W_1)$	$W_2)$
Year	(1)	(2)	(3)	(4)	(5)	(6)	(7)	(8)	(9)	(10)
1948	1.6558	1.0580	−1.0689	−0.8976	1.4620	1.1067	1.0157	1.0094	1.0127	1.0064
1949	0.4420	−0.0658	−2.2210	−2.0722	−0.3382	−0.6323	1.0041	0.9992	0.9972	0.9915
1950	2.9881	2.5704	−0.2676	−0.1414	3.4175	3.1694	1.0286	1.0233	1.0285	1.0238
1951	2.5443	2.2166	0.0551	0.1589	1.8701	1.6819	1.0243	1.0201	1.0251	1.0215
1952	−0.2395	−0.4773	0.6015	0.6827	0.4010	0.2710	0.9976	0.9955	0.9994	0.9978
1953	−1.5834	−1.7311	3.1221	3.1807	0.1145	0.0401	0.9849	0.9843	0.9942	0.9953
1954	−1.8472	−1.9049	1.3273	1.3633	−1.8037	−1.8224	0.9824	0.9827	0.9860	0.9869
1955	1.3789	1.4113	0.9690	0.9825	0.9518	0.9884	1.0130	1.0127	1.0164	1.0169
1956	−1.0249	−0.9025	0.6576	0.6485	−0.5962	−0.5051	0.9902	0.9917	0.9919	0.9937
1957	−1.9688	−1.7563	0.6864	0.6547	−1.8652	−1.7210	0.9813	0.9840	0.9829	0.9857
1958	−3.3326	−3.0302	−1.3444	−1.3987	−3.2578	−3.0621	0.9687	0.9728	0.9638	0.9665
1959	−0.5765	−0.1840	−1.5932	−1.6701	−0.8053	−0.5496	0.9944	0.9981	0.9893	0.9918
1960	−2.2203	−1.7378	−0.5745	−0.6740	−2.5401	−2.2349	0.9790	0.9842	0.9766	0.9810
1961	−1.9641	−1.3916	−0.5529	−0.6750	−2.7297	−2.3710	0.9814	0.9873	0.9791	0.9842
1962	−0.4080	0.2546	0.1811	0.0365	−1.1931	−0.7739	0.9960	1.0021	0.9964	1.0023
1963	0.6482	1.4008	0.5622	0.3949	−0.4855	−0.0081	1.0060	1.0126	1.0079	1.0146
1964	1.4743	2.3170	0.3233	0.1334	1.5529	2.0966	1.0140	1.0210	1.0153	1.0224
1965	2.8205	3.7531	−0.4224	−0.6350	2.8590	3.4668	1.0270	1.0344	1.0264	1.0334
1966	2.3666	3.3893	−0.2487	−0.4839	2.9526	3.6183	1.0226	1.0310	1.0224	1.0304
1967	0.9228	2.0355	−0.6735	−0.9313	0.4718	1.1774	1.0087	1.0184	1.0067	1.0156
1968	0.5090	1.7117	0.3135	0.0331	1.1904	1.9574	1.0047	1.0154	1.0058	1.0162
1969	−1.5649	−0.2722	0.2985	−0.0045	−0.6319	0.1767	0.9851	0.9973	0.9856	0.9972
1970	−4.2987	−2.9160	0.2937	−0.0320	−3.8340	−2.9978	0.9598	0.9738	0.9596	0.9725
1971	−3.1626	−1.6898	0.7618	0.4134	−3.1427	−2.2466	0.9702	0.9846	0.9717	0.9854
1972	−2.6764	−1.1136	0.5624	0.1914	−1.0778	−0.1072	0.9747	0.9898	0.9758	0.9900
1973	−2.8903	−1.2374	1.2733	0.8796	−0.2576	0.7766	0.9728	0.9887	0.9759	0.9914

Source: See "Derivations."

a. Ratios include effects of work stoppages. "Average level" refers to period to which regressions were fitted. See table I-3 for ratios that are comparable for columns 7 to 10.

Table I-3. Alternative Estimates of the Effect of Fluctuations in Intensity of Utilization on Output per Unit of Input and of the Semiresidual, 1948–73

Year	*Estimated ratio of actual productivity to productivity if intensity of utilization were at its average 1948–73 value based on:*[a]				*Indexes of the semiresidual (1972 = 100) when intensity of utilization is based on:*[b]			
	N_1 (1)	N_2 (2)	N_1 and W_1 (3)	N_2 and W_2 (4)	N_1 (5)	N_2 (6)	N_1 and W_1 (7)	N_2 and W_2 (8)
1948	1.0201	1.0089	1.0169	1.0058	65.42	66.84	65.69	67.06
1949	1.0084	0.9987	1.0013	0.9909	66.12	67.47	66.65	68.01
1950	1.0331	1.0228	1.0328	1.0231	68.12	69.53	68.20	69.52
1951	1.0288	1.0196	1.0294	1.0209	68.54	69.89	68.56	69.81
1952	1.0019	0.9950	1.0035	0.9972	70.56	71.80	70.51	71.65
1953	0.9892	0.9838	0.9983	0.9947	72.48	73.65	71.88	72.85
1954	0.9867	0.9822	0.9901	0.9863	72.50	73.60	72.31	73.30
1955	1.0175	1.0122	1.0207	1.0163	73.52	74.68	73.35	74.39
1956	0.9945	0.9912	0.9960	0.9931	75.34	76.38	75.28	76.25
1957	0.9856	0.9835	0.9870	0.9851	76.34	77.30	76.30	77.18
1958	0.9729	0.9723	0.9677	0.9659	77.54	78.41	78.02	78.93
1959	0.9987	0.9976	0.9934	0.9912	78.78	79.70	79.28	80.22
1960	0.9832	0.9837	0.9807	0.9804	79.97	80.78	80.25	81.06
1961	0.9856	0.9868	0.9832	0.9836	80.99	81.75	81.26	82.02
1962	1.0003	1.0016	1.0005	1.0017	82.45	83.21	82.51	83.22
1963	1.0104	1.0121	1.0121	1.0140	83.63	84.37	83.55	84.22
1964	1.0184	1.0205	1.0195	1.0218	86.13	86.85	86.10	86.75
1965	1.0315	1.0338	1.0306	1.0328	87.60	88.32	87.74	88.43
1966	1.0270	1.0304	1.0266	1.0298	89.57	90.22	89.68	90.28
1967	1.0131	1.0179	1.0109	1.0150	90.14	90.66	90.41	90.93
1968	1.0091	1.0149	1.0100	1.0156	92.71	93.15	92.70	93.10
1969	0.9894	0.9968	0.9897	0.9966	94.45	94.73	94.50	94.76
1970	0.9640	0.9733	0.9636	0.9719	95.42	95.51	95.53	95.65
1971	0.9745	0.9841	0.9758	0.9849	96.71	96.76	96.66	96.71
1972	0.9790	0.9893	0.9798	0.9894	100.00	100.00	100.00	100.00
1973	0.9770	0.9882	0.9799	0.9908	102.77	102.68	102.55	102.42

Sources: Tables I-1 and I-2; see "Derivations" and *Slower Growth* for explanation.
a. Ratios include effects of work stoppages.
b. Semiresidual excludes effects of work stoppages.

Table I-5. Index of Effect of Changes in Intensity of Utilization of Employed Resources Resulting from Fluctuations in Intensity of Demand: Years Ordered by Height of Index, Selected Years, 1929–82

| Year | Present index (1972 = 100) (1) | Rank among years covered by former estimates | | Year | Present index (1972 = 100) (1) | Rank among years covered by former estimates | |
		Present estimates (2)	Former estimates (3)			Present estimates (2)	Former estimates (3)
1941	106.56	1	1	1954	101.05	21	22
1950	105.46	2	2	1969	101.04	22	19
1965	105.19	3	4	1957	100.72	23	23
1951	105.06	4	3	1978	100.34	. . .	. . .
1966	104.78	5	5	1961	100.33	24	25
1955	104.19	6	6	1977	100.28	. . .	. . .
1964	104.06	7	7	1960	100.09	25	24
1948	103.82	8	8	1973	100.01	26	28
1929	103.57	9	9	1972	100.00	27	26
1963	103.29	10	12	1971	99.63	28	29
1967	103.20	11	11	1976	99.12	29	27
1968	103.12	12	10	1958	98.78	30	31
1952	102.54	13	15	1979	98.62	. . .	. . .
1940	102.52	14	14	1970	98.43	31	30
1949	102.27	15	13	1981	98.13	. . .	. . .
1962	102.11	16	17	1975	98.02	32	32
1953	101.91	17	16	1982	96.70	. . .	. . .
1956	101.69	18	18	1980	96.49	. . .	. . .
1959	101.54	19	21	1974	96.29	33	33
1947	101.22	20	20				

Sources: Columns 1 and 2, table 5-1, column 9; column 3, *Slower Growth*, table 5-1, column 9.

Table I-8: Comparison of Indexes of Effect of Fluctuations in Demand Intensity on Output per Unit of Input, and Indexes of the Semiresidual, Based on Two Methods, 1972–82

| Year | Indexes (1972 = 100) when intensity of utilization is based on N_1 only (formula 1) | | Indexes (1972 = 100) when intensity of utilization is based on N_1 and W_1 (formula 3)[a] | |
	Intensity of demand[b]	Semi-residual	Intensity of demand[b]	Semi-residual
1972	100.00	100.00	100.00	100.00
1973	99.80	102.77	100.01	102.55
1974	97.00	101.76	96.29	102.52
1975	99.29	98.52	98.02	99.79
1976	99.69	102.48	99.12	103.07
1977	100.62	104.74	100.28	105.10
1978	100.33	106.11	100.34	106.10
1979	98.31	106.75	98.62	106.42
1980	96.59	106.64	96.49	106.74
1981	98.13	105.62	98.13	105.62
1982	96.51	104.63	96.70	104.43

Source: See "Derivations."
a. The series in the columns below are the alternative carried to table 5-1.
b. Excludes effect of work stoppages on intensity of utilization.

Table J-1. Nonresidential Business: Estimation of Index of Gains from Economies of Scale, 1929, 1940–41, and 1947–82

1972 = 100

Year	National income with effects of three irregular factors removed (1)	Income series used to estimate gains from economies of scale (2)	Index of gains from economies of scale (3)
1929	27.05	27.36	86.38
1940	28.36	31.16	87.64
1941	32.60	32.46	88.05
1947	41.43	41.70	90.58
1948	42.73	43.22	90.95
1949	42.16	44.51	91.25
1950	44.71	45.52	91.48
1951	47.80	47.62	91.95
1952	50.58	50.65	92.60
1953	52.95	53.32	93.14
1954	51.89	54.97	93.46
1955	54.58	55.82	93.62
1956	57.36	57.66	93.96
1957	58.31	59.61	94.32
1958	57.96	60.85	94.53
1959	61.23	62.36	94.79
1960	62.58	63.81	95.04
1961	63.34	65.37	95.30
1962	65.98	67.12	95.58
1963	68.06	69.08	95.89
1964	71.95	72.15	96.37
1965	76.17	76.34	96.99
1966	81.12	81.06	97.65
1967	83.47	84.87	98.16
1968	87.85	88.33	98.61
1969	91.99	92.73	99.15
1970	92.59	95.39	99.47
1971	93.88	96.37	99.58
1972	100.00	100.00	100.00
1973	107.09	106.81	100.76
1974	107.93	111.02	101.20
1975	102.51	111.62	101.26
1976	108.56	111.95	101.29
1977	114.76	115.32	101.63
1978	121.43	121.97	102.28
1979	125.99	127.81	102.83
1980	126.13	130.44	103.06
1981	126.90	130.91	103.10
1982	123.70	132.23	103.22

Sources: Column 1, table 4-6, column 5, divided by table 5-1, product of columns 7, 8, and 9; columns 2 and 3, see "Derivations" and *Slower Growth*.

Table L-1. Nonfarm Business: Numbers of Part-Time Wage and Salary Workers Transferred to Full-Time Status to Derive Potential National Income, 1960–82
Thousands

Year[a]	Males	Females	Total
1960	511	276	787
1961	639	363	1,002
1962	333	199	532
1963	263	177	440
1964	157	109	266
1965	−4	28	24
1966	−130	−118	−248
1967	−26	−30	−56
1968	−172	−84	−256
1969	−140	−110	−250
1970	78	65	143
1971	164	203	367
1972	101	162	263
1973	5	85	90
1974	184	219	403
1975	617	573	1,190
1976	437	448	885
1977	379	467	846
1978	244	409	653
1979	213	367	580
1980	587	590	1,177
1981	721	777	1,498
1982	1,384	1,374	2,758

Source: See *Slower Growth*.
a. See *Slower Growth*, table L-1, for earlier years.

Table L-2. Nonfarm Business: Average Potential and Actual Weekly Hours of Full-Time Wage and Salary Workers, by Sex, 1966–82

	Males		Females	
Year[a]	Potential (1)	Actual (2)	Potential (3)	Actual (4)
1966	42.36	42.68	38.21	38.28
1967	42.10	42.20	37.77	37.76
1968	41.96	42.03	37.63	37.60
1969	42.32	42.01	37.78	37.63
1970	42.03	41.50	37.54	37.30
1971	41.63	41.35	37.23	37.12
1972	41.81	41.56	37.38	37.28
1973	41.77	41.48	37.29	37.15
1974	41.67	40.84	37.17	36.83
1975	40.85	40.49	36.71	36.64
1976	40.83	40.56	36.79	36.72
1977	40.49	40.38	36.55	36.52
1978	40.15	39.99	36.71	36.68
1979	40.26	39.82	36.28	36.19
1980	40.26	39.62	36.23	36.18
1981	39.40	39.00	36.03	35.98
1982	39.76	39.27	36.03	35.98

Sources: Columns 1 and 3, see "Derivations" and *Slower Growth*; columns 2 and 4 calculated from the data underlying table 3-7.
a. See *Slower Growth*, table L-2, for earlier years and "Derivations" for comments on comparability.

Table L-3. Nonfarm Business: Potential Less Actual Total Weekly Hours of Wage and Salary Workers, by Components, 1960–82[a]

Millions of hours

Year	Employed workers			Shift from unemployment to employment			Labor force response to demand for labor			All components		
	Male (1)	Female (2)	Total (3)	Male (4)	Female (5)	Total (6)	Male (7)	Female (8)	Total (9)	Male (10)	Female (11)	Total (12)
1960	19.6	7.4	26.9	25.7	12.3	37.9	7.0	12.9	19.9	52.3	32.6	84.7
1961	20.1	8.3	28.5	46.9	22.8	69.7	12.6	23.3	35.9	79.6	54.4	134.1
1962	8.5	4.3	12.8	25.8	13.1	38.9	7.1	13.0	20.1	41.4	30.4	71.8
1963	2.3	3.0	5.4	28.1	14.7	42.8	7.7	13.8	21.6	38.1	31.5	69.8
1964	−3.1	0.9	−2.2	19.5	10.8	30.2	5.5	9.6	15.1	21.9	21.3	43.1
1965	−9.9	−1.1	−11.0	7.5	4.4	11.8	2.1	3.6	5.8	−0.3	6.9	6.6
1966	−11.3	−4.3	−15.6	−6.0	−3.8	−9.8	−2.2	−2.9	−5.1	−19.4	−10.9	−30.4
1967	−2.7	−0.7	−3.4	−3.0	−1.9	−4.9	−1.1	−1.9	−3.0	−6.9	−4.5	−11.4
1968	−5.3	−1.3	−6.6	−7.9	−5.1	−13.0	−2.6	−4.3	−6.9	−15.8	−10.7	−26.5
1969	6.6	0.2	6.8	−9.7	−6.4	−16.1	−4.9	−3.1	−8.0	−6.2	−11.2	−17.4
1970	16.5	5.1	21.6	17.3	10.2	27.5	6.3	10.0	16.3	40.1	25.3	65.4
1971	10.4	5.6	15.9	36.7	21.5	58.2	13.5	20.9	34.4	60.6	47.9	108.5
1972	8.6	4.8	13.4	31.0	18.7	49.7	17.9	11.7	29.6	51.3	41.4	92.7
1973	8.6	4.1	12.7	16.2	10.3	26.5	6.3	9.5	15.7	31.0	23.9	54.9
1974	28.2	10.4	38.7	31.1	19.8	50.9	11.9	17.9	29.8	71.3	48.1	119.3
1975	18.2	11.0	29.2	90.6	54.9	145.5	32.3	50.5	82.8	141.1	116.4	257.5
1976	15.3	9.8	25.0	75.9	48.1	124.0	27.7	42.7	70.4	118.8	100.7	219.5
1977	9.7	9.2	18.8	62.3	41.7	104.0	23.1	35.5	58.6	95.1	86.4	181.5
1978	8.9	8.4	17.3	41.0	29.2	70.2	15.4	23.9	39.3	65.3	61.5	126.8
1979	15.4	7.9	23.3	36.7	26.0	62.7	13.8	21.2	35.0	65.9	55.0	120.9
1980	30.6	12.4	43.0	68.0	43.8	111.8	24.0	37.5	61.5	122.5	93.8	216.3
1981	24.3	15.3	39.6	78.6	52.0	130.6	27.3	43.3	70.6	130.2	110.7	240.9
1982	39.4	26.5	65.8	129.3	82.0	211.2	41.9	68.9	110.8	210.6	177.3	387.9

Sources: See "Derivations" and *Slower Growth*.
a. See *Slower Growth*, table L-3, for earlier years.

Table L-4. Potential Less Actual Labor Force and Employment, 1960–82[a]
Thousands

Year	Potential labor force less actual labor force			Potential employment less actual employment						
				Transfers from unemployment		Adjustment from labor force		Total adjustment		
	Total (1)	Male (2)	Female (3)	Male (4)	Female (5)	Male (6)	Female (7)	Male (8)	Female (9)	Total (10)
1960	594	210	384	638	348	201	369	839	717	1,556
1961	1,088	387	702	1,167	651	371	674	1,538	1,325	2,863
1962	611	219	392	646	378	210	376	856	754	1,610
1963	666	242	424	709	430	233	407	942	837	1,780
1964	468	173	296	495	319	166	284	661	603	1,264
1965	179	67	112	189	129	64	108	253	237	491
1966	−180	−68	−112	−154	−114	−65	−107	−219	−221	−440
1967	−96	−37	−59	−80	−57	−35	−56	−115	−113	−227
1968	−223	−85	−138	−205	−157	−82	−132	−163	−263	−576
1969	−255	−98	−157	−251	−196	−94	−150	−345	−346	−691
1970	527	204	323	448	318	196	310	644	628	1,272
1971	1,121	437	684	959	669	420	657	1,379	1,326	2,705
1972	959	375	584	809	580	360	560	1,169	1,140	2,309
1973	509	199	310	422	321	191	297	613	618	1,231
1974	962	376	586	811	615	361	562	1,172	1,177	2,349
1975	2,753	1,077	1,676	2,400	1,726	1,034	1,609	3,434	3,335	6,769
1976	2,318	907	1,411	2,010	1,506	871	1,354	2,881	2,860	5,741
1977	1,936	757	1,179	1,664	1,314	728	1,131	2,392	2,445	4,837
1978	1,300	508	792	1,107	920	488	760	5,991	1,680	3,275
1979	1,167	454	713	988	828	436	682	1,424	1,510	2,934
1980	2,041	790	1,251	1,822	1,392	760	1,199	2,582	2,591	5,173
1981	2,368	911	1,457	2,124	1,657	875	1,398	2,999	3,055	6,054
1982	3,749	1,427	2,322	3,488	2,606	1,371	2,228	4,859	4,834	9,693

Sources: See "Derivations" and *Slower Growth*.
a. See *Slower Growth*, table L-4, for earlier years.

Table L-5. Derivation of the Excess of Potential over Actual National Income That Is Due to Labor Input, 1966–82
Values in billions of dollars

	Nonfarm business wage and salary workers									All non-	
				Ratio of potential to actual				Potential compensation, not adjusted for education			
	Compensation			Age-weighted hours		Intragroup hours efficiency index				Labor earnings	
Year[a]	Total (1)	Male (2)	Female (3)	Male (4)	Female (5)	Male (6)	Female (7)	Male (8)	Female (9)	Male (10)	Female (11)
1966	337.9	271.4	66.5	0.9862	0.9813	1.002	1.001	268.3	65.3	313.4	69.5
1967	359.1	287.2	71.9	0.9953	0.9925	1.001	1.000	286.0	71.4	331.9	75.3
1968	394.7	314.5	80.2	0.9894	0.9829	1.001	1.000	311.5	78.8	362.1	83.6
1969	434.9	343.5	91.4	0.9969	0.9833	0.999	1.000	342.1	89.8	394.4	95.4
1970	459.5	361.7	97.8	1.0272	1.0387	0.997	0.999	370.4	101.5	416.1	101.9
1971	486.4	382.7	103.7	1.0396	1.0742	0.998	1.000	396.9	111.3	439.7	107.5
1972	537.0	421.0	116.0	1.0324	1.0612	0.998	1.000	433.9	123.0	480.5	121.0
1973	604.2	471.8	132.4	1.0191	1.0334	0.998	1.000	480.0	136.7	539.5	138.8
1974	663.2	513.0	150.2	1.0455	1.0656	0.996	0.999	534.2	159.9	586.6	156.0
1975	694.5	533.0	161.5	1.0924	1.1641	0.998	1.000	581.1	188.0	610.0	164.9
1976	778.5	593.5	185.0	1.0756	1.1352	0.999	1.000	637.5	209.9	673.9	189.7
1977	872.8	661.7	211.1	1.0582	1.1103	1.000	1.000	699.9	234.4	748.9	217.9
1978	995.1	745.8	249.3	1.0387	1.0724	1.000	1.000	774.3	267.4	843.8	256.0
1979	1,125.0	838.8	286.2	1.0388	1.0622	0.999	1.000	870.5	304.0	949.9	296.5
1980	1,230.4	906.3	324.1	1.0750	1.1045	0.998	1.000	972.7	357.9	1,022.0	333.3
1981	1,362.2	997.8	364.4	1.0790	1.1207	0.999	1.000	1,075.9	408.4	1,117.4	372.9
1982	1,422.7	1,033.1	389.6	1.1357	1.1967	0.998	1.000	1,171.4	466.1	1,153.0	397.3

Sources: Columns 1–7 and 10–13, see "Derivations" and *Slower Growth;* column 8, the product of columns 2, 4 and 6; column 9, the product of columns 3, 5, and 7; column 14, column 10 times column 12, minus column 10; column 15, column 11 times column 13, minus column 11; column 16, column 8 minus column 2 plus column 14: column 17, column 9 minus column 3 plus column 15; column 18, the sum of columns 16 and 17; column 19, column 18 divided by

| residential business employment | | | | Nonfarm business wage and salary workers, potential less actual compensation | | | Column 18 as a percentage of column 10 plus column 11 | Labor weight, nonresidential business | Nonresidential business national income in 1972 prices, adjusted to potential utilization | Excess of potential over actual national income due to labor input, 1972 prices | |
| Education index, ratio of potential to actual | | Adjustment of potential earnings for education | | | | | | | | | |
Male (12)	Female (13)	Male (14)	Female (15)	Male (16)	Female (17)	Total (18)	(19)	(20)	(21)	(22)	Year
1.000	1.001	0.0	0.0	−3.1	−1.2	−4.3	−1.113	0.790	608.8	−5.4	1966
1.000	1.000	0.1	0.0	−1.1	−0.5	−1.6	−0.393	0.794	627.7	−2.0	1967
1.000	1.000	0.1	0.0	−2.8	−1.3	−4.1	−0.931	0.803	659.6	−4.9	1968
1.000	1.000	0.2	0.0	−1.3	−1.6	−2.9	−0.590	0.811	690.4	−3.3	1969
1.000	1.000	−0.2	0.0	8.5	3.7	12.2	2.347	0.818	695.5	13.3	1970
0.999	0.999	−0.4	−0.1	13.8	7.6	21.4	3.902	0.822	706.8	22.7	1971
0.999	0.999	−0.7	−0.1	12.3	7.0	19.3	3.205	0.824	751.9	19.9	1972
0.999	0.999	−0.5	−0.1	7.6	4.2	11.8	1.747	0.826	804.3	11.6	1973
0.998	0.998	−1.1	−0.2	21.0	9.4	30.4	4.094	0.827	810.4	27.5	1974
0.994	0.996	−3.4	−0.7	44.8	25.8	70.6	9.106	0.826	771.8	58.1	1975
0.996	0.996	−3.0	−0.7	40.9	24.3	65.2	7.549	0.826	815.3	50.8	1976
0.996	0.997	−2.8	−0.6	35.4	22.6	58.0	6.003	0.827	862.6	42.8	1977
0.998	0.998	−2.0	−0.5	26.5	17.5	44.0	4.000	0.828	911.9	30.2	1978
0.998	0.998	−2.0	−0.5	29.7	17.3	47.0	3.769	0.828	946.1	29.5	1979
0.996	0.997	−4.0	−0.9	62.4	32.8	95.2	7.028	0.831	946.8	55.3	1980
0.996	0.997	−5.0	−1.2	73.0	42.8	115.8	7.770	8.834	957.4	62.0	1981
0.993	0.995	−8.4	−2.0	129.9	74.5	204.4	13.187	0.834	931.1	102.3	1982

(column 10 plus column 11) times 100; column 20, annual data that were averaged to obtain the "labor" column in table G-2; column 21, table 2-6, column 5, plus table 2-4, column 2; column 22, the product of columns 19, 20, and 21.

Note: Figures are rounded.

a. For earlier years, see tables 2-4 and 2-6 for columns 21 and 22, and *Slower Growth*, Table L-5, for columns 1–19.

Table L-6. Average Potential Weekly Hours at Work per Person Potentially Employed, by Sector, 1929, 1940–41, and 1947–82

Average Weekly Hours

Year	Whole economy (1)	Nonresi- dential business (2)	General government, households, and insti- tutions[a] (3)
1929	48.3	49.0	43.9
1940	43.1	43.8	38.9
1941	43.0	43.8	38.3
1947	41.7	42.7	35.9
1948	41.2	42.3	35.3
1949	40.8	41.9	35.2
1950	40.7	41.7	35.2
1951	40.6	41.7	35.6
1952	40.5	41.7	35.8
1953	40.4	41.5	35.7
1954	40.1	41.2	35.3
1955	39.9	41.1	34.9
1956	39.8	41.1	34.5
1957	39.4	40.6	34.3
1958	39.2	40.5	34.0
1959	39.1	40.4	33.8
1960	39.0	40.3	33.8
1961	30.7	40.1	33.5
1962	38.6	40.0	33.4
1963	38.3	39.7	33.3
1964	38.2	39.6	33.1
1965	38.2	39.6	33.0
1966	37.8	39.3	32.8
1967	37.4	38.8	32.9
1968	37.2	38.6	32.7
1969	37.2	38.6	32.6
1970	36.7	38.1	32.2
1971	36.4	37.8	32.0
1972	36.3	37.7	31.8
1973	36.3	37.6	31.8
1974	36.0	37.4	31.6
1975	35.4	36.6	31.3
1976	35.4	36.6	31.3
1977	35.2	36.4	31.1
1978	35.1	36.3	31.0
1979	35.0	36.1	31.0
1980	34.8	36.0	30.7
1981	34.6	35.7	30.7
1982	34.5	35.5	30.7

Sources: See "Derivations" and *Slower Growth* for a description of the series for total potential hours and employment from which these averages are derived.

a. Average potential hours are the same as average actual hours excluding persons on work relief. Military reserves not on active duty are excluded.

Index